SAVOY

MILAN

MONTFERRAND

GENOA

V E N I C E

MANTUA

FERRARA

LUCCA

PIOMBINO

FLORENCE

SIENA

Urbino

PAPAL STATES

Benevento

KINGDOM OF NAPLES

CORSICA
(Genoa)

T Y R R H E N I A N   S E A

SICILY
(Spain)

D1349928

Italia, Italia

Italia, Italia

PETER NICHOLS

MACMILLAN

SBN 333 00930 4

First published 1973 by
MACMILLAN LONDON LIMITED
London and Basingstoke
Associated companies in New York Dublin
Melbourne Johannesburg and Madras

Printed in Great Britain by
NORTHUMBERLAND PRESS LIMITED
Gateshead

To Paola,
Whose Dedication merits more
than a Dedication

Contents

Endpaper maps. Modern Italy, showing the regions, and Renaissance Italy.

Acknowledgements

MANY people have helped me more than they know, some wittingly and some unwittingly. I would like to thank them all even if my gratitude never reaches them, including the burglar who destroyed most of the first draft and notes with the result that much of the book had to be rewritten, probably to its benefit.

Journalism is the least selfish of professions and I have the good fortune to enjoy its generosity most days because my office is with the Rome office of *La Stampa*. No one could have better, friendlier and more helpful colleagues.

Early in my time here I came across an extraordinary anthology (and it came across me) aimed at giving a picture of the Italian mind and character. It was the 1961 special issue of the *Texas Quarterly*, which remains invaluable. I have taken from its pages the quotations from Bacchelli and Alvaro. Through them I met Elena Croce. I have quoted a passage from her contribution and I wanted to add my gratitude to her for making me feel at home in her circle of friends.

I like living in Italy and should acknowledge my debt on this score – for not everyone can say they like living where they live – to the Italians themselves and to my editor, William Rees-Mogg, who allows me to go on working where I feel I can work best.

I could not have had a more sympathetic hand to lead me through the pre-publication processes than that of Teresa Sacco.

I gratefully acknowledge the following books from which brief extracts have been quoted: Corrado Alvaro, *Ultimo Diario* (Bompiani); Riccardo Bacchelli, *Italia per Terra e per Mare* (Mondadori); Bertolt Brecht, *Tales from the Calendar* (Methuen); Isak Dinesen, *Gothic Tales* (Penguin Modern Classics edition); D. H. Lawrence, *Twilight in Italy* (Heinemann).

PETER NICHOLS

For the purposes of conversion, the following rates of exchange have been used: 1465 lire=£1; 600 lire =$1.

CHAPTER ONE

The Centaur

SUPPOSE I had gone to Japan; or stayed in Germany, which I liked; or moved on after two or three years in Italy, which is too short a time to have any clear and accurate ideas about the country. I cannot imagine what sort of a person I would have become, or what I would have felt like, or what I would have wanted to achieve, or what I would have looked for in people, or how I would have judged their motives, instead of what I now am, and how I behave in all these and many other ways. And, of course, I believe that I have seen things in Italy that no one else has seen or in a way that no one else has seen them. This feeling may be right or wrong, presumptuous, self-indulgent; but there is no other excuse for writing about Italy.

For me there is one other. I have hated a lot of the books I have read about Italy. Some people have actually hated the place itself, or despised its way of life to a point not far from hatred, and I do not mind reading their angry bluster though I do not share it. Nor do I share, I hope, the much worse complaint, because it is fatuous but widespread, of falling at the feet of the centaur in a pool of sentimental adoration.

This complaint is chronic among the British and Germans. Italy, their hallucination goes, is where life is lived to the full; this is where inhibitions are cast away; this is where a tubercular cripple dies on the steps of St Peter's happily gasping some line of 'O Sole Mio', living life to the full, to the last, to the last cough. Fortunately, one of the qualities of most Italians is that they are free of sentimentalism. They are a realistic people, very conformist, much more hard-headed than Western Europeans in general. But they do not mind the foreigner thinking of them as soft-hearted, emotional and uninhibited, pastel-shaded souls who die choking with a song on their lips. They know very well they are not. They know that they are more as the unhappy Rolfe described them: 'Italy is and always has been, a land of raw reality, of glittering light, of pure primary colour, of nature naked and not ashamed, of perfectly transparent souls, of rapidest versatility, clearest mystery, ultimate simplicity, steel and brains and blood.'

It is not just the Mafia and the traditional way of righting wrongs in Sardinia that show the relentless side of a nation's character. The southerners have this relentlessness in a more dramatic way than others because it is more essential to the life they know. The vendetta is simply the extreme expression of relentlessness. Fixity of purpose, which is much the same thing, is in the air they breathe, or in the dust of the roads as they move on foot or on mules five miles each morning to the fields and five miles back at dusk. One of the deepest images that can be engrained on the mind, though now it is rarer, is that of scores of peasants, cloaked in grey-green wool, with faces covered to protect them against the bitter night-wind as they solemnly moved through the semi-darkness along a road in the mountains of Lucania. They looked as if no natural obstacle, even in that poor region where nature consists mainly of obstacles, could have stopped the steady, weary movement towards their peasant-towns where by night they gathered to sleep, drawn fatally back and forth each day as if by profound instincts of self-preservation and laboriousness, with a fixity of purpose and of acceptance that is cold beyond belief. The Piedmontese in the far north have a fixity of purpose of just this strength, though owed more to a rigorous climate and a military tradition. That is how Piedmontese officers in the First World War could send thousands and thousands of southern peasants to death against the enemy lines, ill-armed and ill-equipped. It also explains the fanatical sense of loyalty and dedication of the real Piedmontese to their work and their employers. Nothing is more touching than the pride – a somewhat grim pride – of elderly Fiat workers as they gather for an annual celebration or the retirement of a group of their number, and the slight sense of bliss with which an executive will say, 'We have a five-day week here, but I usually like to come in on Saturdays if I can....' Fixity of purpose is not God-given; the Italians have followed it and still do because they have had to labour against powerful enemies, natural and human, in order to create a living and a background to life. Lucania and Piedmont are widely different examples geographically and materially. The first is poverty-stricken, the most nature-haunted of Italian regions, hard and terrible but with a tip of human nobility emerging from the rocky mass. Piedmont rose as a modern state from the devastation of the Renaissance wars and survived despite its exposed position because of the sturdy, often unimaginative, resilience of its people. But both are only examples. Similar behaviour can be found throughout the country.

Romance is simply not very important in the Italian outlook on life. Occasionally there are cases of extreme romantic love, ending in suicide, of a kind that Anglo-Saxon writers customarily set in Italy – wrongly, if the aim of the setting is greater credibility. Italian men appear to be emotionally more romantic than Western Europeans because they are far more at ease with women and take far greater trouble to please them. They have had to: otherwise the family, on which everything has depended in the past and much will depend for the foreseeable future, could not be the powerful unit that it is. The few cases of death for hopeless love are inclined to be more a realistic assessment of the situation. A double suicide occurred near Taranto in February 1970, simply to choose one instance which happens incidentally to illustrate

Italian social customs. He was married, and there was no divorce in Italy; she was about to marry a man chosen for her by her parents, a custom still strong in the south and not easily broken. So he shot her, and then himself. At much the same time, in Rome, a girl aged thirteen threw herself from a fourth-floor window because her parents had forbidden her to see the boy with whom she was in love. But cases of this kind are rare and warrant a good deal of space in the newspapers. They are far outnumbered and quite overshadowed as typical of the race by the regular killings 'for honour', which normally mean that the man kills the seducer of his wife or mistress, or the woman herself or both (and sometimes the seducer of a sister or other close relation whose dishonouring dishonours the family). This is a course of action directly opposed to the romantic outlook. There are only two principal characters in these dramas; the man, and the man's reputation. The woman is simply an instrument, of no importance except for the trouble she has caused. Some people wrongly describe these murders as *crimes passionels*, on the assumption presumably that a French phrase is as good as any because all foreigners behave in the same sort of outlandish manner. But these crimes in Italy are a matter of honour not of passion and are not only coldly executed as a rule but are recognised in the penal code, which lays down light sentences for deaths involved in these triangular settlings of accounts. The article concerned is number 587 and in fact, if properly applied, would not sanction more than a few of these revenge-crimes; but the judges make liberal use of it, and powerful efforts to have it abolished regularly come to nothing. It lays down near-impunity for anyone killing or injuring a spouse, daughter or sister (or the person caught with them) 'at the moment in which he discovers the illegitimate carnal relationship and in the state of ire caused by the offence to his honour or to that of the family'. This article strongly suggests that at least an element of immediate reaction is necessary to justify its use in defence of a killer. But many of these crimes are planned or are the result of a steady growth in resentment. A startling settling of accounts of this kind came to trial in Genoa in July 1971 when a middle-aged man was charged with having killed his wife by stabbing her with a kitchen-knife because, allegedly, he had reason to believe that she had men-friends. The hearings revealed that the woman's death was little more than the culmination of regular beatings from her husband who, on the fatal night, made use of the knife that was at hand rather than mere physical violence.

Probably the classic case in modern times of the Italian version of the *crime passionel* (a crime devoid of passion) happened a year earlier than the Genoa case. A Sicilian called Angelo Ferrara and his wife, Maria, left the town of Pachino, almost on the southernmost tip of the island, to go to Milan where he shot, while she stabbed, a man who had been her lover ten years earlier – four years before she had met her husband. The woman was a schoolmistress. In 1959 she met Sebastiano Fichera, a man well known for loving and eating. He seduced her, left her, married another woman by whom he had two children, abandoned the family and went to Milan where he made a substantial fortune in the fruit-and-vegetable business. In 1963 the woman married Angelo Ferrara. The discovery that she was not a virgin fundamentally shocked him. The thought of an earlier lover obsessed him. He constantly plied her with questions: 'Who was he ...? Why did you allow him to seduce you ...? Do you still think of him ...?' At the elementary school where she taught she was known to be a woman who never smiled, always as if in mourning. Her two daughters appeared to be no consolation. Finally, after seven years, she told her husband the name of her former lover. Both apparently thought by this time that by killing the man they would raise the oppressive curse on their own relationship. They drove to Catania and flew to Milan, asked for an appointment with the victim and shot him three times at point-blank range. The woman stabbed him. Their one mistake, almost laughable in this context of ancient relentlessness, was that they did not quite kill him and he was able to tell the police who his assailants were. They were caught at Alessandria. Pure stupidity, the whole affair? In modern times, certainly; but the impulses which caused it were promptings from some deep, remote past still able to exercise its domination on persons living in a technological age in the world's seventh most important industrial country. The woman's statement to the police included the passage: 'The scoundrel deserved nothing better and he knew that sooner or later I would have my revenge. That is our law. He had destroyed my existence because my husband could never have tolerated the dishonour which had entered our house. I had no alternative.' There was no passion here, just a settling of accounts, like the settling of a butcher's bill because non-payment would bring trouble.

Even less could be said of the most striking examples of the survival of the vendetta, another form of the crime without passion, but pre-ordained and often dramatically premeditated. Eight people died in the feud which tore through the Calabrian town of Seminara for months after its origins in a quarrel in a bar on the night of 17 September 1971. Seminara is a small town of 8000 inhabitants near the motor-highway from Naples to Reggio Calabria, but it has absorbed little or nothing of the modern outlook symbolised by the great road which was supposed to bring fresh thinking to the deepest south. Its main square, Piazza Vittorio Emanuele, had by late 1972 been the scene of forty-one shootings. A few yards away – just to provide an idea of Seminara's background – is the church dedicated to Santa Maria dei Poveri (St Mary of the Poor): a decade ago the sacristan was shot as he rang the bells, shot repeatedly until his killer had the satisfaction of seeing the body fall to the ground at his feet.

The famous feud between the Pellegrino clan and the Gioffre clan began when the two families were already quarrelling about their rival interests in providing contract work for the building of the highway. On the evening of 17 September 1971 a certain Giuseppe Frisina, aged forty-two, belonging to the Pellegrino interests, insulted the nineteen-year-old Giuseppe Gioffre: he was said to have called him *un cretino bastardo*, 'a stupid bastard'. Gioffre came charging at him and Frisina shot and wounded him. Frisina took refuge in the house of a friend, Antonio Pietropaolo. For three weeks nothing happened. Then the Gioffre family decided, as they could not find Frisina, to take revenge on other members of the Pellegrino family, a form of parallel vendetta. Rocco

Pellegrino, aged thirty-two, had a petrol pump near Ponte Vecchio. On 7 October he was shot, and died two months later in Messina hospital. The youth who worked for him was wounded and recovered. On the same day the Gioffre family discovered the hiding-place of Frisina. He was no longer there and so they killed Pietropaolo for having given hospitality to their enemy. The following day shots were fired at Michelangelo Pellegrino, brother of Rocco, who was driving his mother and another brother back from Messina where they had been to see Rocco. There were no deaths, but the enquiries of the *carabinieri* resulted in the arrest of a young Gioffre and the flight of another, Vincenzo Domingo Gioffre, to take refuge in the mountains. This latter Gioffre, known as 'Ringo', made a career for himself as a bandit until his arrest in the autumn of 1972. On 12 November a sixty-five-year-old pensioner called Vincenzo Gallico was shot in Piazza Vittorio Emanuele, apparently for having remarked in general terms that the Pellegrino group were 'basically right'.

Three days later in the same square Rocco Gioffre shot at Arcangelo Frisina. All four shots missed. Both were aged fourteen.

On 17 November a group of Gioffre supporters knocked on the door of a woman known to be friendly with Salvatore Pellegrino and insulted her. The reply from the Pellegrino side was massive. Gaetano Gioffre, aged twenty, was shot and killed in his Fiat 850 while driving with his girl-friend: she was injured, as were two other persons and a child aged four. The killers were Salvatore and Raffaelle Pellegrino. The funeral of Gaetano Gioffre was due to take place on 21 November. As the procession moved through the town led by the crippled drummer who performed at all such occasions (including the funeral of the sacristan), the figure of Salvatore Pellegrino appeared, sub-machine gun in hand. Archpriest and seminarist fled, as did the coffin-bearers. Only the drummer and the bandit remained. It is said that Salvatore then gave the final insult to Gaetano by spitting on his coffin. The coffin had to be moved from the street by the *carabinieri* as no one else dared touch it.

For months there were no new developments after this

macabre scene. Then came a murder ascribed to Salvatore Pellegrino. He shot Domenico Gioffre, the father of the dead Gaetano. This Gioffre was a strange character. One of his children was born deformed and, in a strangely untypical way, he became so attached to the child that its death was a deep shock to him. He vanished into the mountains, returning one night to dig up the body and take it away with him into the Aspromonte. When searchers found him three days later, they had to take away the corpse by force. This was the man whom Salvatore Pellegrino shot at seven o'clock on the morning of St Joseph's Day. The bandit shot once at his adversary and then said, 'Turn round, Domenico. Once, when you were ill, I spared you. Now that you are well I am killing you.' And he fired another three shots. At least ten people witnessed the killing without making any attempt to intervene. At Domenico's funeral a member of the Gioffre family, Vincenzo, aged forty-nine, who had seemingly had no part in the killings, appealed to the authorities to round up Salvatore Pellegrino and his own nephew, Vincenzo Domenico Gioffre. He said, 'We must put an end once and for all to this butchery.' Three days later he shot Pietro Pellegrino. More killings were to come. The next victim was Rocco Suraci, who had helped the wounded Rocco Pellegrino. And on 26 January 1973 his widow Carmela, aged twenty-eight and mother of four children, was killed on her own doorstep.

Women being more practical than men in most matters, and much less likely to be really moved by questions of dignity and status within the community, the woman's form of relentlessness is more closely attached to immediate realities. And by no means limited to the south. The idea is expressed to perfection by Brecht's description of how the wife of a sixteenth-century Venetian tailor goes day after day to the Inquisition building to demand payment for a coat from Giordano Bruno, who had been arrested before he could accept delivery of the garment and had had, in the meantime, all his possessions confiscated. These strange encounters between the sharp-minded old woman and the harassed heretic who was arrested on 25 May 1592 at three o'clock in the morning and was a prisoner until he was burnt at the stake on 17 February 1600 form one of Brecht's *Kalendergeschichten*:

> It was not until two days later that she went to the Holy Office building again, as it seemed only proper to allow the gentleman time to make his enquiries.
>
> She was, in fact, given permission to speak to him once more. True, she had to wait over an hour in the tiny room with the grated windows, because he was at an interrogation.
>
> He came in and seemed very exhausted. As there was no chair he leant against the wall a little. But he came to the point at once.
>
> He told her in a very weak voice that unfortunately he was unable to pay for the coat. No money had been found amongst his belongings. Yet she need not give up all hope. He had been thinking it over and remembered that in the city of Frankfurt a man who had printed his books must still have some money laid by. If this was allowed, he would write to him. He would apply for permission the very next day. At today's audience it had struck him that the prevailing atmosphere was not particularly favourable. So he had not liked to ask and risk spoiling everything.
>
> The old woman watched him searchingly with her sharp eyes as he spoke. She knew the subterfuges and hollow promises of debtors. They didn't give a damn for their obligations and when you cornered them they went on as though they were moving heaven and earth.
>
> 'Why did you need a new coat if you hadn't the money to pay for it?' she asked stubbornly....

It makes a perfect study in relentlessness: the great heretic who is tortured for his intellectual views and harried for money which he no longer possesses: a very Italian situation.

Even the supernatural in Italy has this quality of harsh reality. Normally it takes the form of religious pictures or statues, usually madonnas, which work miracles while weeping or bleeding or giving other manifestations of being other than they seem. But their miracles fulfil specific requests. Sanctuaries are full of gifts for the miracle-worker, some expensive, some simple, depending on the resources of the beneficiary, given in return 'for grace received'. It is not an uncommon sight in the backward parts of the south to see women remonstrating with the image in order to wrest from it a cure for a crippled husband or a sick child. There is very little free-and-easy haunting, manifestations without an obvious point. Such ghosts as there are, such obvious ones as Beatrice Cenci or Nero, who is said to sit some nights in Piazza del Popolo, are apparitions reflecting dire and bloody behaviour. A house with a ghost that goes no further than harmless antics is a cause of immense wonder to Italians, who will sit in silence at the account and try to remember if they have ever heard of such a thing before: 'Years ago there was something of this kind in – where was it? – perhaps it was Via Giulia ...,' somebody would say, just so as not to be left speechless.

This single-mindedness of which so many Italians are supremely capable, this refusal to see the world in any other way than as it is, has its origins in a subconscious feeling, completely justified by history, that Italians have little more to rely on than their individual quickness of wit. A framework of life regarded as normal elsewhere has never existed in Italy. They invented the modern state, but have not been able to make one for themselves; they have explained how successful rulers should behave, without nowadays being able to persuade their rulers to rule them. They became a national state in the accepted, liberal fashion of the nineteenth century but they have not produced a Bismarck: they have no memories of a Louis XIV or a Tudor dynasty to give an idea of patriotic centralisation. They have remained much more themselves. Very little counts for less in Italy than the State. They invented the idea of the modern man who masters all human knowledge, yet the educational system continues to produce graduates qualified in just those branches of knowledge that are rightly not in demand. The traditional education is an open invitation to turn everything into rhetoric and away from practical action. It produces a class trained to speak airily on mighty themes. Anyone from what is quaintly called 'the ruling class' (because it does anything but rule the country), from members of municipal sub-councils to that other Italian invention, the Senate – all of them can talk and talk about Vietnam and disarmament, racial troubles in American cities, arms embargoes in the Middle East, the need to protect liberty, the decline in moral standards, faith in the democratic system; but nothing they are likely to be able to do anything about, or should be doing something about, such as drainage, the price of fruit, or giving justice to the simple citizen. The lack of a frame, or a basic idea, for Italy was put in these terms by Elena Croce, daughter of the philosopher: 'For any other European country, it is possible to cite a more or less established national image; the image may be conventional or even distorted, but it is at least discussable, arguable. For Italy no such image exists: a vague *potpourri* of the collective impressions, enthusiasms and disappointments of tourists and travellers to Italy over the centuries. But there is no generally acceptable Italian image of Italy.'

This lack of generalisation, this lack of a national shape, leads to what many Italians believe to be true: that any and every generalisation about Italians must be wrong because there is no such thing as an Italian. There are only Tuscans, Lombards, Piedmontese, Sicilians, Venetians, Emilians, Sardinians, Neapolitans and so on, all as unlike each other as men from opposite ends of the earth. What, one constantly hears, has a Milanese in common with a Neapolitan? The answer is: a great deal more than they will ever admit. And there is the whole problem of north and south, the real problem not only of finding a collective image of Italians, but the economic thorn, the real national issue, the psychological block towards real nationhood. The south is poor and cannot seem to make itself rich, however much the Government spends, and the north keeps getting richer; hence the gap widens.

Can it be that from the waist down Italy is a different creature? Is the famous boot shape really an elegantly shod hoof, and the top a normal Western country? Sit in Lombardy, in the richest of Italian regions, and they will explain endlessly that without the poor south Italy proper – the north, that is, and part of the centre – would be the richest country in Europe: the factories and business houses in Turin and Milan, the ports of Genoa and Venice, the farms of the Po valley, of Emilia and Romagna, and then the Riviera, the Alps – what more could one country want? And that, too, was what Cavour intended when he set out to unite Italy around Piedmont. He did not want the south.

And in the south the constant sound is of their neglect, their ruin, at the hands of the north. The southerner, they will explain, is a second-class citizen with little or nothing to say in the running of his own or his country's affairs, exploited by the north and doomed to live in want or to emigrate. There is nothing I can do; what could I do? is the continuous lament from individuals in the south. And yet, collectively: the civil service largely consists of southerners, as does the police force. More often than not the local prefect in a provincial city and the chief of police, both with immense power over the local citizens, will have come from the south wherever one meets them in Italy. The one Christian Democratic leader whose period of power rivalled that of Alcide De Gasperi – Aldo Moro – is from Bari. President Leone is very Neapolitan, the second Head of State to come from the old capital of the southern kingdom. At one time, when Scelba was prime minister and Martino the foreign minister, lobby correspondents had to keep their wits about them because both slipped easily into heavy Sicilian accents. The Socialist Party – a northern invention if ever there was one – is led by a Neapolitan; the Republican Party by a Sicilian; the Communist Party by a Sardinian; financial policy within the Government was for years in the hands of a Lucanian, Emilio Colombo, who in August 1970 became prime minister; by far the greatest of post-war trade unionists, Di Vittorio, came from Cerignola near Foggia; the Fiat works in Turin, Italy's showpiece of private industry, originally based on the highly disciplined workmanship of the upright Piedmontese, is now dependent on southern labour. This is an example of how internal migrations on a huge scale have changed the whole aspect of the problem of north and south, in one of the two great revolutions which have transformed Italian life since the war.

Vast armies moved from their homes. Up to ten million people moved in the two decades after the war, many of them illegally because for much of this period the Fascist laws controlling migration were in force and were designed to stop the very phenomenon which grew to dominate Italian post-war life – the shift from the country to the towns, and largely in terms of social significance a shift from the southern countryside to the northern industrial cities. The most dramatic visual expression of this process was the weary climb down from the daily train arriving in Turin from the deep south of southern peasants clasping cardboard boxes tied with cord which contained their possessions as they stepped into a new world and a new life. But many people have simply moved into the nearest town or city, leaving the land behind them, not just because there were difficulties in making a living from it but because they felt a kind of disgust for it, an urgent need to be rid of it, to leave it to its own devices instead of worrying crops from it, while seeking what they think will be a fuller life in the quickly expanding towns. In the quarter of a century since the end of the war the number of Italians living in towns has trebled.

The second great revolution, though the first in order of time, was the political revolution of the immediate post-war years. To identify it one has to leave Fascism aside for what it was, an aberration, and put Communism in its proper place as a challenge not a threat. Many a madonna will weep in the south at such thoughts, and somewhere in some police office files will be shuffled for a new annotation, but the political event of the century, quite literally, is that for the first time in the hundred years of Italian unity the Roman Catholic political forces came to power. And they were a mass force. Italian unity a century ago was shaped by an *élite*. It was anti-clerical and its final act of imposition, that of taking Rome in 1870 by a show of force from the Pope who had temporarily lost his French defenders, drove the Papacy into a bad-tempered voluntary exile. Not only the Pope but his followers too. The black nobility closed its doors against the new state as the Piedmontese royal family (the oldest royal house then still ruling in Europe, with a tradition of piety including an anti-Pope) came to Rome. Catholics were forbidden to take part in political life, and picture-postcards purporting to show an incarcerated Pope were distributed with requests for offerings from the simple faithful. Democracy, such as it was, was still led by an *élite* entrenched behind the myths of the *Risorgimento*. This was the formal position for half a century until, as if by divine intuition, the Popes were proved right: liberal, anti-clerical, democratic Italy collapsed. What else would one expect from a country that had humiliated Christ's Vicar? Mussolini took over the country. The Church made its peace with democracy's destroyer, with a politician who may have been mistaken for many things – the British Foreign Office thought him an important statesman – but certainly belonged to no *élite*. That was one of the reasons why the Vatican was able to come to terms with him. And then he, too, was overthrown, and his overthrow brought political Catholicism in the shape of the Christian Democrat Party into full possession of the keys of the kingdom (and later of the republic).

All this makes for fascination. But not for the clamp with which Italy can take hold of the mind, the grip of an urgent interlocutor with something vital and actual to say; it is all history to a great extent. Moreover, sentiment does not explain why Italy has this power, why it defeats more people than it improves, for the simple reason that, in many ways, it is too good to be true and so the truth requires so much more effort to comprehend. Too many people can make do with the parts that are just too good.

For instance, a traveller on a spring day a dozen years ago walked along Capo Colonna, outside Crotone in Calabria, where a child was sitting by the single classical column remaining from which this cape takes its name, a column of what was once the temple of Hera, the goddess of the earth. The child said, in an unaffected, unrehearsed tone how a column of solid gold used to stand there centuries ago and sometimes now, when the sun and the sea were right, fishermen saw a glint of gold on the sea-bed. And the shrine of the madonna? It was a fair question because there was a small chapel close to the column with a picture in it of the madonna. Oh! that was a miraculous image much revered by the people of Crotone: the madonna protected the place and deflected the bombs, sending them to fall in the sea. But she saw to it that they did no damage to the submerged column of gold, so that still the fishermen see the glint amidst the waves when the sun is right and the sea is right. When this little experience was recounted to an English priest working in Italy, he said with a look of glazed rapture, 'I wish somebody had said that to me!'

Another instance. In a central Sardinian village near to where a few nights earlier a family, including a child, had been machine-gunned to death while watching television, a traveller stopped for food. He asked in a shop where he could eat and was told there was nowhere in the village but he could join them in their meal. He happily accepted and went to close the door of his car. Luggage, notebooks, passport, money, all the means of getting to where he had to go, all were there in the car, and the door was hanging open to reveal all – it was a coupé – like some invitation for an embrace to a thief. 'Don't close the door,' he was told. 'People here will be offended.' He did not close the door and, of course, nothing was touched.

Another instance. One summer evening in 1960 the Palermo left-wing newspaper *L'Ora* reported that workers building a dam a few miles from the city had occupied the site. They had placed a barrier across the path leading to the site where they stopped any visitors and asked them their business. When faced with unusual cases, they went and asked for a ruling from the man who was organising the occupation, a heavily built man with spectacles and a black beret. It was Danilo Dolci whom one would have half-expected to see there. He was happy to explain the importance of the dam to sympathetic visitors and why it had to be finished, doing so with an easy authority because he not only knew the area well but had trained as an architect before settling as a social worker in Sicily. More than one view is possible about Dolci, his methods and achievements; there can be no two views about his gift for making simple people talk from their hearts. He has the world's most generous handshake. His warmth engenders warmth; this at bottom is his outstanding quality, and in terms of social conditions in western Sicily there should be no doubt about its exceptional character. The workmen, about fifty of them, sat at their evening assembly in a half-circle on wooden benches. Dolci with his guest sat at a trestle-table. He told them that he had someone with him who would be interested to hear what was on their minds. He added a hint that, as a friend from a long way away had come to see them, it would be both proper and useful to them to ask him a few questions about how they ordered things, including labour relations, in his country. The sunset was bright red. They ate food brought in parcels from the village. The first of the workmen to speak was a wiry, brown-faced man with a peaked cap and a prison record for banditry. He explained that they had occupied the site because they had been unfairly laid off. The company building the dam was being paid by the Government's Southern Development Fund; the payments had not arrived and, in order to put pressure on the bureau-cracy concerned, the company had stopped work, and because it had stopped work it no longer needed workmen and so they were told to go away with, probably, the hope that their treatment would stimulate them to make trouble and thus apply a little more pressure to the Government's offices. The workmen were having to suffer by not receiving their pay because of a conflict involving a huge construction company and the Italian Government. Given conditions in the south over the centuries, they might have accepted the situation with fatalism and a shrug of the shoulders. But the injustice was clear to them – even more so because of one of the interests controlling the company concerned: 'We are told', a man said, 'it is the Vatican.' They were at least trying to do something about it, to put the claims of humble, extremely humble, humanity amidst a tussle of giants. Southern apathy had momentarily been broken.

These are the successful little snapshots which for many people suffice as a true portrait. And, if attractive instances are to some sufficient on their own, they are not sufficient to account for the mystery of the country's grip on those who know it better. Much can be explained by Italy's past and by its continuity, which the child at Capo Colonna had grasped. Culturally, we are all Italy's children; actually, to see the mother as a geographical expression is in itself an excitement, the type of excitement which Goethe expressed with such emotional accuracy. But the past is not enough. Italians know that simple truth because they more than anyone else have to live with the relics of the past around them. There must be something in the present to turn what could be at best nostalgia into a potent experience. The fascination of Italy is that modern civilisation, the values of Western materialism both good and bad, are here confronted by the sounding-board of an ancient civilisation as well as by the people with the sharpest reactions in Europe. Italy provides a constant checking-process to our suppositions, opinions and myths.

The two types of Italy are not just one in the north and one in the south. That would be too simple an approach. Most of Italy belongs geographically to the Mediterranean more than to Western Europe. It is the only member of the European Community which has all its coastline on the Mediterranean. History has been a distorting process in the sense that it has constantly dragged Italy northward and westward. The accident of the presence of the Papacy in Rome was responsible for this distortion; popes needed secular support after taking over the inheritance of the Empire and were forced to look for it from Franks and Germans, not Greeks or Turks. It is a charming paradox that the policies of the popes have brought Italy to look westward and northward while the Papacy itself, in its ritual and behaviour, is formalistic, authoritarian – in a word, eastern and Byzantine. This strain towards the west happened again after the Second World War with the Papacy's near-recognition of America and the Western powers as the new secular arm. Social advance has since become identified with Italy's European vocation. There is a fear among Italy's more modern-minded politicians of the Mediterranean element in the country's character. Rightly, because it is strong; wrongly, if it is looked on as something to be discarded completely, a shameful trait, like being born in the wrong place or going to the wrong school. Italy has been to two schools and in both did more teaching than learning. Now the learning is being done, and done at high speed. The lesson of testing new fashions and ideals on its own ancient social structure and outlook is both damaging to Italy and absorbing because the final results cannot be foreseen; like a doctor who gives himself a deadly disease to prove that his cure is effective.

CHAPTER TWO

Men and Women

I HAVE known people for ten years or more, known them quite well, as well as you might know your next-door neighbour in the country or your colleague in the next office, before meeting their wives. Still less their mistresses.

This does not mean that the woman is unimportant. It means the opposite. The intimate relationship of the sexes is the foundation of Italian society but it is not based on the fetish of the couple. British and American practice is summed up by the 'You must come and meet my wife' insistence after the first five minutes of a new acquaintanceship, or 'My husband will enjoy meeting you, I am sure.' It would be very near irrelevant to an Italian whether or not his wife was likely to like you, and their outlook is much more rational than that of the West. How many people could genuinely say that they are as fond of their friends' wives or husbands as they are of their friends? Or would not rather see them separately, or just see the one they happen to like, or have something to discuss with, and never the other part of the bargain? The Italians have subconsciously grasped the point; not consciously, because they have not thought about it. But the effect is the same, except that you will not often see their wives separately, or not many of them. Still less, as I have said before, their mistresses.

The Italian male, as far as love, sex, seduction and related matters are concerned, is a much-maligned character. And on the whole deservedly so. There is something ridiculous about the airs of virility which an Italian male will give himself – the endless talk of sex and boasting around the bar-tables on summer nights, which all the listeners know is false or stretched to the point of the ridiculous or, if prospected in the immediate future, is unlikely to take place, however much manly anticipation of enjoyment accompanies the declaration of intentions for the night. Erotic chatter is thicker in the air in the south, and looked on more as *de rigueur* when two or more men are gathered together. A Piedmontese businessman recounts an experience which illustrates both the Italian failure to appreciate irony and this concern with talking about sex. He was in Apulia to visit a factory, and the local manager, an Apulian, drove him around the area while keeping up a constant discourse on sex. The Piedmontese became bored and decided to bring this barrage to an end by ridicule. He began talking himself and took over the conversation with stories, all imaginary, of the most preposterous sexual feats. But his irony was not grasped for what it was; the Apulian pulled in to the side of the road and said that enough was enough, he was too distracted to drive.

Even the suddenly liberated male who finds himself with an empty flat on a hot summer's night, after his wife and family have made their annual move to the sea, is not half the libertine, with no thought but sexual adventures, as he would have his friends, and himself, believe. This sudden disconcerting flash of freedom which most husbands experience as the hot months approach is delicately described by Ercole Patti in one of the stories in his *Roman Chronicle*. He follows the mental processes of a lawyer who suddenly finds a night of freedom before him and decides to use it. The house is empty. The television quiet. There is no reason to stay at home. And so he goes out. The women he encounters are beautiful; they have smart cars, ornamental dogs, deep tans; there is an atmosphere of sensuality as he walks the Via Vittorio Veneto. But his supper gives him indigestion. The second glass of whisky was a mistake. Instead of strengthening his resolve it made his head unsteady. He feels unaccountably tired. And he ends his night of bachelorhood before going off to join his family, in bed, at home, alone, at a quarter to eleven. Patti gives his story a sensitivity, a pathetic sensitivity, which is not necessarily typical of this male element of sexual flatulence when faced with the need for action, not boasting. But it heightens a common predicament and implies that the man is better than his boastings would have us suppose.

After the conversations at the bar-tables, there is the apparent conviction of many an Italian male, difficult for an objective observer to digest, that he is proving irresistible to a girl who is making no secret of her annoyance or amusement. It is another of the situations for which the Italian male is maligned, with good reason. Irresistibility is simply not borne out by the statistics. A survey conducted in 1965 showed not only that eighty-one per cent of Italian males objected to the closing of licensed brothels but that nearly three-quarters made use of prostitutes, which suggests a high degree of resistibility. By 1970 the business of prostitution was estimated to have reached an annual turnover of the equivalent of £65 million ($160 million), and was regarded as the greatest single source for financing other forms of crime. Strange as it may seem, it is true of Italy at least that you cannot be a successful bank-robber unless you have money behind you. The law, moreover, supports male fantasies of virile dignity, less than it used to but still quite heavily.

In December 1966, the ninth section of the civil tribunal in Milan (Milan, not Naples or Palermo) ruled that a wife's behaviour in forcing her husband to wash plates and carry out other domestic tasks gravely injured his dignity and was a just cause for granting a legal separation, there being then no possible recourse to divorce. Male freedom from the kitchen is an immense part of his emancipation, of course. It would still be difficult to recall having seen an Italian husband working in a kitchen, and never in any Italian home, humble or lofty, is there the slightest suggestion of helping with the washing-up, a tradition which in Britain is a fatal leveller of the sexes. The smarter women's magazines, which naturally are written by emancipated women, try to give the impression that since Italy began to become a modern country, around the year 1960, men are constantly in the kitchen, or leaping out of bed to make cups of tea for their wives. There is no reason to believe this, to say nothing of no wish to, and such fantasies can be placed for want of better evidence on the level of the sexual boastings of the men at the bar-tables on summer nights. Anybody can have their dreams.

Support for male superiority in a legalistic society such as Italy's naturally had its place in the legislation on family life. This legislation supported the man's habit of predominance because his status as head of the family was unquestioned until Parliament seriously began a revision of family law, including the granting of equal status to the wife, in June 1971. This revised legislation was unfinished at the dissolution in 1972 but was immediately taken up again by the new parliament and represented one of the few occasions on which public opinion was being led by the legislators. The draft was very advanced in content. The Constitutional Court and Parliament have diminished some of the man's legal advantages on the very proper grounds that they are unconstitutional, but they remain substantial. Until the Court was asked to pronounce on some of the more glaring discrepancies between the Constitution and family law, the husband could send his wife to prison for adultery while he himself could have affairs without number and without risk of imprisonment because marital unfaithfulness was only a crime for the woman. A woman's adultery was punishable with up to three months' imprisonment and could be cited as grounds for a request for legal separation (like that of a man forced to do the washing-up). A man's adulteries were only punishable if it could be proved that he had a lasting relationship with a woman which was cause for public scandal. For twenty years this legislation cohabited with the principle laid down by the Constitution that all Italians are equal before the law. The two articles in the penal code which sent an adulterous wife to prison and punished the husband only if he kept a concubine at home or 'notoriously elsewhere' were finally abrogated in December 1969. This judgement was one of the instances in which judicial action coaxed the more backward sections of public opinion towards a more modern outlook. One has only to bear in mind that charges of adultery could be brought by a man against his legally separated wife; and until the introduction of divorce in December 1970 she could take no further step to be free of her husband unless she managed to obtain an annulment from the ecclesiastical courts. Separations aside, the husband still retained the right to open his wife's letters, to forbid her to see people of whom he disapproved and, in certain circumstances, to strike her legally. And, almost legally, shoot her, because the penal code enshrined the principle of light sentences for 'crimes of honour'. If a woman left her husband, she would not have had the right, until approval of the new family legislation, to take away even her bridal dress. But the man's greatest weapon was that women in Italy, or the great majority of them, are still trained to manage a household and they can only with difficulty leave their husbands because they are not usually equipped to be economically independent. That was why a high proportion of women were against the introduction of divorce – for realistic not sacramental reasons. The woman would be lost without a husband, even if he beat her each evening.

This side of it is the jungle, the thick undergrowth of the collected concepts of traditional, old, largely agricultural, divorce-less, patrician, inflexible and essentially Mediterranean society. It is this undergrowth from which Italy is now emerging, often with great difficulty, and – where honest with itself – not without a sense of loss. Few people positively enjoy losing a feeling of security, and the past habits of mind were not all jungle, not all defects. Certainly the past was not simply raw material requiring reform as the great Italian advocates of progress are inclined to imply; nor is the whole concept of the complete shattering of society now as true as traditionalists, while wringing their hands, are inclined to think. A parish priest rang a funeral peal on the church bells when the divorce bill was approved by the Senate, saying that the funeral was of the Italian family. Things are no longer as extreme as in the Middle Ages when a father was entitled to break the leg of a son who threatened to leave the farm. But an outlook as ancient as the Italian view of the family cannot be quickly demolished. Where it has been there is a feeling of emptiness as much as of emancipation, especially for the women.

For the men, in the traditional outlook, life starts in a special sense the moment they are born. To have a boy-child is still something which the mother can boast of without limit; the blue ribbons fly at the main entrance to apartment houses with a special pride when a boy has been born to one of the families living in the block. Birth for the boy was traditionally the start of a long sentimental education. His life, unlike those of Anglo-Saxons, is lived from the beginning very close to women, and this closeness continues. The first of these women and by far the most influential is the mother. This might be true anywhere but it is nowhere as true as in Italy.

A man's mother is traditionally a composite figure. She lives three lives. She is first the young woman who gives birth to the child. If it is a boy she feels a gale of elation, of completion, of having given something immeasurably precious, a powerful feeling which the priests have managed to express in their talk of the Queen of Heaven which upsets the dour Protestant or the exact scholar of the Gospels; it is no exaggeration of the way a woman wants to feel, defining as it does, with the craft and power inherited from thousands of years of Mediterranean priesthood, the relationship which the woman wishes to establish and maintain. It was no coincidence that the most moving cinematic portrayal of Christ's relationship with his mother was expressed in Pasolini's film which set St Matthew's Gospel in a southern Italian background. The question 'Who is my mother?' gained greatly in poignancy and realism which Pasolini plainly intended as he cast his own mother as the Madonna. The feeling is common to all parts of Italy but its real strength is in southern homes. There the mother may have no rights. She may die unavenged if she damages her husband's precious honour. She may live a life of crushing labour, supported only by superstition. But, where poverty has not crushed away human dignity, she can be made to feel in primitive terms, within limited economic means, the queen of the house. Her span of physical beauty is short. One can listen with awe to the devotion with which a southern fisherman will recount how his wife at twenty-five years of age was ugly, but at the time when he married her she was very beautiful, and there was the feeling that his memories of that short blooming would see them both through the rest of life. It would have to, he was the first to admit.

Her second incarnation is through her son's wife. The mother's own relationship with her son is close and she bequeaths to his wife a vast legacy of understanding on the son's part of an unselfconscious relationship with women. This relationship has a depth which in the Anglo-Saxon world is unthinkable. She will also have taught the future wife during the usually long period of engagement, still customary in Italy, as much as she can of the boy's likes or dislikes, his favourite dishes, his quirks and virtues, how he likes his coffee – the best way, in other words, of giving him a guarantee of happiness and with it a guarantee of the wife's own satisfaction. This is why the traditional family was saddened if a son decided to marry, as is increasingly the case, outside the circle in which the mother may impose her continuing authority.

Her third incarnation is as grandmother. In this final cycle of life, her authority and experience are recognised and so is her usefulness. She feels and she represents continuity. A familiar sight in the depths of a Lucanian village used to be the grandmother of the local potter. The potter himself was aged about forty. He worked in a dusty, khaki shirt with a folded copy of a right-wing Rome newspaper on his head. He was making pots and vases from designs which were quite evidently Greek in origin. Understandably so as that part of southern Italy was colonised by the Greeks before the Romans arrived. The local doctor, for instance, has a fine collection of Greek pieces, an Apollo in particular that was enviable, which had been brought to him by peasants who had turned up these specimens while working their soil and had no money with which to pay him. The potter's grandmother was a tiny, grey-haired woman dressed in black with incongruously large boots. She might have been anything from seventy to ninety years old. The fact that they were potters and had always made what they were making now was the clearest thing in her mind. There had been changes in her lifetime; there was no longer a demand for earthenware dishes and flasks for cooling water because people were now buying refrigerators. It all went back long before even the members of the family whom she remembered as a girl, right back endlessly, she suggested, with the sweep of a bent hand. To complete the account, the potter himself was the last of the line.

It gradually becomes easier to understand why young men in Italy, so spoiled from birth, are so infuriatingly cocksure. Why young people until about 1966, when student unrest began, were quiet, unrebellious and frighteningly conformist. Why the country itself has produced eruptions of creative energy but never stomached a revolution, a 'breaking of the bones' which would also involve a break with familiar customs and lore. The break, but not the revolution, is now nearer than it has ever been. Italians, like everyone else, face a genera- tion gap, sons who take drugs and girls who run away from home. But it is a break more by imitation of others than by conviction. Why, to go back to apparent trivialities, an Italian will never queue (can you imagine the son of the Queen of Heaven queuing?); why they must constantly talk to keep themselves at full inflation. Why, to the southerner in par- ticular, as the south places such great weight on exterior impressions, treachery must be met by death and particularly if the treachery is on the part of the wife or a man's acknow- ledged woman. Otherwise the man will not be seen to have acted out his drama, a drama of retribution and self- justification. He must show to himself and to others, mainly to others, the sort of man he thinks he should be and the sort of man they should think he is.

The worst thing of all is to look ridiculous. A somewhat viciously right-wing newspaper in Rome once published a photograph of a Christian Democrat politician whom they did not like at the time because he was thought to be genuinely left wing (which he later proved he was not). He was small and was photographed from behind the rostrum at which he was addressing the national congress of his party. He was standing on several volumes of the telephone directory.

Palmiro Togliatti, the late leader of the Italian Communist Party, was not the type of man who could be easily subject to ridicule. He was mercurial, highly intelligent and about as soothing to his opponents when at his best as fresh hydrochloric acid poured on to old nails. He was normally adept at slipping out of the potentially embarrassing situations into which the clumsiness of the Russians was inclined to force him. Except once. On the eve of the twenty-second congress of the Soviet Communist Party he was photographed placing flowers on the tomb of Stalin. It was clear to all that Khrushchev had not told him about the impending defenestration of the despot's bones. Fortunately, from the point of view of his own reputation, there was a feeling in Italy that the Russians were impossible people to deal with anyway, especially after the end of the clarity imposed by Stalin's tyranny and the arrival of a man as impulsive as Khrushchev.

From the politicians downward a formidable barrier stands to protect the ruling classes from disrespect and thus from ridicule. This is one of the reasons why political satire is almost unknown in Italy except in a few intellectual clubs. Politicians must first give their permission if they are to be mimicked on television. A member of parliament is addressed as 'Honourable' for the rest of his days even if he loses his seat at the next election; he does not pay on the railways, will have a state motorcar with driver at his disposal for the rest of his life once he has fought his way up to being a minister, and will expect to find constituents in his office bearing well-cured sides of ham, or half a lamb, and can scarcely be expected to lose the savour of all this just because some satirist decides to poke fun at him.

All officials – and the category of public employees includes post-office clerks, policemen and bus-drivers – are protected by laws which punish as a crime the *vilipendio* or insulting of one of this enormous confraternity. It is reasonable to suppose that the Head of State should have protection of this kind as he has no other form of defence and in any case holds a symbolic office, which cannot be said equally of a bus-driver. But the protection goes through all the ranks of officialdom, a long, long list. Once, in a thoughtless moment, a foreigner told a post-office official who was being unusually and purposely unhelpful, 'Remember, you are a public servant!' thinking in some residual Anglo-Saxon way that the man would thus be put to shame. Instead, it was as though the unfortunate member of the public had spat obscenities across the parlour-table at a nun. 'Moderate your tone!' was the outraged answer, and there was nothing for it but to do so and admit defeat, as Italians are constantly having to do in this skirmish with the public powers. There are signs of a more liberal attitude: a Rome court laid down in August 1971 that a policeman in civilian clothes and off duty could not claim his full rights and privileges as a public official when involved in a traffic accident which he himself had caused.

There is frequently a delicate balance between the ridiculous and the non-ridiculous in Italian behaviour. Self-centredness makes people less critical of their own actions and so more inclined to behave in a way that others will think ridiculous. But the moment of actually being made to feel ridiculous is so dreadful a shock that the slight shift from silliness, apparent to all, to feeling silly, realising that one is looking foolish, brings an explosion of rage or shame or indignation or horror out of all proportion to the slight change in the situation visible to the outsider. This is what accounts for the sudden furies, tears, violence, dramatic striking of attitudes, the physical attack on an overtaking driver, the strutting off the stage in white-hot pique. Chaplin was too late with *The Great Dictator* to bring ridicule to bear on Fascism. Italians were not able to see the film until two decades after the end of the war.

On 26 October 1959, in Florence, there was an incident at the national congress of the Christian Democrat Party when one of their leading personalities reacted strongly to heckling. Italian politicians are not used to being seriously heckled, less then even than now. This man was under attack from the young people in the Party on the grounds that he had, allegedly, given facilities at the time of Suez to the British and French forces. He was also accused of being too much to the right, and there was a shout of 'Fascist!'. From a silvery-haired statesman, who at the time was prime minister, he changed in a second to a ridiculous figure, his face white with emotion, eyes wet with tears, running from the stage until he was brought back and given a bunch of flowers, to the cheers of his supporters. Dignity returned, and the rules of how to behave towards the older and wiser patriarchs on the platform came back into force. Despite its ridiculous elements, this was not an incident likely to do grave damage to a career. Memories in Italy are short. This man went on to become president of the republic. Though it is of deadly importance not to be made to look foolish, people will forget about it quite quickly, especially if the person concerned is a politician with power.

The architect of this whole outlook on life is the woman. She spins the skein of Narcissus around her son and makes him all but invincible to the arrows of hurtfulness; but not quite invulnerable, so the penetrating of these defences is that much more wounding and humiliating. The woman does not need the scaffolding of the law like that built around male prestige. Her authority is clear. It becomes so at an amazingly early date. At a wedding near Trieste, which is about as far north as one can go, the young man's bewitchment with the elegance of his bride in a charming white dress was complete: the design of the dress had naturally been kept a secret before the ceremony from him and from members of his family. His sister suggested that perhaps the bride, too, was charmed by the elegance of her bridegroom. 'Oh, no! She chose everything I have on, from my tie to my socks,' he said, not without pride. It is sometimes wrongly thought that attachment first to the mother and then, in somewhat similar terms, to the wife is a southern characteristic. A report on young peoples' behaviour issued in 1970 showed that, if anything, *mammismo* was stronger in the north than the south. What greater rights can women lay claim to? They are the arch-conservatives and, although the more advanced thinkers among them claim much, the majority would have settled for a long time to come for no divorce, a decreasing number going out to work, a steady drop since the end of the war in the number of women in Parliament, the indignities suffered by the rice-workers in the north and the olive-pickers in the south and the mixture of scandal and almost breathless triumph when a Sicilian girl became the first to defy the ancient tradition of the island by refusing to marry the man who had kidnapped and raped her.

The case of the Sicilian girl who became the first 'dishonoured' girl in the island known to have refused to marry her seducer is historic, but in the opposite sense to what was thought at the time. The girl's name was Franca Viola. She was of modest family and lived in the western Sicilian town of Alcamo. She was engaged at sixteen to a young blood of the town, Filippo Melodia, who had the ways of a spoiled bully which Sicilians take for manliness and was said – though without much conviction – to have his connexions with the Mafia. The girl broke the engagement, saying to her father that Melodia expected her to be nothing more than a slave. The young man's attractions were exerted in various ways: the girl's father's barn was burnt down and his vines ruined. Then Melodia and his friends kidnapped the girl, held her prisoner and freed her after she had been raped on the understanding that she could now do nothing but marry her violent lover because no other man would accept a 'dishonoured' girl. Melodia was also confident of coming to no bad end because the Italian penal code – article 544 – lays down that marriage between a raped girl and her assailant extinguishes the crime. Franca Viola refused this solution, and her father backed her. She became almost a national heroine; not quite, because Sicilians saw better than northern journalists the likely result of her courageous decision. She met the Pope; offers of marriage and of work were sent to her. Melodia and his friends went to prison. History had been made, we were all assured; Sicilian girls would now be so strengthened by Franca Viola's example that they, too, would refuse to marry their seducers if they did not happen to love them. She and her father had taken two bold steps: rejecting a fundamental

Sicilian custom and having recourse to the law. In December 1968 the girl married a young man from Alcamo and they moved to Monreale in order to be closer to the husband's office in Palermo. In July 1971 an Italian reporter had difficulty in finding where she lived: for two reasons. People did not like to talk of her because they disapproved of what she had done; and many people had forgotten her presence because she seldom came out for fear of attracting attention to herself. The fear was not of vendetta from Melodia's friends but of the glances and the comments of other women. In the words of a local *carabiniere* she should not have sent Melodia to prison ('What did he do wrong?') and should not have refused to marry him. That was not how to behave in Sicily, and she was Sicilian. And what had she gained by it? 'Now she lives practically a prisoner and has few friends.' Change in Italy is not a natural development. It has to be imposed.

Even education is no sure talisman of social progress, as the case of another Sicilian woman shows. Antonietta Bagarella was born in 1944 at Corleone into a poor family of illiterates. She was intelligent and set herself to study, and eventually became a schoolmistress. On 3 August 1971 the special tribunal in Palermo ordered that she be kept under special surveillance for two and a half years for alleged connexions with the Mafia. She thus became the first woman to be officially confirmed as involved with a criminal organisation regarded as exclusively male. Her experience could be regarded as furthering women's rights, if one's predilections are in that direction, or as disheartening evidence that education cannot alter the traditional outlook of western Sicily. Women work less in the fields, less in the textile mills, less indeed in the whole of industry than seventy years ago; more as secretaries, shopgirls, models, receptionists, a tiny few in diplomacy, some as judges; there have been applications for consideration of women as engine-drivers, and in January 1971 inmates of the dreadful old Ucciardone prison in Palermo were pleasantly shocked to find a twenty-six-year-old girl as deputy governor, though she only lasted a few months before being moved when somebody realised that if the governor were absent the prison would be in the hands of a girl. At the present stage of women's emancipation, the decision can hardly be questioned. A woman deputy governor of Rome's Rebibbia prison caused a scandal in 1972 by being discovered having an affair with a prisoner charged with killing his mistress. She maintained that when he was free she would marry him – a strange echo of the Franca Viola case.

The point of all this is that the impression of emancipation is there because more girls have jobs which bring them into the public eye; not because more are working. Many of them still have to overcome the obstacle of a father who feels dishonoured by having a working daughter, as if he were not able to support her at home. Since the beginning of this century, the total number of women going out to work has dropped slightly, but the proportion of the female population who work has fallen dramatically. At the 1901 census 5,260,000 women out of 16,320,000 went to work – a proportion of thirty-two per cent; at the 1971 census the total was 5,031,000 out of 27,500,000 women – a proportion of nineteen per cent.

Society is still not equipped to provide women with this freedom. It is opposed by prejudice, lack of proper training and lack of facilities such as nursery-schools which would free a young mother to continue working. As these facilities do not exist, a working mother must rely on domestic help. Servants are not only becoming more difficult to find but they are much more expensive, especially after the introduction in July 1972 of the law by which Italy's 600,000 domestic workers became entitled to full social-security benefits. This measure meant that the employers were bound to pay substantial contributions even for part-time household workers.

The Constituent Assembly which met in 1947 to draw up the republican constitution had 19 women members. The first parliament, elected in 1948, had 44 women out of 574 Deputies in the Chamber. The sixth parliament, elected in 1972, numbered 23 women among the 630 Deputies: the Communist Leonilda Jotti, was chosen to be one of the Deputy Speakers; she is also a delegate to the European Parliament. One of the few women to make a name for herself in Parliament was the Socialist schoolmistress from the lower Po valley,

Angelina Merlin. She succeeded in getting legislation passed in 1952 abolishing licensed brothels. She used to complain that women were inferior citizens – a *sottoproletariato* – yet surprisingly, in January 1971, she lent her name to a campaign to abrogate the divorce law. The organised feminist movements are regarded by most Italians as curiosities. In early 1973 there were five main groups; their membership was small but energetic and present in most big towns.

The Italian shopgirl is a delight, if a tantalising one; the Italian secretary is a horror. The latter will take no initiative. She will be sharply demanding on the telephone when asking whether you intend to accept her employer's invitation to drinks next Thursday which she forgot to post to you, and furiously feminine, unable to say, in a hair-tossing mood of really not knowing or not caring much one way or the other, if you ask whether an appointment with her employer is possible within the course of the week. 'How do I know, he's not here. . . .' The shopgirls have fewer pretensions. They hate to sell you things. Often you have the feeling that they know exactly what you want but have no intention of letting you have it. Their salesmanship is amateurism run wild. It is difficult to break into their conversations with each other, animated and obviously of constant importance. If you say that something in the window has attracted your attention they may spare you a second of interest to agree that it is attractive. Ask whether they have it in another size and they will smile magnificently while admitting that they do not have the faintest idea. It would be beautiful to think that their attitude is really a protest by strong-minded young women brought up to know how to sew, and cook, clean the house and smile, against the advance of materialism. Of course, it is nothing of the kind. It is just that they are thinking of other things while being shopgirls. And from about the end of 1969 onwards labour troubles began affecting the department stores, and protest against what was felt to be exploitation joined a natural lack of aptitude for organised selling.

Italian women on the whole are much less brilliant than their men. This is a consequence of the mother's influence. The men from the start of their conscious lives are flattered into showing themselves off, and this includes talking. The results can be marvellous. In all classes and in all regions, Italians talk wonderfully well, with an ease and an unconsciously rich use of the language. There are none of the inhibitions of the Anglo-Saxons who avoid a pretentious or elegant vocabulary for fear of actually seeming pretentious in character or knowledgeable. This difference is one of the reasons why Italians read very little by comparison with, for instance, Britain. The total daily sale of newspapers was 5,200,000 in mid-1973; in Britain with much the same population daily sales are three times this figure. At least three-quarters of all newspapers are bought by men: the Milan newspaper *Il Giorno* estimated early in 1973 that women accounted for less than ten per cent of its daily sales. The five million when worked out in relation to the number of inhabitants places Italy near the bottom of the European scale as a consumer of news. Italy is ahead only of Spain, Portugal, Yugoslavia, Albania and Turkey. Even the reading of a newspaper requires a degree, however brief, of solitude, of not talking. Given the choice, most Italians will prefer to sit with others and turn the pages of an illustrated weekly and talk rather than sit and read. 'I have not read the book,' a woman says in a well-known cartoon, 'but my friend read me the summary over the telephone.'

In some ways this taste for talk is a great blessing. It has meant that television has not had the disastrous effect on conversation that it has had in Britain or in the United States. Italians enjoy watching television. They enjoy it more if they watch it in a bar than in the sitting-room. They are in company. They can talk it down. And do. There are moments when they are prisoners of their sets: the annual San Remo song festival used to be one of these events; a vital football match in a country obsessed with watching sport. The World Cup semi-final in 1970 attracted a larger audience than the first landing on the moon. But it is seldom that one hears, as in Britain, a conversation opening, continuing and ending with a reference to the television programme of the night before. Also, perhaps, because yesterday in Italy is deader than yesterday in the Western world. And tomorrow holds far higher hopes than today, whether of business triumphs, winning the lottery, erotic pleasures, or being able to provide the family with a reasonable meal. There are still many who rise in the morning not knowing the answer to the basic question of feeding hungry mouths. The active population of Naples, for instance, is between thirty and thirty-five per cent, and it is said that about one-fifth of the income of Neapolitans comes from smuggling. And still more people are far from clear on the first of each month where they are going to find the money for the rent, the grocery bill and the hire-purchase payments due at the end of the month.

Most wives still shop in small businesses rather than in supermarkets. There are far too many small shops in Italy on any rational count in relation to the population. This has always been so and the tendency is increasing despite the concentration of people in towns and cities, which ought to help the process of devising a more rational system of retail selling. At the end of 1970 there were 1,100,000 retail shops in Italy, 300,000 market stalls and 250,000 bars and restaurants. Each shop can, on paper, have 50 customers as opposed to 1000 in the United States. The average takings of an Italian shop is 25 million lire a year as opposed to the equivalent of 80 million in France and 100 million in Germany. An official American report on Italian food distribution, referring to the situation at the end of 1966, stated that the United States with a population of 200,000,000 had 227,005 retail food-shops and about 2700 food wholesalers. Italy with a population of 53,000,000 had 499,966 food shops including 600 supermarkets and 43,939 food wholesalers, or about one for every eleven retail food-shops. Since that date, the number of shops has slightly increased but fundamentally the situation remains the same. Rome as late as 1972 had a food shop for every 93 inhabitants: the national average was one food shop for about 110 inhabitants. Both shopkeepers and customers are paying the price of an inefficient marketing system. This system came under its closest scrutiny in August 1972. Prices rose steeply during the holiday weeks. The Government's attempt to freeze prices brought angry reactions from shop-keepers, especially in Rome where shops and markets closed in protest, leaving the field open to the supermarkets and to the theorists who began to explain to a now more responsive public why the whole system required overhauling. The move from the country contributed, in one way, to bolstering the old system instead of imposing an essential reform. Men and women who move in from the land, especially if they are elderly, can adapt themselves to running a small shop better than to working in a factory, and so try to face a new life by opening the traditional type of grocery shop or a tobacconist's.

But the housewives are also respecting an ancient tradition. Too much is sometimes made of the continuity of Italian civilisation from classical times. But a glance at Pompeii or at the ruins of Ostia Antica shows that the small shop with its slate recording credit is one of the continuing elements in life. Political parties, including the Communists, support the small shopkeeper. The small shop has two huge advantages over the supermarkets. The first is that credit is a natural part of dealing with small businesses and to the shopkeeper an outstanding bill is a form of assurance that the customer is tied to this one shop. It can be embarrassingly difficult at times to pay at a shop where one is reasonably well known. Credit in Italy is a way of life. For some, the only possible way of life. There is a habit of paying something at the end of each month which may well not cover the outstanding account, and the final settlement, as the monthly gap widens, is left until the husband receives his double or treble salary in December or some stroke of luck comes the family's way. The second great attraction of the small shop is that the housewife can talk to neighbours and friends, see what they are eating and buying. Life is still a public matter in Italy and privacy is seldom respected and seldom wanted. There is no Italian word for privacy.

An Englishman's home is his castle. An Italian's home is where he goes to eat and sleep. He seeks an occasional respite there, not a permanent refuge. And when inside he will probably have no way of avoiding members of the family. The result is that Italians spend a large part of their day in the company of other people and know a great deal about their neighbours and friends. This semi-public living has been the habit in the Mediterranean since the first civilisations around its shores. Public living can be studied, just as it was in the ruins of Pompeii, of Ostia Antica, in the daily life today in the old quarters of Naples and other southern towns. One of the reasons for this is the climate. But there is a temperamental difference which cannot be explained by climate. Loneliness is a greater problem in northern countries than in the south, especially among elderly people. But solitude, the idea that a man or a woman can voluntarily and contentedly prefer to keep themselves to themselves, or at least keep the public part of their lives to a minimum is, except in such rare cases as religious solitaries, a characteristic of the north.

Italians eschew solitude. Semi-communal living brings its own problems to relationships and tolerance. Italians are always being accused of having no civic sense but they have a strong communal sense of the group to which they belong. They are also much more at ease with people and so give an appearance of greater affability and spontaneity. Their natural situation is in company and so they function smoothly in company with others. To do so they require gifts which to the Anglo-Saxon mind are defects as much as qualities. The very art of talking and behaving easily is inclined to be suspect in the more reserved atmosphere of the non-Mediterranean reaches of European civilisation. Italians have a fatal fluency and, if transplanted to an Anglo-Saxon background, would be forced to break up the streams of words with innumerable hums and ha's and hesitations if they did not wish to pass for glib. And they bring to a fine art a quality which to their northern neighbours is once again on the frontier between quality and defect, that of saying what they think will please. It may be near the truth, or just a gentle distortion, or it may bear almost no resemblance to the truth at all but will give pleasure. Absolute truth, in any case, is not particularly attractive to the Italian mind.

The most important outcome of public living is the lesson it gives in secretiveness. What you do not see of Italian life is extremely fascinating. The private proportion of life, small though it is, is jealously guarded. That is why the newspapers have few advertisements for lonely-hearts' clubs but a wide choice of private investigators. Italians know that their life is an inverted iceberg, if such a thing were physically possible, of which the nine-tenths above the surface is engaging but means little: what matters is the tenth which is out of sight. That is why the place abounds in secrets, and in people trying to find out more than meets the eye. Conversely, the average Italian takes for granted that the truth may never be revealed about scandals, assassinations, plots, the intriguing by which certain political prisoners are not brought to trial: all this and much more belongs to that small proportion of life which perforce must be kept in the shadows because so much else is public knowledge.

The talk of the women is much more mundane than that of the men. In most cases they do not expect to be judged by their intelligence and wit, with the exception of a few fine talkers who have the social position and background to demand attention. Most Italian girls will have grown up in an atmosphere in which their brothers were given more attention and they know that the centre of the stage is a male province. In the north, it is being taken more for granted that husbands and wives may both work. This is partly because the pay of an industrial worker is not enough to provide for his wife and family. On the whole women still prefer to run a household than to have a job. At the same time they have their frustrations. In ten years the columns of women's magazines specialising in help with readers' worries have received five million letters. It is clear that the talks with friends, the visits to the confessional, advice from the family, are not enough for a great number of women. At the end of 1970 reports began to appear suggesting that the consumption of alcohol was increasing, in particular among women. In Italy it is still a rare sight to see a man drunk.

Alcoholism is an increasing problem, but the average Italian is not a great drinker either by comparison with other countries or with Italians' own past practices. Italians in late 1972 were drinking an average of 106 litres of wine a year, 11·8 litres of beer and 1·7 litres of spirits. The respective French figures were 112, 41·3 and 2·3. In the decade 1900-10 the then population of 33,500,000 drank nearly 120 litres a year each. The present average comes to about a quarter of a litre a day. Though the greatest producers of wine in the world, the Italians are third in order of average consumption: Portugal comes first and France second. Italy is nineteenth in the order of the average amount of spirits drunk and fortieth as a consumer of beer. Italians treat alcohol with respect and despise drunkenness as shameful. In women it is judged still more severely. The slight rise in their drinking is presumably explained by the additional pressure which modern living places on a woman who has not yet discarded the habits and duties imposed by older standards.

This accounts for the growing indication – including a substantial proportion of letters to the women's magazines – of objections to the Italian male's claim to sexual virtuosity. These signs had reached such a point that in April 1971 as serious a newspaper as the *Corriere della Sera* devoted a long article to 'the Waterloo of the latin lover'. And the illustrated weeklies were busily printing interviews with psychiatrists, gynaecologists and similar experts to explain why Italian women, always regarded in the past as elect among women, if for no other reason than that they marry Italian men, were proving for the first time unruly wives, discontented, dissatisfied and, by natural reaction, inclined to blame their husbands for failing to live up to the legend woven around them – mainly by women. The Italian male is his own worst advocate when dealing with the Italian female. He is inclined unconsciously towards superiority or a certain patronising kindness; he has been manipulated but without his knowing it, by his mother, his sister, his mistress or his wife and so is at a loss when genuine problems of relations with the opposite sex require rational elucidation. The extreme nature of his predicament was described by the *Corriere della Sera* in the following terms: 'Exhausted by work, derided or insulted in the matrimonial bed, humiliated by reports in the illustrated press which goad him to the point of drawing blood, snatching from his grasp the last shreds of what he believed to be a national flag, what does the future offer for the poor ex-Latin male?' Things look bad. But the real point, which neither side is likely to face, for totally different reasons, is that an account has now to be settled with reality. The male by his upbringing and by the examples of one or two renowned symbols, of which Casanova and Valentino have been the most influential, believed quite honestly and completely in his virile superiority in international terms. The Italian woman used to regard herself as the passive but grateful beneficiary of his affections and mother of his children, however many there should be. Both are now having to adjust their standards to a truer average. It is a point of interest that in 1973 only about two per cent of Italian women took the pill, and ninety per cent according to a survey regarded fidelity as essential to marriage. But one change was being felt. The old distinction between wife and lover was breaking down: wives were demanding more of what would in the past have been reserved for the lover. The critical sense was increasing on both sides. For the woman, marriage had to be less of the final aim to be achieved and more the beginning of a life together. The men grasped the point much earlier than the women. But it was the men, after all, who had to stand eight hours a day in a factory while the women on the whole awaited them at home. And it was they who felt the strains of the technological age which was making life easier in general for their womenfolk and much more strenuous and tense for the men. The women in many cases simply did not possess the knowledge to diagnose what was wrong nor the imagination to understand what both now required. They had never been brought up to pry – indeed, had been severely discouraged from prying – into the more scientific notions of sexual partnership. But suddenly the magic had gone and there was nothing in its place. Neither the men nor the women could fairly be blamed, and they were both at a loss to face their predicament because of the almost total lack in Italy of instruction in sexual matters.*

Italian women are fanatical about physical appearance. Not because, as with the men, they fear to look ridiculous, but because they fear looking half a degree less than their best outside the home. It is not just personal pride, though they

* The naval base at Taranto shocked local opinion in June 1973 when the first course ever given to Italian sailors in sex education was tried out experimentally there, not so many miles from the birthplace of Valentino himself.

are almost as vain as the men, but pride in the good name and good standing of the family. The women in this sense are perfectionists. An open sports car with a girl in it will as likely as not have a hairbrush behind the windscreen so that she can put herself in order at each traffic light or traffic jam. The allure of the walk of Italian women is due to the advantage they take of never walking any distance unless it cannot be avoided; sensible shoes, in the Italian sense of the term, are not those that help them to walk with greater comfort, but shoes which show them off to better advantage. Their dress sense is conventional but usually impeccable. They somehow manage to adapt either fashions or themselves to innovations. They used to depend on local dressmakers to copy a modish dress but lately have been buying far more ready-made clothes. No one would have believed that Italian girls would have worn the mini-skirt. It went against their training, against what their priests have been telling them of feminine modesty (Padre Pio, for example, the late allegedly miracle-working friar of the Gargano, specified the exact length of the skirt to be worn by women coming to him to be confessed, and Vatican guards refuse entry to St Peter's to women in short skirts or sleeveless dresses), and, more important in the final analysis, against what seemed most suitable for the typical Italian frame. But they took to short skirts with surprising grace and dignity. The fashion was not regarded as a symbol of emancipation. It was a new way of looking attractive. That is also why they managed to change with equal skill to long dresses; because they regard fashion as embellishment, not as fashion for its own sake.

Female emancipation was one of the high ideals with which the air was full, along with other strange noises, in the immediate post-war years. The explanation is that women had gone to prison for their beliefs during the Fascist period or had shared exile. They played their part in the Resistance movement. Pavese's beautiful novels of the period are unfair about the conduct of the women during the German occupation; they were proud of what they had done in the national liberation movement. The left wing in particular pressed for the rights of women. At the end of the war women did not have so much as the right to vote. They were given the right in 1947. It was the Christian Democrats who were most anxious that they should have the vote. Women were the arch-conservatives, after all; they listened to the priests; they were afraid of hell; in the final count they meant the most because they were the pivot of the family and brought up the children. And certainly they have been a stronghold of votes for the Christian Democrats. The left was inclined to be more radical in the matter of women's social rights. Immediately after the war, a Socialist deputy, Umberto Calosso, argued that women should have full equality, and be allowed the initiative even in sexual relations. No suggestion, however heady the air in the immediate post-Liberation days, could have been more doomed, not just because it was plainly unacceptable but because of the potential damage the thought of such an idea would have on Italian society.

The truth is that the women have the future if they want to take it but will certainly not do so. At the beginning of 1970 more than half (sixty-two per cent) of pupils in primary and secondary schools were girls; they accounted for nearly three-quarters of the enrolled students in the liberal arts. In character they are more determined than the men. But they are still the man's inferior, beginning with fundamental inequality before the law. 'The law is equal for all,' it says in every court in the country; but everyone knows that it is not equal for rich and poor, not equal for anarchists who are continuously rounded up for interrogation after political violence, not equal for the Mafia who seem to be able to slip out of sentences of guilt like an illusionist from the centre of the stage, and, finally, it is not equal for women. They did not make it their business to press for reform of family law which was promised them by a succession of governments and finally pushed forward in Parliament.

They have the whole of Italian manhood to look after; and that they certainly accept as their business. Almost every Italian male above the age of about twenty has some sort of fixed relationship with a woman; a fiancée, a wife or a mistress. There is nothing to compare with the tradition of bachelorhood in countries further north. 'Shall I never', asks Benedick in Messina, 'see a bachelor of three score again?' The answer is 'Most unlikely.' The men will sometimes go to immense lengths to show the value they place on their chosen woman's affections. A young painter once took a very youthful widow to live with him. He not only kept her child as well but gave her everything that she asked for, without question. He had a small amount of property which he was forced to sell. He found her a job, and she put her entire salary into a savings account and continued to ask him for more money. What should I do? he would ask as a total breakdown in his finances came nearer. It was clear that he would do nothing, and would face ruin rather than a break with this dictatorial beauty.

The view that Italians are emotionally superficial, exploding with rage, dissolving into tears, striking dramatic attitudes, totally overlooks the deep reality of personal relationships which are in no way superficial. Personal relationships are extraordinarily personalised; it is a commonplace that Italians love children, and indeed they take an unusual interest in them, but their generalised regard for children has nothing to compare with the love they feel for their own children, and it is much the same with the women in their lives. Generalisations about Italian conduct are usually correct because Italians are a conformist people (not the great individualists they constantly claim to be). Generalisations such as: though loving children, they are cruel to animals; though setting an immense value on physical beauty in a man or woman, they feel no pangs for an exquisite landscape spoiled; though extremely courteous under a roof, they jostle on the streets and drive with no consideration whatsoever; they are capable of marvellous feats of personal bravery but reject fighting as the pursuit of fools. Judgements of this kind are easily made and nonetheless true. But they do not so much as hint at the emotions involved in what seems a commonplace situation.

Society is naturally built around the realities of Italian feeling in a way that administrative life is not. This is the chasm between the two. It is often said that every country ends with the police it deserves. This cannot be entirely true of Italy. Italians have the holidays they deserve; there are many of them and each celebrated for itself, very fully with its proper meaning. They have the shops they deserve, small, inefficient, too expensive, pleasant to deal with. They have the language they deserve because Italian is a language urgently wanting to be talked not written; there would be nothing for it to do if people stopped talking it. They have the personal relationships which they deserve, in which hatreds can run deep and feuds may still continue their relentless way; but there is a deep fund of humanity in their personal relationships which is naturally at its deepest between men and women. It is the most precious essence, the sacred deposit left after centuries of experience. 'Once Italian humanity is lost,' Corrado Alvaro wrote in his *Last Journal*, 'everything is lost.'

CHAPTER THREE

Figures in a Landscape

I LIVED off the Via Appia Antica for two years and began a novel there which opened with the sentence: 'It was the day the sun set behind a peacock posed on a haystack.' As indeed it was, and not so remarkable at that because if the peacocks were not posing on the haystack they were strutting through the pergola of roses or eyeing, one foot in the air, the pump-house which quivered with rhythmic impulses when the electric motor was in use. But the difficulty with this novel was to show some connexion between this apparently exotic (though accurate) description of the background and the very unexotic people living in it who would be involved in a rather bloodthirsty but earthy plot that I had in mind. The effort to make the connexion taught me a good deal about place, about the spirit and meaning of place in Italy.

They were not my peacocks; the peacocks and the haystack belonged to a peasant farming a few acres of the Roman *campagna* (the countryside around the city which astoundingly reminded Dickens of the Home Counties) on a share-cropping basis. He had the house next to mine. He gave a proportion of the crop to the landowner; and paid as well a small rent; his life was frequently taken up by finding ways of convincing the owner that once again the harvest was virtually nothing. Share-cropping is now approaching extinction in Italy but for centuries has been the main form of land-tenure in the central regions. It is a typically Italian arrangement. The law lays down the percentages to go to the landowner and the part to be retained by the farmer. Each invariably wanted more than his due and very much more than was being proposed by the other partner to the bargain. There were no absolutes: there seldom are in Italy. Who can say, after all, exactly how much better or worse the harvest was this year with all the usual uncertainties attached to agricultural life? The farmer is in the best position to know and also knows that his interests are to conceal the truth if things are going well and to exaggerate misfortune into disaster.

The man with the peacocks had moved to this farm from Subiaco, a town in the hills south of Rome famous as the retreat chosen by St Benedict from the licentiousness of the city. And famous in another way as the birthplace of Gina Lollobrigida, who by coincidence lived across on the other side of the Via Appia Antica. The peasant was later to leave the farm and move on to Rome itself, setting up a stall in the big open market near St John Lateran, thus becoming a fully fledged element in the huge process by which Italy in a few short years changed from a nation made up largely of country-dwellers to a nation predominantly of city-dwellers.

Another of his, and my, immediate neighbours was part of the same process. This fellow was a stocky, moustached Sicilian dressed invariably in a cotton singlet and cotton trousers which changed unobtrusively with the seasons to a woollen singlet and woollen trousers. He had large blue eyes which shone with good humour until something went wrong, when they froze into an impossible combination of ice and lava, like the snow on his native Etna. This Sicilian lived more modestly than the peasant. He had found his way northward with a wife and two children and was living in one room of a half-collapsed, probably medieval, outhouse at least half of which was rubble, but fertile rubble because weeds grew thickly in it and his chickens found enough to eat from it to keep them alive and laying. One had the feeling, too, that their energetic laying was a response to the slight air of menace which surrounded this household, not altogether unwarranted because the man was known to beat his wife. He made some money by going off on his motorscooter to mind a petrol-pump. At night, when he was in, the motorscooter stood on its stand in the middle of the one room.

Both he and the peasant from Subiaco would talk for hours about where they had come from; neither would ever become prosperous because the world was against their types at the time. They were just statistics, or would have been if the collecting of statistics in Italy were not so haphazard a business. But wealth would have been no recompense for having had to leave their homes in the search for economic improvement. They used to sit on benches improvised from beautifully inscribed slabs of Roman tombstones (the Via Appia like all the consular roads was lined with graves) beneath one or other of the overgrown rose-pergolas covered with semi-wild blooms, in the midst of a patch of vines, each man with a glass of wine in his hand which was about as semi-wild and wholesome as the roses themselves, each with the sun setting behind him and the peacocks taking their final stretches which would have swept Horace Walpole into a delirium and have brought marvels of silver prose from Pater. And there they were, talking about Subiaco's fame as a supplier of wet-nurses to over-burdened Roman families. Landscape was a background accorded no importance at all. They might just as well have been in the local pin-table hall or the Wimpy bar on the Via Veneto which a British ambassador was later to have the temerity to declare officially open.

The place that mattered was the birthplace. The immense pull it has will last another generation. All this partly explains why many Italians feel no pain when some magnificent land-scape is destroyed for the benefit of a building speculator. They are not particularly worried when they hear that swimmers on a deserted beach along the magnificent coast of Calabria emerge covered with oil. And a really successful citizen who makes money in America, or becomes a minister in the Government or a *monsignore* in the Pope's court comes back to the village or town where he was born to build an ugly villa for himself, or sees to it that the local post office is rebuilt, at public expense, in the most dreadful pseudo-Fascist style which is still the Italian style for official buildings (a commentary in itself on what they think about officialdom). The benefactor who has ruined the main *piazza* will have a plaque placed on the awful new building expressing the gratitude of the townspeople. Or, if he becomes really powerful, he can wreck the whole place from top to bottom. Ample funds combined with quick, unplanned expansion frequently destroy the last remnants of local character.

Italians ask each other where they come from in the same way as Englishmen talk about the weather. And for the same reason. There is such a variety. An Italian who comes from the mountains of southern Calabria, the Aspromonte, and an Italian from the Lombard plain are divided as far as any two people from the same continent could be divided by purely geographical differences of environment. After the family, the place, the birthplace, is the next most powerful idea in the formation of character and outlook. One example sums up the genius of place. Italy has been ruled since 1963 almost without a break by coalitions based on an alliance between Christian Democrats and Socialists – an unlikely alliance on paper because it meant bringing together Marxists and Roman Catholics in the same cabinet-room and thus much depended on the holder of the office known as the Presidency of the Council of Ministers, the equivalent of prime minister. These governments were led at different times by three very different prime ministers. The first was Amintore Fanfani, a dynamic, sharp-minded, abrasive, highly intelligent and blazingly energetic little man without self-doubt (as far as I know). Then there was Aldo Moro, a large, slow-moving, slow-smiling, courteous, tormented-looking figure said to suffer from low blood-pressure, with an attractive quiff of silver hair which, combined with his pained expression, made him popular with women for his television appearances, a man of great manœuvring ability concealed beneath tortuous rhetoric (he invented the description of these centre–left coalitions, which is so utterly Italian in its logical nonsense, as 'converging parallels'). He was followed by Mariano Rumor, a friendly, quick-witted, devout, mercurial talker, hospitable, tense behind his ready smile, painstaking in trying to deal with difficult colleagues (and no prime minister had more-difficult colleagues) but never ponderous. The first is a Tuscan, the second an Apulian and the third a Venetian. Each stamped his administrations with the spirit of his own place. I ventured in an article published by an Italian newspaper to talk of a Tuscan centre–left, an Apulian centre–left and a Venetian centre–left. The only partial objection came, I was told, from Moro himself who wrote a letter to the editor of the newspaper concerned, in his own deliberate longhand, seeking reassurances that Apulian was not meant in any pejorative sense.

Of course, there is a massive difference between north and south, even if it is sometimes exaggerated. History and geography have played impertinent tricks on the peninsula. The Mediterranean for most of the course of civilised human history has been the centre of life. Reaching it is still, in the full Johnsonian sense, the real object of travel. I never cross the Alps southward without excitement for the descent. The accounts of medieval pilgrims, with the ink freezing as they wrote, or the wild sledge-runs which eighteenth-century gentlemen made in crossing the Piedmontese Alps, still make evocative reading. Looked at from the Alps, Italy sweeps out like a huge pier into that primary and now increasingly polluted sea. This peninsula contains some of the most beautiful sights in Europe and the most beautiful works of man's genius. Throughout much of Italian history, the urge northward has meant a vocation towards greater vigour, a more modern outlook at every point in history and, increasingly nowadays, a sense of belonging to a more quickly developing civilisation. Italy regards membership of an integrated Europe as an assurance against falling back into the static ways of Mediterranean life, as unprogressive in the modern sense as the tideless sea itself. Seen from Rome, and even more from north of Rome, the Mediterranean is a temptation not a stimulus. Apart from Israel and Malta, Italy is the only functioning democracy in the area. It functions uncertainly but the machinery has so far been preserved. The task of Italian politics is to find the energy to do more than keep the machinery in existence; it is to find the conviction and means to make it work. This is the real importance of the European idea. As far as political development is concerned, the choice is Europe or a secondary place, and the perpetual threat of falling back into a Mediterranean mortmain.

The first impertinent trick of history was to set the Holy See in Rome. The presence of the popes meant, in the first place, that a city and a country which ought to have gone the way of all seats of vanished empires were forcibly kept alive and dragged into European affairs. Ozymandias refused to be dismembered. The idea of this special visitation on the part of St Peter is not limited to Rome. At opposite extremities of the peninsula there are legends of a possible presence of Peter: from the Piedmontese Alps, where his passing is still recorded in humble villages, to the southern stretches of Apulia. At Otranto a beautiful little Byzantine church is pointed out as the first Catholic church to have been built in Italy. It is dedicated to St Peter who, according to pious tradition, landed there on his way to Rome. And slightly further north a coastal village has the strange anomaly of a sixteenth-century tower built for defence against the Saracens, just like other towers lining this coast, with the difference that a chapel has been added to it dedicated, again, to St Peter. On the morning on which I saw it, the walls were plastered with slogans: 'Long live the Prince of the Apostles.' At whatever date these legends came into vogue, they suggest a relatively early – probably early medieval – concurrence in the special place given to Italy and not only Rome in the pursuance of the story of the Gospels. The presence of Christ himself in Italy, except in visions, plays no part in Italian legend. The nearest example of his actual physical intervention that I have encountered was his allegedly miraculous part in giving the lakes at Avigliana, outside Turin, their curious formation. He came to the place as a poor man and was turned away from each house except that of the poorest woman in the community. The village was destroyed in a tempest of divine wrath and covered by a lake, except for the house of the poor woman which next morning stood alone and unhurt on an isthmus.

The popes as religious heads of western Europe and successors of the Roman emperors secured for Rome its continuation as centre of the civilised world. In doing so they assured three separate existences for Italy itself: the south, the centre and the north. The split between western Christianity and the eastern Christianity of Byzantium made its contribution to these differing outlooks by its continuing influence in parts of the south. The eastern empire which Constantine had planted in Constantinople continued for another thousand years after the western empire fell in 476. Its influence was strong in Sicily, Calabria, Apulia and Sardinia for some four centuries after the collapse of Rome, and briefly in Justinian's revival of imperial power at Ravenna in the sixth century. But it was much less the Byzantine presence in the south than the papal presence in the centre which imposed different historical destinies on the three parts of the peninsula. The popes constructed a state of their own across the centre of Italy which effectively cut off north from south. Involuntarily the popes were arbiters of Italy's compartmented growth.

History is by no means everything in explaining Italy. But some aspects of the past cannot be ignored. The south was great and flourishing long before Rome was thought of as a power in the world, imperial or ecclesiastical. The south was Greater Greece, *Magna Graecia*, colonised by Greek cities, a faithful extension of one of the fundamental civilisations to arise around this sea which has taught man everything except modern technology. Their temples were huge. Like colonists everywhere they built much larger public buildings than they needed and in a grandiose style. For later generations they are perfect because they make such impressive ruins. One of their new towns – Neapolis – still boasts of being older than Rome, and Neapolitans still reproduce what must be the nearest equivalent to daily life in classical times. Naples is one of the great tests. Some people hate it and some people love it. I think that people who do not like Naples are afraid of something.

The break between north and south came near to being corrected only once between the fall of Rome and the rise of the modern nation of Italy. If this development had been completed Italy would, of course, have been the heart of the system, and physically undivided as a heart must be. The prime mover, the great would-be corrector of history's impertinences to Italy, was the Emperor Frederick II. He was half-Norman and born and bred in southern Italy and Sicily. Frederick's failure is normally rejected with such excuses as that he was ahead of his time, a doctrine comfortable to the mediocre and, when applied to him, more hollow than usual because the times have not caught up with Frederick yet. The answer is simple indeed: he ran foul of the Papacy. His outlook was not simply intellectual, or probing into the future: the recent history of the south, up to his time, gave him ample justification for what he was trying to do. The Saracen conquest in the ninth century followed by the imposition of a form of Norman feudalism in the south had already sketched a solution to Italy's eternal problem, the dilemma of how to humanise the centaur. Frederick was an amalgam of European and Mediterranean qualities. His experience was of an enlightened despotic rule in Sicily which he aimed to apply to the whole of Italy. His Sicilian upbringing gave him a Mediterranean attitude, though a very vigorous one – a vigour perhaps inherited from his German forebears; his birth as a member of the House of Hohenstaufen gave him the Empire, which he inherited from his father Henry, son of Frederick Barbarossa. His father was crowned in Milan with the iron crown of Lombardy in 1186, and Frederick was born in Jesi in Apulia in 1194. The Mediterranean element was perhaps stronger in him than the northern strain – though a Hohenstaufen, he spoke Arabic and not German – but he might have achieved the splendid European edifice standing on the twin pillars of Italy and the German Empire. These ambitions were defeated by a combination of the Papacy and the French. The popes had no intention of losing their position as arbiters of Italy's fortunes and can hardly be blamed for that, otherwise they would have surrendered the process of history which had made them masters of Rome. For this perfectly understandable reason, the popes wrecked what Europe should have been. With one of the ridiculous paradoxes which history can so readily supply, the representatives of a religion which was nothing if not Mediterranean in its origins filtered its influence through the country which should have been the bridge between the two parts of Europe and in the process left Italy split for centuries. Frederick of Hohenstaufen's house was destroyed by Urban IV, a French-born pope who brought Charles of Anjou, the French king's brother, into Italy. In 1266 Charles of Anjou defeated and killed Manfred, Frederick's illegitimate son, and two years later defeated Conradin, the last of the line. Frederick's failure, first to unite the country as it had been united under the Romans, and second to make Italy the second pillar of the secular empire (instead of just the seat of the spiritual power) could only be followed by fatalistic acceptance of permanent division.

The seal was placed on this fatalism by the direct rule of the Spaniards in southern Italy from 1559 to 1713. The sixteenth century may seem a long leap from Frederick II, but the main lines of Italian history are in fact closely connected over varying lengths of time and for this reason lend themselves to synthesis. The Spanish hegemony meant for southern Italy a long period of bad government combined with religious bigotry, out of keeping with the Greek outlook which had been preserved there with some faithfulness as Italy's natural inheritance from the Mediterranean. Spanish officials imposed heavy taxation and held back Italian intellectual initiative. Their presence coincided with the full force of the Counter Reformation. Inevitably the Counter Reformation was a restrictive force on intellectual enquiry even if, as in Italy, there had been no Reformation to precede it. At its best it represented a popular reaction to the intellectual fervour and pseudo-classical hedonism of the Renaissance. Some such reaction was inevitable because in artistic as well as social terms the Renaissance spirit left little room for advance along its own lines. What is there left to do after climbing Everest? The Renaissance as a 'marvellous form of paralysis', in Guido Piovene's words, explains the cultural and aesthetic meaning of the Counter Reformation in Italy. In Rome the Inquisition was bad enough. It broke Galileo, and burnt Giordano Bruno before he could pay for his coat. But the austere Spanish approach was more mystical and, in terms of free enquiry, far more damaging, and it was the Spanish version which fell with full weight on southern Italy. The south was dominated by a power which was admittedly Mediterranean but not in the Italian sense. The defects of southern Italy were enlarged and the dispiriting historical load became heavier.

The effects were to be felt long after the Spaniards left. The naturally strong family-ties of a Mediterranean people were not only reinforced but turned in on themselves as protection in face of an unjust and insensitive state. The client-system, the regular acceptance of fatalism as a complete outlook on life, the seemingly infinite patience in face of injustice, the deadly slowness of the bureaucracy, the brief but vicious intensity of sporadic uprisings such as the Sicilian Vespers when life became intolerable (there were echoes of this feeling in 1969 during the riots at Battipaglia when police shot two citizens and in the Reggio Calabria rebellion in 1970 and 1971), the distrust of others, a distrust of the State amounting to hatred, the fashioning of tight associations for self-protection of which the Mafia is merely the best known, the constant feeling of being exploited, the sharpness of wit where there is a prospect of gain (early in 1970 the Cardinal-Archbishop of Naples introduced identity cards for his priests because American tourists were being increasingly robbed and swindled by thieves in ecclesiastical dress), the economic decay – all made a precocious advance during this period, and most of these elements are present in southern society today. What used to be called the Kingdom of the Two Sicilies, with Sardinia, which was also under Spanish rule, knew no sustained period of good government after the end of the Roman Empire, and for its real greatness had to look back to pre-Roman times. There are still connexions with the great past in humble life. Croton, the Greek city of which only a single column of the temple remains, was protected by Apollo, and Pythagoras taught there. It was he who first taught musical therapy, practising what he called 'purification' or healing through music, doctoring the soul by means of harmony. Peasants in the south still use ancient incantations as cures, and they frequently mix Christian and pagan symbols and ideas. A Lucanian cure for a headache still in use a few years ago, and probably continuing, depends on the incantation begging that the pain 'be raised, as the sun rises, and God our Holy Saviour rose'.

The central regions of Italy have had different sorts of deities. There was not so deep a conflict between Christianity and pagan religion, and most of this area was governed after the fall of the Empire by that delightfully unpredictable system by which a usually mature, if not elderly, man is chosen pope. For about a thousand years successive popes ruled central Italy as part of the responsibility for being Christ's Vicar on earth. They preserved the *mystique* of Rome. They were the main thread connecting the classical world with modern civilisation. But it was not the direct connexion with the Greek world which the south still possesses. This connexion, however, in the European context owes most to the Papacy's acceptance of the imperial heritage and the general refusal of Italians to countenance revolution as a solution to their problems. There have been plenty of revolts in the face of intolerable injustice; there have been uprisings caused by the transient attraction of a particular personality: never a desire to begin again, not even after the fall of Fascism.

The popes had no interest in seeing Italy united, and when national unity was achieved had to be forced out of their capital, of which they had made, from the Renaissance on, so lovely a city, so demanding in its requirements on the individual, so cynical in rejecting whoever cannot come to terms with it, that no greater mistake could have been made in terms of objective judgement than to put the capital of a young and uncertain nation within its corruptingly sacred walls. Romans are often referred to as the least attractive Italians, the least courteous, the least charitable, the least ready to help, the least Christian in a word. They are, in fact, warmer than they seem, but the impression they give is of real products of a city misgoverned for centuries in the name of all that is sacred by a semi-divine priest-prince. In his *Last Journal* the Calabrian writer Corrado Alvaro wrote of Rome:

> On the bus a man who was selling Red Cross stamps for the tuberculosis drive gave me stamps for half the money I paid him, taking advantage of the fact that I was about to get off. At the post-office, a wretched, anaemic female clerk with vulpine features denied receiving the thousand-lire note that I had given her a few seconds before for the purchase of stamps. And you have to be perpetually on guard, even in public places, against the customary attempts to cheat you of fifty, or a hundred or five hundred lire, or sometimes as much as a thousand lire.... You are constantly compelled to regret having been decent, kind, compassionate. You are forced constantly to defend even your smallest pleasures because there is always somebody lying in wait to exploit them....

Alberto Moravia once said that Rome's greatest quality from his own point of view was that it had taught him common sense. That is to say, in a kinder way, in the way of a man to whom Rome is home, and a more constructive way, what Alvaro was trying to express.

Rome should obviously have been left as a kind of European sacred city, a Mecca, a Benares, under the rule of the popes. Instead, the capital of Italy was grafted on to it, and with civil servants and immigrants it grew horrifyingly fast. In 1870, when the Italians took it from the papacy, it had 230,000 inhabitants, in 1940 one million, in 1967 2,500,000 and by the end of the century it is estimated that it will have four million inhabitants.

Such a fate might have overtaken Florence, which was briefly the Italian capital before the move was made to Rome. Florence is the other peak of the central Italian genius. It is brilliant and assertive; argumentative and self-assured; it still has sparks of the old Renaissance genius but no longer the material around them to burst into flames. I confess I have never deeply enjoyed Florence apart from the possessions in its buildings and museums. But I have never met a Florentine who has not assured me that I have only to spend ten days in the city in his company to emerge converted. I have not so far done so. I suppose because I do not want to be argued out – and none argue more insistently than Tuscans – of an instinctive impression. But, Florence apart, there are few experiences more beautiful than travelling through Tuscany in the spring. It is the greatest garden in Europe, part naturally made and partly the work of man (who decided where the cypresses should grow, man or nature? and who, indeed, thought of cypresses at all as they give no harvest, not even shade), apart from Venice, which is the supreme example of how men correct and exploit nature and nature co-operates or submits. (And, like Naples, Venice is a test; those who claim to dislike it usually blame the tourists but what they really mean is that they cannot stomach a dream come true.)

This co-operation on the part of nature ought not to count. Italians refuse to be landscape poets. Chateaubriand remarked that French landscape-painters discovered the Roman *campagna*. They will not regard natural beauty as worth preserving, they will allow oil refineries to be placed in their country under less stringent conditions than elsewhere and ignore shameless building speculation which has disfigured their finest cities. But the co-operation between man and nature is there and was not in origin meant to provide scenic beauty. The man-made element in the scenic beauty of central Italy is the result of centuries of the use of agricultural methods intended to favour the fullest possible exploitation of hilly and mountainous land. In one respect only is the co-operation fully intentional; in cooking. Central Italy by general agreement has the best food in Italy, just as central Italy – Siena, to be exact – speaks the finest form of Italian. Cooking in Italy fundamentally consists of serving something exquisitely fresh with the least amount of modification in the process of preparation. The kitchens of Florence or Bologna or Arezzo or almost anywhere in Tuscany or Emilia or Romagna follow the same principle. Emilians are the heartiest of central Italians but there is a natural sturdiness about central Italy north of Rome which to the south falls away into fatalism and northward vanishes into fogs and industrial haze.

The crown of the Lombards now kept at Monza in a double-doored altar-safe was known as the Iron Crown. The iron is, in fact, provided by the flattened remains which it incorporates of what is said to have been a nail from the true cross. It is right that the north should have such a symbol. Lombardy and Piedmont provide the industrial weight, the effort which since the end of the war has made Italy the seventh industrial power in the world. Its lifeline, unlike the rest of Italy, is no longer the sea and its backbone is no more the mountains.

About one-third of Italy is covered by Alps or Apennines, which share with the sea the geographical domination of the peninsula, and have made it a difficult part of the world to inhabit. By centuries of labour men have managed to make something of this unhelpful legacy. Long before the rise of Rome the formula had been devised for making the best agricultural use of the land. Grain was planted on the comparatively tiny amount of coastal plain, then olives on the higher ground and vines up to 3000 feet. Fertility is in general confined to the coastal plains, such as the plain around Naples, another around Foggia, or narrow strips carefully tended, like the plain of Metaponte, with new zeal since the post-war elimination of malaria, or reclaimed land like the drained lake of Fucino and the Pontine marshes south of Rome (which were settled by Mussolini in Roman fashion with ex-soldiers who took life easily until the boom of the black market in Rome during the war really provided an incentive to hard work).

The north has a completely different shape and geographical character. Its life-line is the Po, the one navigable river in Italy. The great northern plain along the Po valley is limited by the mountains not cut by them, the Alps on one side and the Apennines on the other. They are extremities not dominating factors. In this strictly geographical sense there is a north and a south. The river is the centre of life in the valley, cutting across the country instead of up and down with the mountains attempting to enclose it from both the Mediterranean world and its immediate European neighbours. Once over the plain, the traveller is in the familiar background of an Italy rising from two seas, the Adriatic to the left and the Tyrrhenian to the right, with a mountain chain down the middle.

The mountains have succeeded in keeping the two geographical schemes apart. Mountains are complacent edifices. They make man sorry if he tries to exploit them. At best his efforts are puny and depend not only on the grace of the mountains in letting him live without disaster but also on his acceptance of their mark on whatever he may produce. In the Piedmontese Alps, for instance, the few remaining peasants (the sub-Alpine civilisation is now nearly dead except where ski-ing provides a dash of fresh prosperity) will still explain in their slow, deliberate manner, as if speaking is not natural to them, that the flavour of their potatoes differs according to the height at which they have been grown (like the variation by altitude in the taste of wines, or Sardinian or Alpine honey) and that anyone from the area worth his birthright can tell where a potato comes from by its taste. Now, of course, nobody wants their tiny, hard-grown, variously flavoured potatoes. In many parts of Italy potatoes are traditionally regarded as fit only for pigs and in any case nowadays it is much easier to grow large, inflated Dutch potatoes and much easier to sell them. In any Alpine village in the autumn the outhouses of the few remaining farms still inhabited will be full of unsold potatoes, and a man with a black cap and a puzzled, tanned old face will mutter on about Dutch potatoes: 'They have no flavour you see....' And soon he and others like him will be dead, and no one will remember the flavours anymore.

But the mountains have their weaknesses, their vulnerable heels. The Alpine passes have, historically speaking, been far more important than the mountains themselves. In fact, the Latin word *mons* was first used to denote a pass and not a mountain and survives in the names of such passes as the Moncenisio. The first known word for a pass was *mont*, and it was a long time before the name was applied to the peaks. Passes seem to have a pull of their own, as if the narrowness drags travellers, and armies, into the fissure as the Danube waters did when the Iron Gates closed in on them. The strategic value of the passes accounted for the importance in European history of Piedmont, the far north-westerly region, which for no other reason was to become the prime mover in the creation of national unity and would annex the rest of Italy to its own royal house and administrative system.

Turin, the old Piedmontese capital, is now Italy's greatest industrial city. Since the war, the northern industrial cities have been settled by hundreds of thousands of men and women from the countryside and the south. They look for any work at all which does not mean continuing to work the soil; to an incredible extent, the move from the land was not a calculated move taken after much rational argument across the kitchen table, but due in many cases to a deep hatred for the soil, for the farms, for life in the country, as if suddenly the peasants were aware that they were regarded as second-class citizens, unattractive to women, socially inferior to the Fiat workers. Others came in search of a safe job, in a background which they think will be what they have seen on television. Italians in general and young Italians in particular seek security with an alarming insistence. From the moment their schooling comes to an end, and sometimes sooner, they begin to apply themselves to the task of finding security.

The former agricultural workers have inflated the population of Turin as they have most of the northern cities. In twenty years its population doubled largely through immigration. Social problems as a result are huge. A slight indication of what this movement means can be seen in the old centre of Turin, around the cathedral and the Roman gate. Throughout Italy the historic centres of the towns and cities raise problems. They are not suited to modern conditions of living unless the inhabitants are willing to invest a great deal of money in improvement or are ready to endure privation. In Rome the first solution is gradually taking over the centre: people with the financial resources, and this mainly means non-Italians and frequently Americans, are taking the inside out of the centre, installing lifts and mock-antique surroundings while leaving the outer walls standing; in Turin it is the second. The seventeenth-century houses have been taken over by southerners and the whole dilapidated area has been turned into a southern town. The washing across the streets, the menacing-looking men in striped shirts who stand around the market-stalls, the atmosphere of vice born from poverty, the plaintive wails of the women; it has nothing to do with Western Europe. And yet Turin is nothing if not a European city.

The modern-minded Italian looks on the southern heritage as a burden, too much connected with the ancient, static, semi-oriental civilisation of the Mediterranean – a civilisation which has done nothing to try to adapt itself to contemporary living, untouched by the modern movements of *Risorgimento* and Resistance on which Italian democracy is supposed to be based. The whole outlook of the south is regarded as inimical to the European vocation, seen as an effort to bring Italy firmly into the industrialised society of the West. Democracy has scarcely been tried there, and where it has it has collapsed into dictatorship. The vigorous communal life of the north in the high Middle Ages had no counterpart in the south, and its subsequent history has been of foreign occupation and, for long periods, of bad and oppressive government which prevented any tradition of relationship between governors and governed. Sardinia is the extreme case (even if geographically it lies less to the south than Sicily or the southern mainland), but if other parts of the south were unable or unwilling to keep their ancient ways as intact as the pastors of the Barbagia they have remained stoically faithful to the tenets of Mediterraneanism: a fatalism, a mysticism, an ability to look after their own immediate wants in the face of cruel invaders and a cruel nature. But, unlike the centre and north, southern Italy has somewhere deep in its mind the idea of political unity, however faint. It was a united kingdom from the time that the Normans took Sicily from the Arabs in 1061: it is five years older in its Norman Conquest than Britain. Although it has been occupied, stifled, sacked and oppressed, the south has a tradition of unity in diversity which the makers of modern Europe are inclined to overlook.

Intellectually the south has always more than held its own. This strength continued after the unification. Pirandello and Croce, Bellini, Verga, Tomasi di Lampedusa are an impressive group to come from one part, and that the backward part, of one country. And the sheer granite substance of the southern mind, its relentless search for the sources of real power, remains unsoftened by moving to the north away from a southern background. This immovable quality combined with the southerner's natural sense for conspiracy brought into being the famous societies for self-protection – the Camorra, the Sicilian Mafia, the Calabrian Honoured Society. This mentality has proved extremely adaptable to conditions elsewhere: indeed, it has every chance to grow in an atmosphere where it is barely understood and ineffectually opposed. This mentality is not like truffles or true Chianti: it can and does spread where the need is felt and yet remains genuine, its dreadful self. The accepted date of the unmistakable mark of southern delinquency in the north is 21 June 1970, when an old peasant found the body of a man on the outskirts of Turin. The man had been burnt to death with petrol as a punishment for having given information to the authorities. It was the sign of the ultimate contempt and at the same time a warning to others.

By their mere presence in massive numbers in the north, the southerners are having a decisive influence on the siting of industry. The huge growth of the northern industrial cities brought congestion: physical congestion, not simply congestion of the social services. From the autumn of 1969 the workers themselves showed that they were no longer willing to accept the social conditions in the industrial cities. These two factors provided the strongest stimulus the northern industrialists had felt to look towards the south as the destination for future investments and industrial development. The pressure of the southerners forced a move which intelligent planning should have suggested a quarter of a century ago. It may have come too late. It would be ironic, the final moral triumph of *laissez-faire*, if the resources were no longer there to carry it out and the will of the south to continue as part of modern civilisation had wilted. At least the southern proletariat ceased to accept the crowded northern cities as models. This rejection must in part have been due to a vital resource which they had themselves, the only vital resource which the southerner has and the northerner has not: something of the Mediterranean in him and an awareness, often dimmed, of a proper dignity to be insisted on whatever the form of current oppression. Industrial civilisation is killing the Mediterranean and soon it may well be little more than a surface mass of oil and plastic. But people who have had direct contact with it have something to offer to western and northern Europe. The real southern problem has nothing to do with north and south. It has to do with poverty, which should be dealt with in all areas whether in the depressed Piedmont countryside, in the decay of the sub-Alpine civilisation, or in what was once the kingdom of Naples.

One of the glories of the old kingdom is the baroque Apulian city of Lecce. There is an old-fashioned hotel there, wood-panelled with large, heavily framed looking-glasses, elderly people at the reception desk and a restaurant where the head waiter is proud to be able to offer local food cooked in the traditional manner: a restaurant and hotel that are provincial and pleased to be so. A woman entered, aged about fifty or so, with a commanding face and powerful physique. She wore a short-sleeved cotton dress as if she had come straight from the kitchen. Three men were with her, one of whom was obviously, from his silence, her husband. The other two were brothers. The waiter asked them what they wanted. The woman replied in a voice with a heavy Emilian accent that they wanted wine and bread and mineral water. 'And nothing to eat?' they were asked with an air of southern patience. The woman ignored the waiter and opened a parcel which she had brought in with her. She began cutting up the home-made sausage which it contained, giving a slice to each man. She stood throughout this ritual and, knife in hand, said to each man, 'È buono ... ?' in a tone of voice midway between a question and a statement of fact. Each of the men went through the motions of tasting it and said, one after the other, 'Yes'. To have said more or less would have been impossible. Eating with solemn faith in the wholesomeness of the sausage, under the eyes of an overbearing housewife, they had suddenly transformed their table in a southern restaurant into the kitchen of a northern farmhouse. It was a splendid evocation of regionalism in which north and south as such do not matter. People are different and they do better to relish what they are with no offence to those not like them.

Place is as important in the north as anywhere else, for the north is not just industry and smoke. It has its beauty: the lakes, the hills of the Langhe between Turin and the Ligurian coast, the mountains themselves, the Venetian countryside, above all the misty romanticism of the Po delta, which is the one fairy world to which Italy can lay claim, a pervasive atmosphere because there is more than just the mist above the waters. The wine and the eels of the delta combine with a delicate earthiness, and the nets and the marshes are delicate and grey; and the delicacy meets its high point as one moves north from the delta to Venice and its lagoon. Yes the north is not the industrial monster that it is sometimes made out to be – the north industry, the south agriculture and soul. The north has its regrets, is aware of the process, unique probably in its force, of seeking to throw off the whole sense of the old life, as though, in Alvaro's words, 'youthful intolerance had made headway in the mind of one of the oldest peoples on earth'. It is a painful period for many Italians. At times they seem to be holding on almost desperately to the civilisation that they know and which their innate conservatism calls on them to abide by; at other times they seem desperate to shake it off, like a farmer who aches to drag off his boots and his old, earthy jacket and have nothing more to do with the soil and crops and animals.

Mantua is on the Po and a beautiful city. Riccardo Bacchelli, author of the novel, *The Mill on the Po*, wrote with a fearful power of prophecy of unhappy change and worse to come, after stopping in the city in the autumn of 1942.

Now as I stand looking out from the vantage point of the grassy promontory of the church of the Angeli, I can see a luminous fog covering the whole human and natural phenomena and investing it with an almost dream-like quality. The very sounds of the roads of the ancient city, near and far, seem part of the dream. And the horns of the passing cars seem like the trumpets of a phantom hunting-party or a tournament which has been dead for many years. At times breaking through the wintry fog, they seem like the sharp peals of the brass trumpets in the overture of Monteverdi's *Orfeo*.

What remains of the past? A patina of gold and faded purple covers the shimmering stagnant water, the yellow reeds on the river's edge and morning snow. Vainly and foolishly I cannot deny the fact that I would willingly be part of any age other than today's.... If my sadness seems immoderate and uncontrolled, I can only say that places and ideas such as Mantua and Italy are of such enduring nobility and ephemeral loveliness that grief at their destruction is incurable. And therefore I feel no shame because, standing here on the shores of the Mantuan lakes, or anywhere in Italy, the memory of Italian greatness and beauty moves me to tears.

There is nowhere better than Mantua to have such thoughts. There are plenty of other places in Italy, in the centre, north and south, just as likely to bring such pained sadness to mind.

CHAPTER FOUR

Beauty and the Past

THE sensitivity and the foresight of Bacchelli are rare. But his combining of greatness with beauty is typical. The idea would be accepted unconsciously by most Italians, though in a distorted manner, which makes one wonder how justified are the claims – to be fair made exclusively by non-Italians – that Italians have an inborn grasp of beauty and are its great practitioners. Trying to define what beauty means to other people is always an impertinence. In the case of the Italians, however, the attempt must be made because the relationship between them and beauty is the most revealing relationship of all and, because of its intimate character, the most difficult to comprehend unless one is content to accept the theory that the sense of beauty is inborn and go no further, as if a sense of beauty were like the pagan opposite of original sin.

Among other uncertainties, the theory of an inborn sense of beauty leaves unexplained why so many Italians appear quite oblivious to the damage done in the name of progress to so beautiful a country. At times they seem consciously intent on destroying splendid scenery, or allowing the Continent's finest collections of artistic treasures to be neglected, and the

archaeological wealth to be untapped – except by the illegal
diggers and the expanding trade of thieves specialising in works
of art. The process of destruction has been propelled
monstrously forward by the pollution attending industrial
advance, and this problem only became a political issue in
early 1971 when it was taken up vigorously by Amintore
Fanfani, then presiding officer of the Senate. In November
that same year, the Communists organised a conference to
debate man's relationships with nature in a social context.
Commissions and discussions were frequent. Their usefulness
was questionable. Italy in 1973 had eighty-one laws which
could be applied to limit pollution. With rare exceptions, they
were simply not applied.

There is no limit to the value placed by most Italians on
physical beauty. A beautiful woman or a handsome man are
immediately admired for their good looks and elegance: and
there the matter stops. No other qualities or defects are worth
worrying about if physical beauty is evident. 'She is right to
be jealous, her husband is a *bel uomo*.' This sort of remark is
constantly heard; it is of no account that he might be greedy,
or selfish, or kind, or intelligent, or thoughtful, or sulky. He
is handsome. If he is rich, all the better because then he will
be in a position to buy beautiful clothes for his chosen woman
and show her off to best advantage from a beautiful car.

The repetition of such a remark over the centuries is one
of the reasons why the Italians do indeed make the best of
themselves: the farm-labourer washing his one white shirt in
the running spring so that he will be elegant for Saturday
night; the constant attentions which a girl will apply to her
make-up and the correct fall of her long hair; the unabashed
scrutinies of themselves by both men and women in any mirror
that happens to be close. 'What a piece of work is man!' is in
their hearts if not on their lips for much of the day. 'You are
looking well,' one girl will say to another. 'How do you think
I am looking? Tell me ... tell me ... how do you think I
am looking ...?' That is really what she wants to know.
Indications of this attitude constantly spring to mind. One
afternoon in a modest restaurant in southern Italy, so far south
that the sea which lay almost at the door, motionless in the

torpor of the sinking sun, was a mixture of the waters of the Adriatic and the Mediterranean, an elegant woman with red hair and an emerald ring sat at a table with her mother. Her style was Milanese but her voice still slightly southern so that no great detective skill was necessary in assuming that she was a southerner who had married some reasonably prosperous businessman in the north. She got up suddenly and took another seat at the same table so that her back instead of her profile was towards a man seated across the room with a younger woman. 'That', his companion explained, 'was because you did not look at her.'

The reverse is also true. The malformed, the ugly, the unsound of mind, all the unfinished creatures born under an unlucky star or maimed are best hidden away, put out of sight, if possible not thought of, as if there were something shaming about having produced them. They are looked at pityingly and scornfully as they sit on the steps of the parish church, better left to the nuns who have voluntarily abandoned this beautiful world.

At the 1972 Biennale, a young mongoloid worker, Paolo Rosa, aged twenty-seven, was put on show as part of an exhibit. The public indignation was great, and no doubt to a great extent genuine: this was no way to treat this poor fellow, and the man responsible was accused by artists and critics of Nazi tendencies. But there was also the feeling that such ill-formed creatures should be kept in the shadows – for everybody's sake, not just their own.* Only when physical handicaps are put to practical use is acceptance felt to be due. Here is an instance. Some years ago a hunchbacked dwarf made a name for himself in the back streets of Naples by his extraordinary skill in making two suits out of one. He would obtain cast-off or surplus American clothes, take them apart and make two suits or jackets, each much smaller, of course, but fit for children. This tiny magician's fame spread, and an organisation grew for laying hands on the clothing sent to Naples by the Americans. An entire little street of the old city lived from

---

* In May 1973 the inhabitants of Borgio Verezzi in Liguria objected to the opening of a home for spastic children on the grounds that it would harm the tourist trade.

this man's work helped by a circle of pupils all thin and small like him. Then he went blind. He could no longer sew. His pupils went out and attempted to start similar organisations in other streets and alleys of the city. But they all failed. They did not have the dexterity and the touch of the pale little hunchbacked dwarf.

One of the great acts of Italian sanctity was the foundation in Turin in 1828 of a hospital for all those whom organised society either rejected or made totally inadequate provision for – the cripples, the chronically sick, the mentally retarded, the deadly travesties of unfinished human forms. It is called the Cottolengo after its founder, and the first two syllables have entered the Piedmontese dialect as *cuttu* meaning 'an idiot'. Giuseppe Cottolengo was part of the nineteenth-century Piedmontese tradition of practical sainthood – John Bosco was another – and the compassion of his work cannot be over-rated because it struck at genuine Italian sin. A foreign visitor who knew the world recounted his pain and embarrassment when his taxi-driver, who was driving him past the Basilica of Santa Maria Maggiore on the way to the airport, relent-lessly hooted at a cripple in an invalid chair until the unlucky fellow was forced to pull in to let him pass. This was the outlook which deeply shocked Cottolengo. He refused to accept that the sick and the poor should suffer without help in the midst of a prosperous city.

From the beginning of 1970 onwards, the wounded of the last two wars, the blind, and those hurt in accidents and permanently crippled began their own agitation for increases in their meagre pensions. They organised several demonstra-tions, and traffic in the centre of Rome was brought to a stop as the halt and the lame and the blind walked or were led or wheeled to Parliament Square to demand better treatment from the Government. No sight could have been sadder, and nowhere else in Europe could it have been as sad.

One of the leading Italian dictionaries defines beauty as 'perfection of form'. So long as it is understood that in most cases this perfection is applied to persons, not things, the definition is correct as to what Italians think beauty is. This outlook places more restrictions on artistic expression than many people will allow. In the visual arts the Italians are supreme, but it is a supremacy heavily based on the classical pose and the splendidly proportioned body. Kitchens are given poetry by Dutch painters and so are superficially unattractive women. It is unimaginable that an Italian painter would penetrate the humble reaches of the kitchen in his search for acceptable subjects, and if he has to paint an ugly woman he makes the best of her.

Italian supremacy in painting has left them with a financial heritage of which the value is huge but difficult to calculate, so huge that its extent must be guessed at because it is so important to Italy's resources. Attaching monetary values to works of art can at best only be approximate, but the effort was made after the 1966 floods which damaged, among other places, Florence and Venice. Estimates varied from 10,000 million lire (£6,300,000,000; c. $17,000,000,000) to three times that sum, taking into account the State's artistic, archaeological and historical property. By law all Italy's archaeological resources are the property of the State, except for private collections created before 1939. Their movement is also the exclusive right of the State, a right frequently challenged by illegal export.

The means devoted to caring for this huge treasure are painfully few. Ancient monuments are looked after by a department of the Ministry of Education, despite the fact that the colossal value of the artistic heritage and the income derived from them in foreign exchange brought by visitors would logically call for a minister who would have a dominant voice not only in the care and availability of artistic masterpieces but also in the problems of pollution and the destruction of beauty. But most Italians do not act as if they were aware of living in Europe's most beautiful country surrounded by Europe's finest works of art, or that the past has left them with a total of 607 museums of varying importance. The expenditure which goes into caring for the world's most important archaeological heritage is less than that spent by one museum in the United States – the Metropolitan – or the Hermitage in Leningrad. The amount spent on the Fine Arts in Italy each year would build only thirty kilometres of motor-highway. A law approved in August 1965 allowed for the increase by 2000 of the number of attendants in museums and archaeological sites; 750 were enrolled without having to sit for any form of examination because they were physically disabled and existing legislation favours the employment of the physically disabled in, of all places, the country's museums. There could be no more eloquent illumination of what Italy thinks of its museums than to put them under the watch of cripples, and it says a lot about what they think of cripples as well. There are 75 local superintendencies of the fine arts; in 1970 they had between them 95 archaeologists, 92 art historians and 107 architects. The average was 3 qualified officials for each superintendency. Education, moreover, is regarded as one of the most unwieldy and obscurantist of the ministries. The *Corriere della Sera* included the post of Superintendent of the Fine Arts in a series of articles devoted to professions in decline. This decline was hastened by a measure introduced in late 1972 by which certain higher grades of the civil service could retire early on pensions higher, in many cases, than their salaries. Superintendents, being among the most discouraged of the State's officials, were expected to take advantage of this provision. The full plight of the museums, libraries and archaeological sites was brought home to the public, and to foreign visitors, by the great strike of Fine Arts employees in spring 1971. The unions claimed that ninety-five per cent of the 7623 employees joined the strike. All the country's most important art collections and archaeological sites were closed at the beginning of the tourist season. The custodians were rebelling against their inadequate salaries – their starting wage was the equivalent of £44 ($104) a month – and the sheer lack of manpower. On an average, museum custodians were responsible for looking after six or seven rooms each; one man on the archaeological sites was supposed to keep watch over ten square kilometres. There was even less protection for paintings and other works in parish churches, especially in country areas.

Another shock came in the autumn of 1972 when heavy rains dangerously affected ill-maintained monuments. On 14 September the Roman Forum and the Palatine were closed; on 26 September the Colosseum was closed and wooden barriers placed around it so that motor-traffic could not come near. The most famous of Rome's classical monuments were thus out of reach of visitors and no one was in two minds about the cause, which was simple neglect. All were soon partially reopened. But there could now be no denying the inadequacy of the means provided by the State to care for its monuments. Italians then suffered the humiliation of having offers from America to buy the Colosseum in order to take it off their hands. One good result was that the Prime Minister, the Roman, Giulio Andreotti, began talking publicly about taking away the Fine Arts department from the Ministry of Education and making it the principal concern of a newly devised ministry.

It was altogether an unfortunate autumn. According to press reports, the number of monuments and archaeological sites in bad condition was no less than 3000. Still it was the famous sites and monuments which attracted most attention. Apart from the Roman monuments (which included worries about the bronze equestrian statue of Marcus Aurelius in the centre of the Capitol Square and Trajan's Column), the condition, to name only the outstanding cases, of the doors of the Florence Baptistry was declared serious; similarly the four bronze horses on the façade of St Mark's in Venice were suffering from damp and atmospheric pollution, whilst the neglect of Pompeii had long been causing concern. And, finally, the tower of Pisa, the monument which most fascinates tourists and is said to attract more of them than any other of Italy's monuments, persisted in its tendency to lean a little more each year.

The trouble with the Rome monuments and with most of the archaeological sites suffering decay was not specifically pollution, traffic and other features of modern life. Venice suffers far more from pollution; and Milan Cathedral, also declared at the same time to be causing anxiety, appears to be a victim of surface and underground traffic. The archaeological monuments apparently suffer most from physical conditions – heat, cold and damp – and from biological incursions such as plant-growth, grass and lichens. Then comes atmospheric pollution and traffic.

Pisa, of course, is a case entirely on its own. The Tower now leans about seventeen feet from centre at the top balcony. The load on its base at its maximum – its tilted side – is ten times what is allowed under existing Pisan building regulations so that there is an element of the miraculous that it stays up at all. The list is increasing at the rate of something less than a millimetre a year. In no sense could the Italians be criticised for doing nothing. The first modern attempt at intervention which involved the pumping of cement into the foundations in 1936 only quickened the movement alarmingly. Galileo's phrase *eppure si muove* was not made about the tower from which he was supposed to have conducted some of his experiments, but it might well have been. The original mistake was presumably made by the Florentine architect Bonanno, who began work on the Tower on 10 August 1174. He was regarded as technically very expert and needed to be because the task was difficult. The firm soil was near the surface and if he dug at all deeply for his foundations he would have come across waterlogged soil of mixed consistency as might be expected of deposits brought by the Arno. He went down about nine feet and kept his foundations light. He had to, because if the soil immediately beneath the building should give way there would be little to support it. He miscalculated because the foundations shifted at an early stage in the building but nevertheless, mistake or not, the base on which the Tower rests has proved extremely resistant.

Exactly where Bonanno went wrong is still a subject for conjecture. Modern Italian opinion has naturally produced the idea that he economised on his materials for his own profit. He was shown in a cartoon as saying, 'I cut a few corners on the materials, but no one will ever know.' The most convincing theory is that he made a mistake with the placing of his pumps. Water would have flowed under the site from the Arno. As he was constructing a circular building (the present height of 179 feet is three times the diameter) he probably put his pumps in the middle, as far away as possible from the walls on which the men were at work. Water would thus have flowed through half of the foundations but missed the other half because it was pumped clear. The Tower does, in fact, lean towards the Arno, which gives some support to the theory. In any event, work was stopped in 1185, when Bonanno had reached the third storey: probably there were already signs of sinking and inclination. The work was resumed in 1275 by Giovanni di Simone who completed another three and a half storeys and gave the tower an unmistakable tilt. In 1350 the bell-house was added by Tommaso Pisano, and the list was 4 feet 10 inches from true. Vasari took for granted that Bonanno had made a mistake. By Vasari's time, the middle of the sixteenth century, the tower leant more than twelve feet. About fifty years later a German architect called Schikardt was told by the Pisans that the Tower had been made to lean purposely 'with particular care and with great art' ('*mit sondern Fleiss und aus grosser Kunst*') but he did not believe them. Italian governments give the impression that they are in two minds about whether to act or go on trusting in miracles. A commission produced detailed studies in February 1972 and initiated an international competition. But its report was not sent to would-be solvers of this historic puzzle. A belief in miracles does at times seem to be the main inspirer of official policy on the arts.

One result is a huge trade in illegally dug archaeological pieces and paintings robbed from churches or sold by priests to make money for the parish. (This illicit selling of works of art – usually works of secondary importance but some great works among them – increased when liturgical reform was introduced by the Roman Catholic Church and worship greatly simplified.) The illegal diggers, known as *tombaroli*, are traditionally unemployed or under-employed farm-workers with a long history of tomb-robbing in the family. It is an ancient trade which depends on a fund of specialised knowledge about the archaeological remains in the area in which they live. Like truffle-hunting, it is both a science and a knack. Nowadays the equipment is modern, including powered drills, electric saws and helicoidal saws for removing painted panels. Activities still fall off during harvest and sowing because primarily the *tombaroli* regard themselves as agricultural workers. The damage which they cause to Italy's archaeological wealth is estimated by the Lerici Institute of Milan's

Polytechnic at about the equivalent of £2,000,000 ($4,800,000) a year, an estimate largely calculated on the basis of sales at auctions openly organised by Swiss art-dealers. Something between ten and fifteen per cent goes to the diggers; the rest is taken by the receivers, exporters and dealers.

The sale, against the law, of works of art may be reprehensible but selling at least keeps the pieces intact even if they vanish abroad or disappear into private collections. It might well be argued that Italy does not have the resources or the apparent wish to look after the treasure that her painters and architects have left behind and that a wider distribution is no bad thing, particularly as a person willing to pay large sums for paintings or architectural pieces will probably take care of them. But actual destruction of the artistic and natural heritage (it is often difficult to divide the two) is something quite different. The irreparable has been committed with seeming alacrity whether on the comparatively small scale of a house built illegally or a monstrous undertaking such as pollution of the Venetian lagoon, destruction of the beauty of the bay of Naples and of the city itself, indiscriminate building in Rome, ribbon development of much of the coast: the list is long and dreadful. But only because it is happening in Italy and because countries such as Britain went through this aspect of industrial advance a century or more ago and are beginning to learn their lessons from the destruction caused then. It would be unfair to say that no Italians care; some do. Some are organised within Italia Nostra, a private body which draws attention to cases in which a famous landscape is about to be ruined or a historic centre disfigured.

Less-publicised forms of ecological upsets afflict the country. Fire destroys 40,000 hectares of forest a year, and some 25,000 hectares are replanted each year. The lack of trees is the principal reason why 50,000 square kilometres of land are subject to serious erosion. There have even been whispers that some of the forest fires have been started by persons intent on developing the area but prevented from doing so by regulations protecting the trees. And then there are the animals. Italians are constantly criticised for the senseless manner in which they destroy wild-life. 'Hunting' is so popular a pursuit that every year 600,000 men put on green jackets, load their double-barrelled shot-guns and fire at almost anything that moves. In 1971 it is reliably estimated that 50,000 million lire was spent on cartridges, giving an average of 50 shots for each 'hunter': at least 50 million animals died and probably 200 million birds. The most justified complaint is not simply against brutality. Birds have their part in keeping down parasites. Because they are shot out of the sky, the Italian farmer must use artificial insecticides. He does so with too much enthusiasm: it is estimated that the amount used each year is about thirty-eight per cent in excess of what is required. The result is that the amount of D.D.T. in Italian adipose tissue is high: 1·8 per million as compared with 0·6 in Denmark, 0·4 in Britain and 0·5 in West Germany. Yet the only complaint of a vaguely ecological kind concerning foodstuffs that one hears from average Italians is that battery chickens may limit one's virility.

Most Italians do not feel strongly on these matters: or, if they do, are convinced that nothing can be done. The tragedy is that Italians have not only failed to learn from the mistakes of other countries but insist on running ahead of the contemporary world in accepting industrial damage, pollution, wreckage of landscape as part of the process of feeling modern. Oil refineries, to give one example, are remarkably numerous in Italy. In 1971 there were at least 40 of these 'black cathedrals' of the technocratic age, double the number in France (19) and Britain (20). One-third of the 100 million tons of crude oil treated in Italy is exported. Italy is content to pay the price for others in pollution. Yet no country stands to lose more from indiscriminate destruction of the natural balance – atmospheric pollution, the poisoning of rivers and lakes and the fouling of sea-coasts – and for that matter the neglect of its works of art and monuments which, if nothing else, attract visitors and confer prestige.

The explanation seems to be simply that Italians, particularly since the war, have sought to shake off their formidable past. Nothing can be more disheartening to a young nation – Italy is a century old – than to have monuments around it which are part of a spectacular history. They have tried to rival these monuments. Once Rome became the capital, the Government built that huge altar to inept national pride, the Victor Emmanuel monument, intended to equal the grandiloquence of the Forum and the Capitol. Many of them no longer want the link with their historic heritage implied in architectural emulation; that phase ended with Mussolini. Italians have consciously decided – humble Italians, that is, not the sort of people who made the decisions earlier in the country's history – that their future as a modern, technological country depends on forgetting the past and following instead the more advanced societies of industrialised states. The past in Italian eyes can mean twenty years, or 200, or 2000.

They are masters, however, of creating the beauty, not of the present, but of the moment: of seeing the whole world in a moment of time. Look at Piero della Francesca's 'Resurrection of Christ' at San Sepolcro. The risen Christ is there before your eyes but gives the impression of not having been there a matter of seconds earlier. The momentary inspiration is completely captured, held in the paint on the wall. Or take a more tangible example. Twice a year the Tuscan city of Siena reaches the height of vital inspiration, of the communal experience, with its Palio, the horse-race around its main square. The horses represent quarters of the city. The race is three times round the cobbled square. It is a dangerous, bare-back contest in which fewer than half the jockeys are likely to finish. There are no rules. Each jockey has a whip, and prize-money as well as the adulation of his supporters if he wins. The race is preceded by a procession lasting two hours, accompanied by constant drumming, the skilful flag-play practised since the sixteenth century and the regular tolling of the bell in the municipal palace. All these devices contribute to the tension which reaches its height as the horses and jockeys ride into the square and the starting-gun sets them off on the actual race which lasts scarcely more than a minute, but for that minute the lives of the crowd are joined to the contest and explosions of grief, joy and relief mark the end. It is a great historic survival and extremely Italian: a moment of life caught in a vortex. The same feeling was present, though perhaps misplaced, in Toscanini's whirlpool interpretation of

Beethoven's Ninth, a completely Italianate reading.

The conscious aim of shaking off the past, and the extent to which it succeeds, is the foundation of Italy's modern problems. A great deal of easy talk is heard of Italy's growing pains, that social tension, violence, apparent contradictions in development are the result of a young nation's process of growing up. Yet what could be older than Italy? And how could so mature, so ancient, so cynical a people only now begin the process of adolescence? They are not growing pains, they are the pangs of a civilisation which has digested whatever the past imposed on it but is having serious trouble with technological society. There would be no problem at all if all Italians were convinced of the need to shake off the past and be entirely modern. But they are not. And often in the same individual one finds the conflict of the pull of the new and the claims of the old. And the claims of the old do not by any means come simply from what one would expect to be the conservative voices, such as the Church and the political right and the mothers. The writer Nicola Chiaramonte took up two columns of the Turin newspaper *La Stampa* in December 1970 to attack the idea from an intellectual's viewpoint of 'the tradition of the new'. His argument was that tradition, in the Latin heritage, was derived from the word *tradere* which meant to pass from hand to hand and that tradition in this sense meant mobility and movement whereas the throwing-off of all of the past and acceptance of only that which was new must by its nature mean stagnation. 'The idea that the intelligence, the sensibility and the ability of man are all the more free the more they are liberated from the "mists of the past" is stupid and barbarous, indeed the very essence of stupidity and barbarism.' There are no harsher words to be used by an intelligent Italian against a concept which is bothering him. He is right to be bothered. He has more right to be than the vested interests which wring their hands at the sight of change because change weakens their position. Italy once gave the rule to the West. It has been taking the rule from the West, and was tempted to take it on the understanding that in a modern world the West is right and traditional society hopelessly inadequate to deal with technocracy. The bitterest of epilogues would be that the West was not right and that much remained to be said for what had been destroyed. Italians are relentless largely where personal matters are concerned or in fields, such as the pollution of Venice, where money is being made and society as a whole, which has few spokesmen, is paying the price. In facing social questions, the relentlessness is inclined to slow down, or be ready where necessary to slacken, because experience has taught Italians that living in society – sometimes living at all – requires a degree of compromise. That is why there are promptings of doubt about the way society is heading, even if for the moment these promptings are a small cloud on a bright sky of frank destruction. And regard for beauty itself can hardly have been totally lost. The peninsula has been buffeted by human tempests just as it has suffered its series of natural disasters but, for all that, there has been a certain continuity of life and outlook through the ages. Where this has been interrupted, the interruption was caused by invasion or war, not by the will of the Italians to change their ways. Now they certainly are changing their ways; it will be a long time before the whole country has been transformed because the traditional outlook is still strong and views may alter before what now looks like an inevitable process is complete. Italian braking-power is at least as impressive as Italian acceleration. But while enough of them feel the drive towards a Western, technological civilisation, and their governments leave them to thresh the old forms of society for nothing but immediate gain, there will inevitably be destruction of beautiful objects and places and customs.

Throwing off the past proved to be the perfect gospel for the building speculators. As a result, Italy's cities with an average of 2-3 square yards of green for each inhabitant are worse off in this respect than the cities of any other Western country. (New York has 18 square yards, Stockholm 80, Moscow 11, Paris 11, London 30 and Amsterdam 20.) Mestre, which is the industrial part of Venice and the area causing much of the pollution, has 260,000 inhabitants and an average of 26 square centimetres of green for each of them, and atmospheric pollution at such a level that in 1973 some

50,000 workers were ordered to work with gasmasks. The motive was entirely profit, but materialism was the air that everybody breathed. And it was slightly ennobled, if you like, by the idea that change was progress, that progress was everything and that too much time had already been lost. Whole centuries indeed. That is why there is nowhere better than Italy to see Western values most clearly put to the test as they are accepted with Italian enthusiasm and frankness, if at times with a superficial frankness.

This frankness is possible because the Italians are so little governed. The protection of beauty – or lack of it – is one example, but only one. There was no attempt at planning industrial expansion in the great days of the boom and little enough at dealing with the social consequences of expansion. The attempt is being made now but with little conviction in a country where what matters is the immediate; yesterday is gone and tomorrow may never come. But this feeling does not explain why the politicians have so markedly kept their distance from the country's problems. The explanation lies in the whole system of political life.

CHAPTER FIVE

Politics and Presidents

To say that Italian politicians are a class apart is like saying that Chianti is a sort of liquid: not a half of the truth and no real indication of its significance or effect. They live in a world of their own which has nothing to do with the world at large, and this they recognise. They cannot speak its language. Years spent in political life have robbed them of this ability. They do not share its problems though its problems are constantly being put before them for solution. Their contact with the masses is to bestow favours (usually in the form of rights denied by bureaucratic clumsiness or political discrimination) in return for which they take votes. This trade replaces the democratic conscience, the genuine popularity and the representative function which is expected of members of parliament. The politicians are the complete products of the system by which self-centredness from the cradle and concern with one's own affairs become a way of life.

Since the fifties Parliament has passed astonishingly few bills of any importance, though scores of little or no importance which are intended to satisfy some local interest. The fourth legislature (1963-8) dealt with 3576 bills, of which 790 were approved, most of them of minimal constructive value. At the beginning of every government the politicians promise fundamental reforms: years and several governments later, nothing having been done in the meantime, they can still look without flinching at a demonstrator – an earthquake victim, a senior civil servant, a dustman, a student, a dweller from the shanty towns, a building labourer, a doctor, a cripple, a schoolchild – carrying a banner with the slogan 'Deeds not Words'. A leading lawyer in Rome likes to recount a personal experience. When in London he parked his car on the edge of Hyde Park where parking was forbidden. A policewoman told him to move on but relented when he explained that it would be for a matter of minutes only, a reasonable plea if he had been in Rome where nobody has any idea of time and public clocks are usually wrong or have stopped long ago. Several hours later he went back to his car. He was relieved to see a different policewoman on duty. But she bore down on him and asked him curtly if he was the gentleman who had said to her colleague that he would be back in a matter of minutes. He admitted that he was and, shamefaced, asked what fine he should pay. There would be no fine, she said, adding – and this is the line which brings rounds of delirious laughter in the sacred city whenever he recounts the story – 'You should keep your promises!'

What most people overlook is the reverse side of this non-existent contract. The country resolutely seals itself off from its governors. Well-intentioned Anglo-Saxons constantly carp about the lack of confidence accorded the State by the ordinary Italian. This leads, so it is sanctimoniously argued, to a dangerous gap between rulers and ruled which is the cause of Italy's internal troubles. The truth is the exact opposite. The gap has been Italy's saving grace. Without it the State would not have lasted. The performance of the State from about the early fifties would scarcely have been tolerated except by a people healthily believing that, as nothing was to be expected from the governing classes, there was no reason to complain when the rulers failed to do not only what they ought to have done but also what they had solemnly said that they would do. In a sense democracy has survived because it has fulfilled so few of its promises, fewer and fewer as the period of post-war reconstruction is left further and further behind.

Even when facts deny them, and the State really does something, the old mental clichés remain. I remember standing on a building-site in the deep south – in Calabria – where a hotel was being built. Almost all the capital was coming from the State's Southern Development Fund established in 1950. The man who had been provided with his capital and would soon have a profitable hotel, which would eventually be his own, stood on the site watching every stage of the work. He would turn back every now and again and say, 'We are abandoned down here, the south has always been neglected....'

The problem is a profound one and by no means limited to the south. It is wrong to suppose that there is no contact between the citizen and politics. The break is between citizens and government. Politicians are constantly plagued by their constituents to do favours for them. A deputy from the south, where the client-system is stronger than in the north, can expect about 4000 letters asking for favours each year, of which about three-quarters would be requests for his help in speeding up some matter in the hands of the bureaucracy which, without intervention from an authoritative person in Rome, would remain blocked for years in the antiquated machine. A deputy from the north would expect to get far fewer, probably not more than a tenth of the total of requests for favours, and he could never expect to be addressed by his constituents in the same servile tones as a southern deputy would be. In both cases the deputy is regarded as his constituents' intermediary with power and, to a greater extent in the south, is judged not by what he says or does in the Chamber but by how much he can extract from the central government for the benefit of his own people. The way of showing his tireless efforts on behalf of constituents, if immediate results cannot be forthcoming, is the parliamentary question. Questioning, both in writing or orally, is naturally intended to give Parliament a means of control over the executive. To a large extent it is exploited as a means of giving proof of a deputy's efforts on behalf of his supporters. In the course of the fourth legislature a total of 27,000 questions requiring written answers were put down and 7000 calling for oral reply.

The Italian parliamentarian (members of the two houses are treated in the same way) is the most highly paid in Europe, earning the equivalent of well over £500 ($1250) a month (after tax). The exact figure in late 1972 was a gross salary of 1,175,386 lire a month and a net income of 953,067. Salaries are tied to those of a senior judge so that there is no unseemly wrangling when a member of parliament is given more money: his salary simply goes up when the judges' income is raised. He has free travel on the railways and reductions on air travel, but potentially far more valuable is his legal immunity. A parliamentarian cannot be arraigned before a court on practically any offence without the consent of the chamber to which he belongs. The original idea of this immunity was to protect the parliamentarian against an undemocratic executive seeking to silence tiresome members through judicial proceedings. Again the shadow of Fascism was heavy on those drawing up the regulations. The system has been abused. Cases have occurred of local politicians who, when threatened with some sort of scandal, or known to be guilty of crime, are pressed into Parliament before proceedings can be opened. But its greatest drawback is symbolical: it suggests that the parliamentarian is a different race of person from the people whom he is supposed to represent.

Modern politicians are not entirely to blame. They are behaving as the country's rulers have behaved in the past. Before Mussolini came into power, government was by an *élite*. In one sense they are open to real criticism: they have not faced the challenge in their own behaviour of the change from dictatorship to democracy since the end of the war, or the changes in society marking the two post-war decades. With more effort they might have drawn on that twist in their country's history to bring about a new relationship of rulers and ruled. Insistence would have been necessary: too many interests were pressing the country towards conservatism, continuity and an easy transition instead of the sharp break, an act of renewal, that there should have been. The least that could have happened, and was expected, would have been behaviour showing that the twenty years of Fascism were an unhappy aberration. This is not to suggest that many of Italy's present politicians were Fascists or retain Fascist philosophies. This is not so. But they seem to find ample reason for retaining, a quarter of a century after the fall of Fascism, legal codes drafted during the dictatorship and heavily bearing its stamp in terms of curtailed personal liberties.

It is wrong to see this problem simply in terms of Fascism and democracy. The reasons why Italians do not feel part of the body politic are much older than Mussolini; indeed, some people will honestly say that Mussolini gave them more of the feeling of participation than they had had before or since. There are two main reasons for the diffidence felt towards the State. The first is that the nation is young, little more than a century old. The second is that the experience of foreign rule and, in some parts of the country, long periods of misrule is lengthy. As far as the south is concerned it continued after unity. The forms of government throughout the peninsula varied very widely. Direct Spanish rule in the south was obscurantist, and the rule of the Spanish Bourbons who followed in Naples was obscurantist and weak. The Dukes of Piedmont built up a militarist little state based on such virtues as hard work, privation when necessary in the State's interest, and the paying of taxes. The Piedmontese administration was famous for its incorruptibility. A high degree of administrative honesty was part of the later Austrian rule of Lombardy and Venice, but these virtues were understandably overlooked by patriots who regarded the imperial presence for what it was, rule by a foreign country. (In November 1966 a greater respect was shown for the Austrians because they were found to have paid attention to the defences of Venice against the sea in a way that Italian governments since the end of Austrian rule had failed to do, a point of some substance in the wake of the floods of that month.)

The one political denominator common to all the varying experiences of government in Italy was power itself, and remains so. The civilised study of the ideology of power is an Italian preserve. Machiavelli is the master. His outlook is a clear-headed admission of the failure of natural morality, or religious teaching, as a force in politics, another field in which the Italians are paramount both in experience and in theory. There is little that Italy has not seen, from such city-states as Mantua to the temporal rule of Christ's vicar. And from all this filtered knowledge, this supreme exercise in the endless adventure, power is what remains. It is the essence of a polychromatic set of studies in political practice.

Power has one drawback as a principal aim. In itself it does not corrupt. Indeed, seekers after power, as a presently active Italian politician justly pointed out, are usually pleasanter people when they have it than when they are without it. In a democracy there can be no question of corruption through absolute power because absolute power cannot be achieved. At least not in Italy; as soon as any politician begins to feel comfortable in office, he is about to be removed. But the search for power is viciously limiting and time-consuming. Its seekers cannot relax with each other. They cannot keep their eyes away from the next step towards its achievement, or their thoughts away from the danger represented by their rivals; hence their minds are distracted from such mundane matters as legislation or consistency, because power might easily come nearer to one's grasp by sharply moving right, or shifting suddenly to the left.

Few people seem to grasp what the Italian political system is about. Except that it has a freely elected parliament, it bears no comparison with the British and American systems, and this is one of the reasons why there is frequent misunderstanding and quite often alarm about what is happening to Italian democracy. This is not to say that there is no cause for alarm; just that alarm for the wrong reason is unhelpful.

The British and American electorates go to the polls to choose the next government. Italians go to choose the next parliament, with not the remotest idea who is likely to be prime minister, a consideration which, for most electors, is secondary. They know very well that, as soon as the count is in and the strength of the various factions within the parties clear, the struggle for power will begin among the leading Christian Democrats whose preserve it is to supply prime ministers. The system seems devised to nurture factiousness and give full play to the relentless power-game. The people vote by a complicated system of proportional representation. As a result, Parliament is far more representative in the wide range of views which it contains of a far more varied country than the House of Commons is representative of Britain. With one exception: the mental and human quality of the average Italian parliamentarian is regarded as below the national average, and some of the more advanced parts of the country – Lombardy is an outstanding example – send a meagre supply of their able men to Parliament. But the British have eased the problem of forming governments by paying the price of reducing the representative nature of Parliament. This is the meaning of a system with two parties, each having a recognised leader. The Italians have paid no such price and have no intention of doing so, however much they praise the British solution and pretend that they wish to emulate it. The result is that their Parliament has, and for the foreseeable future will have, seven or eight parties in its halls, varying from the Communists, on one extremity of the horseshoe lay-out of the Chamber of Deputies, to Neo-Fascists on the right. The fact that elections are regarded as having no direct relevance to government is shown by the repeated refusal to call a general election when a government falls. Part of this reluctance is due to purely mercenary considerations. Winning a seat is expensive because the campaign is costly; the equivalent of £20,000 ($50,000) has been given as a fair estimate. And the investment is expected to last the full five years which is the statutory maximum term between one general election and another. Until 1972 no general election had ever taken place since the war before the natural life of Parliament had come to an end. General elections are called by the President of the Republic after consultation with the presiding officers of the two houses. But, money aside, the main reason for avoiding recourse to a general election was the full knowledge that it would settle nothing – a point ironically reinforced by the results of the May 1972 election, which was the first time the rule was broken. A shift of a million votes in Britain would mean a landslide for one party or the other, or at least a sharp correcting of an abnormal situation. A shift of a million votes in Italy could quite well be absorbed without noticeably altering the basic balance. Parliament, moreover, is not the principal seat of political decision. The two houses have to give their approval to every new government but the main decisions are taken by the parties. Until 1972 no government fell because it had suffered a parliamentary reverse: governments are dismantled by the party secretaries.

Isolation of the politicians in their governing capacity, the search for power as the one common denominator in political life, the separate existences of Parliament, governments and party structures are concepts not to be found in the Italian Constitution. This does not mean that the Constitution is an irrelevant document. In many ways it is more a set of aspirations than a description of public life in the Republic. A good case could be made for arguing that the real division in Italian affairs is not between north and south, rich and poor, right and left, but between Italy of the Constitution and Italy in which its principles are flouted or ignored. Gradually the document is being more faithfully applied, which is important because, despite some lapses, it sums up the thinking of patriotic Italians of all parties, including the Communists, about the State they wanted after the Fascist experience. Ideologically, Italian democracy is based on anti-Fascism. It is not just anti-Fascist; it found its inspiration and its return to the path indicated earlier by the *Risorgimento* in the liberation of part of the country by Italian democrats from the Fascists and the Nazis before the Allied military advance. The Constitution is an attempt to create the blue-print for a state which ought to emerge from these experiences and is deeply marked by the lessons learned under the Fascists.

The document was drawn up by a constituent assembly and approved on 22 December 1947 by 453 votes to 62. It came into force on 1 January 1948, replacing the Albertine Constitution, the 'Statute' which Charles Albert of Savoy gave to Piedmont in 1848. When unification was achieved around Piedmont, this Statute was applied to the whole of Italy and later, under Fascism, underwent modification to increase executive powers and reduce personal liberties. The idea of calling a constituent assembly to write a new constitution should have been inspiring in itself, especially as it would be a republican constitution, representing all the more a new start when one considered that the House of Savoy, the Italian royal house which was rejected by popular referendum in 1946, had ruled for longer than any other family in Europe. Strangely enough, the Constitution was to offer the general lines of a fresh approach fundamentally different from what Italians had hitherto known. The document has its defects. But a convinced constitutionalist in Italy is a man of advanced thought and his unquestioning devotion to the document could in the present atmosphere well lead him into trouble.

The Constitution opens with the statement that Italy is 'a democratic republic based on work'. This assertion might sound un-Italian. As a way of expressing a truth so curtly, it is un-Italian. But it is nevertheless a truth. The Italian ability to work is one of the nation's outstanding qualities. Surviving prejudices that Italians dislike hard work are absurd. Italians refuse to make a virtue of work for its own sake – except perhaps among traditionalist Piedmontese, but even there the deciding factor is less the value of work than loyalty to an employer or a firm. Working to the average Italian is not praying: it is not the main reason why we are here. The more saints' days and holidays the better (there are seventeen recognised public holidays a year, which is more than anywhere else in Europe, and in a reasonably progressive-minded factory an Italian worker could expect to work about 220 days out of the 365). But work as a means of gaining what one wants is taken with alacrity. When they are at work, Italians work with great concentration and will. The tragedy of unplanned economic advance was that conditions both inside and outside the factories brought about a revulsion to organised labour much like the earlier revulsion towards labouring on the land. But this was a protest against inhumanity, not against work as such.

In November 1970 an investigation was made into the standard of living of a factory-worker. Alfa Romeo was chosen because, as a state-controlled company, it should have provided the highest level of working conditions and is indeed considered by the unions as a company ready to respect the dignity of the worker. The pay was scarcely enough on which to live, especially for a man with a family. It was not unusual for a factory-worker to do some other job in his free time. One man made money in the evenings by taking jobs as a skilled carpenter, quite apart from growing vegetables in the garden to lighten the housekeeping budget. Another, a young southern immigrant with wife and child, was subsidised monthly by his family. Similar results came from a 1973 survey in a privately owned factory: skilled workers did not earn enough to provide for their families. All this brought to mind a remark by Giuseppe Saragat when he was still President. After listening to what people were saying was wrong with Italy, he commented: 'Italy is the one country in Europe where the people still work *con amore*.' It is a massive asset, but one which became heavily overshadowed as the first flight of industrial enthusiasm passed. The outbreak of serious strikes in the autumn of 1969 marked the breakdown of the traditional style of labour relations.

The Constitution goes on to say that sovereignty belongs to the people, who exercise it in the forms and within the limits prescribed in the document. Citizens have the right to equality before the law, irrespective of race, language, religion or political opinions. All religions are equal before the law.

And then comes the famous Article 7. This is the most questionable article in the whole Constitution. It says simply: 'The State and the Catholic Church are, each in its own sphere, independent and sovereign; their relations are regulated by the Lateran Pacts.' The principle enunciated in the first part of this article is perfectly good; but the second half of the article goes far beyond principle. The Lateran Pacts were the series of agreements – an international treaty, a financial accord and a concordat – made in 1929 between Mussolini and the Holy See, which were supposed to settle, for the first time since 1870, relations between Italy and the Papacy. On balance these agreements were favourable to the Church at the time. They became more so. They were designed to be applied on the Italian side by a heavy-handed dictator whose background was anti-clerical. Mussolini had sufficient instinct for power to know that in Italy power without the support of the Roman Catholic Church is half-empty. But in his time the Pacts had no connexion with the Constitution. In 1947 they became, by virtue, if such a phrase is appropriate, of Article 7, involved in the Constitution. And Italy's political affairs were for the first time in a century in the hands of a Catholic party, dependent on the Church for its popular support.

To judge this arrangement one has almost to be Italy's family doctor. Clericalism and anti-clericalism are both sicknesses. They do not between them make a constructive amalgam in the way that, for instance, romanticism and the classical tradition were combined in Brahms, or patriotism was transmuted into operatic art by Verdi, or such a genius as Botticelli could at one stage in his career express the delicate paganism of the Renaissance and later turn to religious mysticism. The two strains in modern Italian thinking are mutually antagonistic – destructively so. And Article 7 of the Constitution enshrined the conflict. Mussolini's concordat made over the whole institution of marriage to the Church: a marriage in church was given full civil effect and the monopoly of ending marriage was left to the deliberations of the Vatican's Sacra Rota court. Hence, when the Italian Parliament introduced divorce on 2 December 1970, this initiative was presented as violating not only the Concordat but also the Constitution. At the same time, the reliance of the governing Christian Democrat Party on votes collected by the clergy meant that the clauses of the Concordat, insisted on by the Fascists, that the Church's secular arm should not engage in politics became a dead letter as soon as Catholic politicians took charge of Italy's affairs. Article 7 brought a new physiognomy of the centaur divided between a vision of Italy which saw the Church predominant in public affairs and the efforts at creating a lay state in which the young nation could establish itself as a part of modern European civilisation. Italy emerged from the Constituent Assembly as that strange hybrid, a confessional republic: all this thanks to Article 7 which, ominously enough, was supported by the Communists as well as by the Christian Democrats.

The Constitution's proclamation, already quoted, that sovereignty belongs to the people 'who exercise it within the forms and limits of the Constitution' is a neat enough way of establishing two principles. The first is political, that of popular sovereignty, and the second juridical with the insistence on the supremacy of law and the law's inviolability. The sovereignty of the people is expressed through their parliamentary vote. Recourse can also be had to a referendum but only for the abrogation of laws approved by Parliament, the creation of regions and changes affecting them and, in certain conditions, constitutional modifications. Parliament would not be able to regard itself, as does the British Parliament, as sovereign in itself but it is the central institution in what is in effect a parliamentary, not a presidential, democracy.

There are two houses: the Senate and the Chamber of Deputies. They have equal powers and functions. Every piece of legislation has to be approved by both. If one house modifies substantially a measure approved by the other, it must go back to be debated again. Hence, there is no question of the Senate's having a moderating influence on the Chamber, except in the sense that the Senate has a slightly older electorate than the Chamber. The explanation of the choice of two houses is that put forward by John Stuart Mill: 'The same reason which induced the Romans to have two consuls makes it desirable there should be two chambers: that neither of them may be exposed to the corrupting influence of undivided power.' In practice the system is a great consumer of parliamentary time. Each house has a term of five years. Until 1962 the Senate's term was six years but this was altered so that elections to both could take place simultaneously. Both are elected by direct, universal suffrage. There is one deputy for every 80,000 inhabitants, or a fraction superior to 40,000; the Senate is organised on a regional basis and every region has a senator for every 200,000 inhabitants, or for a fraction superior to 100,000. The electorate for the Chamber consists of all citizens of twenty-one or more, and to be eligible for election one must be twenty-five; for the Senate the minimum age of the electorate is twenty-five and forty for membership.

Executive power is exercised by the Council of Ministers

under a prime minister designated by the President. This designation is one of the principal powers accorded the President. The others are that he can dissolve Parliament, or only one house, after having consulted their presiding officers, except in the final six months of his term of seven years when this faculty is denied him. The last six months are known for this reason as the 'white semester'. He may send messages to Parliament and he has the task of promulgating laws approved by Parliament. If he dislikes a law sent to him, he can send it back to Parliament and, giving his reasons, ask that the measure be looked at again. If it is approved once more he must proceed to its promulgation, whether or not he likes it. He has thus a right of suspension but not a veto. The President in Italy is neither a figurehead nor an active politician, or should not be one. The President is elected by a joint session of Senate and Chamber with representatives of the regions. Because of the quality of compromise in the way this post was elaborated, the presidency has changed character with each different incumbent. As an indication of the power, direct or indirect, of the presidency, it is worth saying that rivalry to reach these constitutional heights is intense and each election is more indecorous and difficult than the last. One indication of the increasing difficulty is provided by the number of ballots necessary to elect each president and the amount of time spent in actual voting. Luigi Einaudi was elected on 11 March 1948 after four ballots, and ten hours and twenty minutes of voting; Giovanni Gronchi on 29 April 1955 after four ballots, and eight hours and forty minutes of voting at an election which was the first to be marked by deep hostility; Antonio Segni on 6 May 1962 after nine ballots, and fifteen hours and thirty-five minutes of voting; Giuseppe Saragat on 28 December 1964 after twenty-one ballots, and forty-six hours and forty-five minutes of voting. Giovanni Leone was elected on 24 December 1971 on the twenty-third ballot, but much time was wasted in a series of pointless votes because of Christian Democratic abstentions; he missed by one vote being elected on the twenty-second ballot, the result of which brought a burst of admiration from those hoping to keep him out: 'What perfection of aim!'

Recent presidential elections have been unbridled displays of ambition. The prospects of candidature cast their shadows before, and for three or four years, if not more, in advance of an election politicians regarding themselves as candidates openly manœuvre to improve their chances.

The increase in the intensity of the fight for the presidency can be explained by the disturbing increase in speculation as to whether the office should be left as the constitutionalists shaped it. In a word, the difficulties of keeping parliamentary democracy functioning prompted thoughts of a Gaullist solution for Italy's troubles. The argument is centred around Article 83 of the Constitution, which lays down that the President is elected by Parliament in a joint session. The vote is secret, and a candidate must win a two-thirds majority on the first three ballots. From then on an absolute majority is required. Technically, the President does not have to be a politician. He should be a citizen over fifty years of age 'enjoying full civil and political rights'. But the chances now of electing a man from outside political life are remote; the one thousand or so politicians who gather to elect the President could hardly be expected to look outside their own number to find a worthy Head of State. The great electors at the 1971 election numbered 1009, of whom 321 were senators, 630 deputies and 58 regional councillors. The proposal of those who prefer presidential rule was simply to modify article 83 so that the President should be elected by the people. The advocates of this change argue that it would end the indirect connexion between electors and the executive which, under the present system, denies to the electorate any feeling that it has a hand in choosing its governments. The objections are obvious: that Italy would be threatened with a disguised return to a form of dictatorship; that presidential rule in Rome would more closely resemble that of Latin America than that of the United States.

Fears that the modification was seriously being considered caused a stirring of the constitutional waters in December 1970. Presidential rule had for years been the slogan of small groups of discredited politicians. It was revived in an interview to a periodical called *Rinnovarsi* given by Mauro Ferri, secretary of the Social Democrat Party. His excursion into constitutional thinking might have been overlooked as another of his characteristic comments on the Italian scene. But a left-wing Christian Democrat news-agency implied that the proposal had come from President Saragat himself, who was a Social Democrat. This insinuation brought a denial from the presidential palace in unusually forthright terms and a rejection of methods by which 'falsehood and calumny were made instruments of political struggle'. Eminent parliamentarians came to the support of the Constitution; Sandro Pertini, presiding officer of the Chamber, described it as a delicate mosaic dangerous to touch because by moving one segment the whole might be displaced; Pietro Nenni pronounced the Constitution a machine which should be modified the least possible adding: 'And, if it is true that the occasion makes a thief of a man, it is better not to put temptation in the way of a president even if he is the finest person in the world.' An additional worry as the 1971 election drew nearer was that one of the leading Christian Democrat candidates, Amintore Fanfani, was suspected of nursing Gaullist ambitions and had actually been heard to speak of himself among his fellow-Christian Democrats as 'the only cock among capons'. Fears on this particular score were laid at least temporarily at rest when Fanfani narrowly failed to be elected in December 1971 and Giovanni Leone was chosen.

Intense though the struggle may be among personalities, the general public refuses to follow it with interest. According to a public-opinion poll taken by the Doxa Institute at the request of the *Corriere della Sera*, 62·5 per cent of those asked in May 1971 when the presidential election would take place replied that they did not know or gave no reply at all, 44·4 per cent admitted to not knowing who elected the President (39·4 per cent had the right answer) and 37·8 per cent did not know whether the presidential powers were strong or weak – an open invitation to an ambitious man to try to strengthen them.

In an un-Latin-like way, the presidency has been left to what the incumbent will make of it. Luigi Einaudi, who was elected on 11 May 1948, the first elected president, was ready with advice which was valued. He was an economist of international repute, an anti-Fascist and a former governor of the Bank of Italy. He remained above politics. His successor was Giovanni Gronchi, a Christian Democrat trade unionist from Tuscany whose election in 1955, with the backing of the Communists, came about by his defeating the official candidate (Cesare Merzagora) of his own party. The Prime Minister, the conservative Sicilian Christian Democrat, Mario Scelba, was seen to burst into abundant perspiration when the result was announced. As a matter of routine, Scelba submitted his resignation to the new President, and had it accepted. The style at the Presidency changed. Gronchi was frequently to be challenged on the grounds of overstepping his constitutional powers. He enjoyed playing a part in foreign policy, through his friends in the Cabinet or by initiatives of his own which at times clashed with the policy of the government of the day. In domestic politics, his preference was for encouraging the Socialists into government, but this basically useful element of his presidency is generally overshadowed by his astonishing involvement in one of Italy's most celebrated shifts rightward. His interest in internal affairs brought accusations that the presidency was involved, if not the inspiring hand, in the disastrous experiment of the summer of 1960 when Ferdinando Tambroni, a former Minister of the Interior, became the first Christian Democrat prime minister to try to lead a government with active Neo-Fascist support. Ten people died in riots in Genoa, Rome, Bologna and Reggio Emilia as a reminder that anti-Fascism was not dead before Tambroni, who for most of his short time in office appears to have had the confidence of Gronchi, was removed. It was a vital moment in Italian politics because it demonstrated that the country at large rejected reaction as a way of approaching its political problems. It was one of two vital moments for Italian democracy. It will keep returning as a point of reference, which is why it was better to introduce it at this early stage.

Gronchi's successor, Antonio Segni, was a conservative Christian Democrat from Sardinia, deceptively frail in appearance and disconcertingly tense. His white hair and gentlemanly appearance made him outwardly an acceptable candidate, but the reason for the choice was completely political. The Christian Democrats in January 1962 formally took the then very controversial step of inviting the Socialists to support a government based on the 'opening to the left'. This policy worried the more conservative members of the Party. They objected when supporters of the 'opening' proposed a candidate for the presidential election in the following May who shared their views on this new approach, and the name of the Social Democrat leader, Giuseppe Saragat, was put forward. In order to placate the conservatives, Segni was elected after a hard-fought campaign. Segni appeared to be more discreet than Gronchi in his contact with the active political world but he suffered a stroke in August 1964 after only two years in office.

His presidency was the most controversial, less for his own character than for the allegations which surrounded his tenure and provided the second basic moment in Italian affairs comparable with the Tambroni adventure. Long after illness had removed Segni from the Quirinale, allegations in the Press began to the effect that he had been involved in plotting emergency measures in the summer of 1964 which could hardly be regarded as constitutional. The instrument of these plans was said to be General Giovanni De Lorenzo, Commander of the *carabinieri*, later Chief of the Army Staff, who in the midst of a series of enquiries into his conduct and a number of legal actions became a Monarchist and later a Neo-Fascist member of parliament. He died early in 1973.

Two points have been proved beyond all reasonable doubt about De Lorenzo. The first is that during his time as head of military counter-intelligence and then as head of the *carabinieri* the counter-intelligence service became an instrument of internal politics. The collection of files was greatly enlarged so that, among the 174,000 in the filing cabinets under his supervision, he had information, some of it disagreeable and most of it, apparently, out of date, on almost all leading figures in public life, including the Pope when he was Archbishop of Milan and Saragat before he was elected president. The second allegation against De Lorenzo proved in a court of law is that in the difficult summer of 1964, when the experiment of alliance with the Socialists was making heavy weather, he prepared lists of persons for arrest by the *carabinieri* in an emergency. He omitted to inform the Ministry of the Interior, which is responsible for public security, what he was doing and kept his preparations strictly within the high echelons of the *carabinieri*. The report of the parliamentary commission of enquiry into these events concluded that no *coup d'état* had been planned. But even the governmental majority on this commission, obviously intent on putting the best interpretation on De Lorenzo's actions, accused him of 'inadmissible' conduct. The left-wing minority on the Commission was much harder. Few people know how much Segni was aware of all this except that he did not like the alliance with the Socialists and there is evidence to suggest that he favoured an alarmist view of what was happening to the country under its centre–left rulers. De Lorenzo's plans were made in July 1964; in the following month Segni suffered his stroke. Except at the beginning of the scandal, Segni's name had scarcely been mentioned in the alleged plot, whether out of respect for the office or respect for his integrity is less easy to say. Curiously enough there is a personal connexion between De Lorenzo and Tambroni: De Lorenzo gained the gratitude, so it is said, of leading Christian Democrats who were in favour of a Socialist alliance because during the Tambroni troubles he made sure that the *carabinieri* protected them.

The departure of Segni cleared the way for the arrival of Giuseppe Saragat at the presidency, the first Socialist to hold the post. It was by far the most difficult election of any president till then: twenty-one ballots, including one on Christmas Day 1964, until the best man, as it was said at the time, won in the worst possible way. Objectively there could be no doubt that Saragat, with the badges of his anti-Fascist exile and the comfort of his anti-Communist background, had the experience and integrity to make an excellent president. But many Christian Democrats would not accept a Social Democrat because in a small-minded way they regarded the office as their due, as their man, Segni, had not finished his term. About a hundred of them handed in blank papers, thus making sure that this constant anti-Communist would be elected with the help of the Communist vote.

Appropriately enough for a Social Democrat, Saragat was at his best in warning about the need for social reforms and in showing the alertness and political energy necessary to maintain democracy. The experience of his predecessors with Tambroni and De Lorenzo was a warning that the draught of Italian democracy is inclined to be shallow. Saragat expressed Italian aspirations in a series of dignified addresses which will make a fine volume for future political students. His misfortune was that, during his presidency, Socialist affairs first offered high hopes of solid achievement but then became unusually bitter and complicated, so much so that the presidency could still not be seen as above politics despite the fact that, according to his advisers, President Saragat made up his mind whether or not to take a certain action on the simple test: 'Would the Queen of England do it?'

Saragat's fundamental aim was one of indisputable rectitude: he wanted to see the formation and growth in Italy of a lay, left-wing, non-Communist, democratic party which could serve as an alternative to unending Catholic rule. Of course, he was right. Even the more intelligent Christian Democrats admit that an alternative to themselves would be in Italy's interests. But it is a dream which would require the lamb and the wolf, the hen and the fox to settle down happily together before rival Socialists would make a common cause. Personalities were involved. Saragat before his election was leader of the Social Democrats, a party which he founded after leaving the main Socialist party in 1947 because he objected to its close ties with Communism. His old leader, Pietro Nenni, gradually came round to dissolving his pact of unity with the Communists in favour of joining Christian Democrats and Social Democrats in government. The process began when the two men met at Pralognan in the Alps in August 1956 and talked of the possibility of reunification. While both were active politicians, little could be done; Saragat's election to the presidency eight years later meant that Nenni was the one undisputed leader of Italian Socialism and he became president of the reunited party at an emotional ceremony held in Nervi's great Olympic stadium on 30 October 1966. But unity was superficial. The Party performed poorly at the general election in May 1968. Saragat felt that they must come to terms with the extent of their failure and the responsibility their leaders bore for having betrayed the aspiration of a new, numerous, lay force in Italian life. They left the coalition – which was a mistake. In government, they would have had some cohesion simply as ministers sitting in the same cabinet room. Out of government, they fell apart once again into a Socialist Party and a Social Democrat Party. The vision was more distant than ever. The Communists were far outstripping the Socialists as either an alternative government or an alternative coalition ally. Socialists in Italy hate each other when a split occurs, as if the other side were a traitor; Christian Democrats hate each other personally with a kind of medieval loathing but never split. It is not an easy situation for a prime minister or for a president and what, for Heaven's sake, would the Queen of England do?

To the ordinary Italian, the presidency comes to life when a new government has to be found. Probably that is right, by the criterion of the writers of the Constitution. The presidency can hardly complain about being left out of affairs. Since the war Italy has had more than thirty governments and the accumulated space between them adds up to a long stretch. One of the features of President Saragat's period in office was his intention to bring more before the public eye the part played by the presidency in the search for a new prime minister.

The resignation of a prime minister brings a grand procession of public dignitaries to confer with the President about whom he should best invite to take over the Government. The leaders of parties go to the Quirinale; so do the chairmen of the parliamentary groups in Senate and Chamber, the corps of ex-prime ministers, surviving ex-presidents (who automatically become life-senators), the presiding officers of each house of Parliament and of the Constituent Assembly. After hearing all these views – Communist, Socialist, Social Democrat, Republican, Independent, Christian Democrat, Liberal and Neo-Fascist – the President makes up his mind whom he should ask to form a government. Except for two short-lived governments immediately after the war (those of Parri and Bonomi) every administration has been led by a Christian Democrat. The problem facing a president is which Christian Democrat to choose. This is hardly a limiting factor; from 1946 to 1973 the Party managed to find twelve different personalities to fill the post, several of them more than once, and with varying allies including (reading roughly from right to left) Neo-Fascists, Monarchists, Liberals, Social Democrats, Republicans and Socialists, with a left-wing minority within the party pressing for years for an understanding with the Communists. Never was a party such a centre party.

After the President has consulted everybody and contemplated the situation for a night or two, he will send for some personality who rushes to the palace (the Quirinale is the old summer palace of the popes on one of the seven hills) to hear what is to be offered to him. He may be asked simply to form a government, in which case he will normally accept 'with reserves'; this is a customary phrase meaning that he will try his hand and report back to the President later to say whether or not he is in a position to shake off his 'reserves' and to accept the invitation. If he has found the necessary support he will, at this second interview, produce his list of ministers for the President's perusal. This is an act of politeness; the Prime Minister has the right to choose his own ministers in consultation with leaders of the governing parties. The President decides whom to choose for prime minister, and his constitutional duties finish there. In effect, he can do little else but accept what the Christian Democrats want. Some presidents, notably Saragat, have insisted on inviting their candidate for the prime ministership to aim at a certain form of government; in Saragat's case, invariably the centre–left coalition. This behaviour bought some growls of unconstitutional behaviour from the left-wing opposition. Another variation is that the President may ask some political personality to undertake an exploratory brief, to see what the chances are of forming the Government which the President has in mind. The person he nominates for this task may or may not be asked to form the Government if the outcome of his exploration is favourable.

Saragat liked the presidency's part in dealing with political problems to be given its full due. Arrivals and departures of those politicians called for consultation were televised and political leaders encouraged, by the presence of a large corps of journalists, to make statements. These statements would normally be comprehensible only to other politicians and journalists specialising in the political scene, but the style is suitable for the Byzantine labyrinth into which the search for a prime minister can take the political class. The ordinary person would have the greatest difficulty in following each step in the ritual. Some tried. Interest, even idle curiosity, dropped sharply after the muddled general election of 1968. The results of the election on balance strengthened the centre-left coalition, yet the coalition promptly fell apart because of the Socialist withdrawal. The Socialists came back, split and brought the Government down again. In June 1970 regional elections were unexpectedly in favour of the coalition, which in the meantime had been put together again. Within weeks the Prime Minister, Mariano Rumor, resigned. He did so without first telling some of the members of his own government. For the first time the ordinary public not only did not know, or very much care, who would be the next prime minister, but did not know why the departing prime minister had decided to go. This period of the summer of 1970 may well have been the nadir in terms of relating public awareness to the functioning of democracy, rivalled by the presidential election of December 1971. Things could hardly get worse. A study of young peoples' opinions published early in 1970 included answers to the question of which institution or persons youth looked to with confidence. Mother, of course, came easily first. The politician was last, with one-half of one per cent.

CHAPTER SIX

Parties and Politicians

I COULD have given the answer myself, more or less; but as I was sitting talking with the most agreeable of the Communist leaders I said, 'When do you expect to be in government?'

He looked at me with a touch of kindly pity in his eyes and went on to point out that he could control affairs better for the moment in opposition than from the Prime Minister's office. In terms of real power he was right. This was the period in the summer of 1970 of Mariano Rumor's third government and very near its sudden end, which came on 6 July. His coalition could give only the barest impression of governing. The acute differences among its partners had by then reached the point where the Prime Minister was ringing the party secretaries separately for consultations because feelings were running too high for them to be brought to the same table, especially feelings between Socialists and Social Democrats. The unions were unprecedentedly militant; demonstrations contained an unpleasant element of violence; morale among the police was low, and there had been news of one serious mutiny in a Milan police barracks. On 12 December 1969 a bomb placed in a Milan bank had killed sixteen people. Arrests were made and the procedures used both by the police and judiciary brought credit to neither, including, among other unexplained enormities, the death of a man held for questioning who later, it was admitted, had had nothing to do with the horrible business. This was one of Italy's bad moments. The bombs were a shocking outrage. They were, moreover, un-Italian because foreign to the behaviour of even extremist political groups: bombs are used with some frequency but not for the indiscriminate killing of innocent citizens. The Prime Minister called together his allies in what he genuinely felt would be an attempt to sink their differences and face an ugly situation. The result was another bout of quarrelling. Who would be prime minister when he could be leading the compact parliamentary opposition of the left, and the main strength of the trade union movement? The opposition's most potent weapon is that it cannot be accepted as an alternative government. Even the Communists themselves do not really believe in the prospect of an alternative majority except as a distant aim. As a result, the non-Communist parties of the centre led by the Christian Democrats have had to take the responsibilities and the fruits of power without a break almost since the end of the war.

A brief profile of Italian political history since the war is relatively simple. In the early post-war days an attempt was made under three prime ministers, Parri, Bonomi and De Gasperi in his first administration, to maintain the anti-Fascist alliance. Hence, Communists and Socialists were in government with Christian Democrats. The split came in 1947, in part under pressure from the Americans. The Christian Democrats emerged from the 1948 election with an over-all majority in Parliament and De Gasperi, who continued as prime minister until 1953, insisted that the democratic lay parties, the Social Democrats, Liberals and Republicans, join his own party in supporting a series of centre coalitions. His successors attempted to follow the same pattern. They did not have his authority and they were forced to face an uneasier internal situation. This was the background to the development, fraught with strange inhibitions, known as the 'opening to the left', the bringing of the Socialists into government. What might have seemed a simple switch among minor alliances was carefully prepared in the later fifties and came about in August 1960 when the Socialists abstained in the vote of confidence on a government led by Amintore Fanfani, which included Social Democrats and Republicans but not Liberals. On the surface the change appeared merely to be the replacement of the Liberals by the Socialists, and in December 1963 the Socialists actually entered the Government. But it was a historic change. Traditionally the Socialists had been in opposition since the founding of the Party in the late nineteenth century. From 1934 until well into the post-war period they were allied with the Communists. The series of centre–left governments, as this alliance based on the Christian Democrats and the Socialists was called, dominated political life for a decade. It emerged from the general election of May 1968 in a critical condition. The centre–left parties had done reasonably well at the polls, but internal difficulties were making coalition government impossible.

In June 1968 Giovanni Leone, who was later to be President, led a Christian Democrat minority government intended to prepare a new coalition. It was followed by three administrations led by Mariano Rumor, the first including all the centre–left parties. This government lasted until August 1969 when the recently reunited Socialist Party split and the coalition collapsed. Rumor was once again left with a minority Christian Democrat government with which to face the serious strikes of 1969 and the Milan and Rome bombings. He resigned in February 1970 claiming that Italy was becoming ungovernable unless his allies would agree to a new coalition, and this he managed to put together again in April. But on 6 July he gave up, telling a hastily convened cabinet meeting that he had had enough.

The Christian Democrats are not just Italy's largest party: they are the rulers, the arbiters, the setters of standards in public life, the creators of what is indeed a régime. They have presided over Italy's immense economic expansion which followed, in Alcide De Gasperi's time, the refurbishing of

Italy's reputation abroad. With a quarter of a century of uninterrupted power behind them, they could look forward to the prospect of keeping power for the foreseeable future unless by their own weakness they should let it drop from their hands, through sheer corruption, confusion and *malgoverno*. It could scarcely be taken from them. The real power of the party runs deep into everyday life. The Christian Democrats are the most adept at dealing with a vital institution of Italian life known as the *sottogoverno*, which must be understood to be believed and even then may seem far-fetched. It is the network of 'interests' cultivated and to some extent created by the Christian Democrats; it is the means by which favours are dispensed, how jobs are obtained in the apparatus of the State or any of its near relatives, directing an opera-house, a licence to run a tobacconist's shop, keeping the parish priests happy by granting small requests, bending the knee in exaggerated servility towards the local bishop, a job in the state radio and television corporation, presiding over the local tourist office. It is the way the ordinary citizen can be equipped to deal with the official administration, because a letter recommending him to an official may well solve his problem: in return for which, of course, he will vote for the party which helped him. The *sottogoverno* is post-war Italy's greatest contribution to the art of keeping a country running when government in the accepted sense of the term is lacking. In Britain, normally speaking, there is a government with sufficient power and authority, whether used well or badly, to maintain the rhythm of administration; in France, when governments before Gaullist times used to fall frequently, the highly trained civil service could govern by itself. In Italy governments, even when they have substantial parliamentary majorities, do not fulfil the minimum requirements of government, and the civil service is an incredible combination of secret society and genuine administrative antique which in part is still regulated by laws dating from the latter part of the nineteenth century. Its ritual is mysterious and narcissistic and has little or no connexion with public life. The instrument of public administration which at any time functions in Italy is the *sottogoverno*, and it has no legal or institutional basis;

but official organisations have to set up entire departments to deal with the 'letters of recommendation' which proliferate in the shaded soil of the 'under government'.

The Anglo-Saxon conscience might be inclined priggishly to call it corrupt. At its most blatant it is a method of purchasing votes. The purest practitioners of the system use it simply for this purpose. The Christian Democrats are the masters in its use. This became very clear at the beginning of the sixties when the Socialists came closer to government and finally joined the coalition. One of their earliest requests was for a share in the *sottogoverno*. They were given a share. A highly intelligent left-wing Christian Democrat, who had been strongly in favour of having the Socialists in government, was soon heard to complain about the hopelessness of the Socialist attitude to this marvellous font of power. 'You can call us Christian Democrats corrupt if you like; but we do favours and give jobs with the aim of getting more votes. The Socialists enjoy the favours and enjoy the jobs for themselves without caring about votes.' Wasted patronage to an intelligent Italian politician is like pouring away one's life-blood in some obscure and useless cause. There is constructive corruption and plain corruption. Italian public life knows both of them well but the aim of the more respected and respectable politican is the first rather than the second.

The writer Ignazio Silone had some wise words to say about the relationship between democracy and the granting of favours which is essential to the Italian system. He is speaking of peasants, but his words could be applied to a large part of Italian society. 'Actually the very word politics fills most poor peasants with disgust. More than elsewhere by atavistic tradition they are refractory and distrustful, conceiving of public life as nothing but fraud, theft and intrigue, no matter who is in power. And they are therefore profoundly sceptical of the possibility of effective democracy and laws applied equally to all. The only advantage of a democracy based on popular vote is that the vote, conscientiously used, permits the poor also to share in the intrigue. Then the letter of recommendation – that sacramental document which allows the poor man to make contact with the bureaucracy – costs less and becomes more effective. These prejudices are surely not favourable to the development of free democratic institutions, but it would be a mistake not to examine their historical origin, to consider them simply the product of human wickedness.'

A thought which might seem, but is not, irrelevant: Would Italians really prefer an efficient civil service and a smoothly working executive supported by a rationally operating legislature, all of which combined would make the *sottogoverno* unnecessary? And, indeed, if all this had happened in the past, would it have made unnecessary alternatives to the legitimate authorities, such as the Mafia, the exaggerated regard for the family and the semi-conspiratorial attitude adopted in any dealings with officialdom? The answer is not so easy as it should be: it should be 'yes' and that should be the end. But a national character is formed as much by what has been done to people as what they are basically like, what history has done to them, the climate, the Church, the geography; and all these influences have taught Italians the great lesson of the inevitable imperfection of institutional life, the acceptance of gross injustice as a matter of course (a shrug of the shoulders accompanies the news that an elderly lady has been held in prison for not having paid her television licence while notoriously no serious tax-evader has ever been put into prison) and the pointlessness of trying to insist on change. The immobile functionary, the bland, priestly smile, the respectful Communist, all weigh against any faith in the efficacy of effort, as does the Italian genius for obscuring the truth. Truth is like the tiny piece of the bone of a saint concealed within a vast baroque reliquary, which the faithful are allowed just fleetingly to discern once a year when the saint's particular feast-day is celebrated. For every other day of the year, it is the sumptuous, rich, irrelevant casing, not the real content which matters. It is not that Italians are basically untruthful, but their flair is dramatisation, not simple exposition. They are not much concerned about facts. Their world is not the world of black and white; it is a world demanding improvisation and a sleight of hand to suggest that two ends are really meeting when in fact they are not. Regard for efficiency in everyday

life is alien to this world. Some of them are aware of this
scant regard for the truth. A cartoon in a leading weekly
showed a witness testifying in court: 'He was a tall man,
rather short, with fair hair practically black and would have
been about seventy but looked twenty.'

Hence, it is difficult to know whether most Italians find
rhetorical complication and confusion preferable to a well-
ordered system of public life or just the best they can expect
to obtain in an imperfect world. The one clear element is
that the proportion of Italians who are driven to indignation
by incompetence should increase as a natural result of the
quick advance towards what is thought to be a modern society.
A more involved form of life naturally means more contact
with the public authorities: the clan can no longer keep to
itself as an almost self-sufficient unit. Yet fundamentally there
is the feeling that imperfection is a more natural state for man
than a perfectly run system. This basic feeling is another of
the graces which has saved the politicians; they could have
done a great deal better (heavens above, they could!) but no
one expected it of them and many Italians did not hope for
it with much conviction.

The Christian Democrats themselves are the standard-
bearers of this outlook. It is not confined to them but they
have made it their own, in part because of the moral teachings
of a party of Catholics which implies that the bad things in
this life lead to the good things in the next, another perfect
alibi for the politicians to do nothing substantial or disturbing and for the public at large to take the situation fatalistic-
ally.

This party is by far the most remarkable as well as the most
powerful element in Italian politics. It is a post-war creation
which took its name from a party formed at the end of the
nineteenth century by left-wing Catholics, which was distrusted
and finally suppressed by the Vatican, and its leadership from
the Popular Party, another Catholic political party which was
also distrusted by the Vatican but actually suppressed, along
with all political parties, by Mussolini. It was refounded after
the war with no clear idea of what it should be except to keep
Communism at bay, but like so many impromptu creations it

has become the most important political instrument in the country and is fully supported by the Church.

Its relative strength in the Chamber of Deputies is shown better in a chart than in words. This chart gives the results of the 1946 election to the Constituent Assembly and of the six subsequent general elections.

The Christian Democrats reversed an entire historical process by their conquest of power immediately after the last war. Their victory meant that the Catholic forces were now for the first time in Italy's history as a nation in charge of the Italian state. The liberal *élite* which ruled Italy until Mussolini came to power had, after the interlude of Fascism, been replaced by Catholics enjoying mass support, including the support, one need hardly add, of the overwhelming majority of the women. It would be difficult to find any more radical change by democratic method in a country's life. The Labour victory in Britain in 1945 is by comparison a ripple on the waters of Lake Avernus.

Did the religious element make any difference? The answer is: overwhelmingly so. Immediately after the war, the Christian Democrats had two massive advantages over all other Italian parties. The first was that their post-war leaders had all known political life before Mussolini's dissolution of the parties, as members of the Popular Party, and most of them stayed in Italy during the Fascist period. It is fair to say that many of them did not like Fascism but were not actively anti-Fascist. They lived in Italy and went about their business during Mussolini's two decades rather than go into exile like many of the Socialists and Communists, or to prison, or to a form of internal exile (still adopted) by which men thought to be dangerous were sent to live in some remote place, as the writer Carlo Levi was sent from Turin to Lucania.

The result was that the Catholic leaders remained more closely in touch with their own rank and file than the exiles could possibly have done. They appeared to provide a greater continuity despite their lack of a share in the heroic side of political life. But who in a democracy wants heroes? Certainly not the Italians. Democracy – and Italian feeling as a whole – is the negation of hero-worship. They want to worship

	1946	1948	1953	1958	1963	1968	1972
Christian Democrats	207	305	261	273	260	266	267
Communists	104 ⎱	183	143	140	166	177	179
Socialists	115 ⎰		75	84	87 ⎱	91	61
Social Democrats	—	33	19	23	33 ⎰		29
Liberals	41	19	14	16	39	31	21
Republicans	23	9	5	7	6	9	14
Monarchists	16	14	40	23	8	6 ⎱	56
M.S.I. (Neo-Fascists)	—	—	29	25	27	24 ⎰	
Others	50	11	4	5	4	3	3
TOTAL	556	574	590	596	630	607	630

footballers, pop singers, the older people worship leading opera-singers, but never politicians. To some extent this feeling was, and is, due to the experience of Mussolini, who was a caricature of a hero but had been accepted by many Italians at his face value. But it was not just reaction. Italians since the war have had plenty of good reasons for concluding that democracy might just as well be done away with or adapted more exactly to the Latin temperament. They have resisted the temptation. They realistically judge democracy as good in the sense that the available alternatives are worse, and its results have on the whole brought material benefits.

To this Christian Democrat advantage of continuity and willingness to accept democratic practice after Mussolini's disastrous experiment was added support from the Allies and backing from the Church. In simple political terms this combination meant economic help and votes. And, as the world's standards go, a stamp of respectability. American aid was assured with which to reconstruct the country. The full weight of the Catholic Church was brought to bear on Italian affairs with some good, some questionable and some appalling results.

The wisest of the Christian Democrat leaders and the head of the Party from the end of the war was Alcide De Gasperi. He died in 1954 after having been prime minister in a series of governments from 1946 to 1953. He was an outstanding man by any standards, but his wisdom had its limits. He was an old-fashioned type of statesman. As foreign minister immediately after the war he saw Italy's humiliation at the peace conference. As a result his main energies were spent in bringing Italy back into international polite society. Given the catastrophic state of the country immediately after the war, friends, and in particular generous friends, were urgently needed. He gave little time to party organisation and in his day the Christian Democrats depended almost entirely on the Church and its secular organisations, such as Catholic Action, to bring their voters to the polls. A party machine of sorts, never particularly effective, was a later invention. He was an honest Catholic himself and appeared to expect the Church's support of his efforts as something that was his due. But he had more Nordic than Latin ideas on how far the Church should be allowed to go in dictating policy. De Gasperi was born in the province of Trent when it was still under Austrian rule and sat as a young deputy in the Vienna Parliament. This experience helped to give him the personal strong sense of the state which marked his own outlook. The Vatican never understood him. During the bad years of Fascism they had given him (through the efforts of his friend Monsignor Montini, later Paul VI) a humble job as a cataloguer in the Vatican Library and regarded this favour as sufficient to place him in their debt for the future. But as prime minister he insisted on showing a disconcerting independence of mind. He would not, for instance, obey Pius XII in 1952 when the Pope urged the Christian Democrats to form an alliance with the extreme right, including the Neo-Fascists, in the Rome local elections. But De Gasperi's internal policy was insufficient: his vision was of an Italy forming part of a united Europe but he did not do enough to bring Italian institutions, such as the educational system, taxation, justice, up to the level required for membership of a socially advanced community and he left a heritage of unfulfilled aspirations towards social reform. At the same time he turned a blind eye towards the corruption practised by some of his colleagues, the rush towards personal enrichment at the cost of the State. Italy from the immediate postwar years onward was constantly producing scandals. Sympathetic critics of De Gasperi say that his religion served him badly in this respect. He was too deeply convinced of the sinfulness of man as a natural condition for him to feel inclined to call a halt to peccadilloes.

Whatever his faults, De Gasperi was a great man by political standards. His colleagues had his faults without the central core of independence. In particular they did not have his personal independence of the Vatican and the Italian hierarchy. Since his death the Christian Democrats have never had an undisputed leader, one of the reasons for the divisions within the Party.

Leave aside for one moment the whole question of the Church's electoral influence and the fact, for fact it is, that in many parts of the country a Christian Democrat who offends the Church can quite simply be kept out of the next parliament. Leave aside as well the honest respect devout men will have for the earthly embodiment of the religion which they try to practise. The Christian Democrat politician at every level is under constant pressure, sometimes unintentional, sometimes intentional, from the mere presence of the Vatican. One of the best of the Christian Democrat prime ministers once remarked privately that Rome was an impossible city from which to govern. The influences on ministers were too great and the greatest was the papal court across the river.

This outlook is worth the deepest examination because it is fundamental to Italian life. Sometimes it looks like cowardice but it is not that. One might ask: Why can no Christian Democrat rise to his feet and crisply, without gestures or drama, take note of some example of ecclesiastical interference in Italian political life (now admittedly less than in the past) and assert the unique competence of the Italian Parliament to deal with such matters? Would he drop dead? Possibly, in Italy; in 1956 a merchant of Prato brought the first legal action against a bishop since the Concordat of 1929 (the bishop had attacked him and his wife as 'public sinners' for marrying in a registry office), won his case, lost on appeal and was brought low by a stroke and financial ruin.

Is there some genuine fear of the supernatural consequences of an act, not of rebellion, but of independence? This is delicate territory, far away in character from the inflated rhetoric which swirls around Italian political life like the mists of the Po delta. It involves a feeling which is more than respect but less than fear. It has elements of the cautious and of the abject, of insecurity about the resilience of the Italian state and wonder at the continuing strength of the Church in Italy, the one constant element in more than a millennium and a half. Even the Communists have something of this feeling and are most reluctant to offend the Church. After all, the anti-clerical state which ruled in Italy from national unity until 1920 failed abysmally, a failure which could be ascribed, like that of the merchant of Prato, to impertinence towards the ecclesiastical authority. No better answer is given to this subject than that it can really never be understood by those who come from a different background, unless one accepts that relations with the Vatican and with the hierarchy – the distinction must be made – are just an example of Italian respect for power and the effective way in which the Church knows how to use it.

One must in fairness say that it weakens Christian Democracy's handling of affairs, and not only that of Christian Democrats, because the Catholic mentality goes far beyond the surprisingly limited ranks of practising Catholics. It subtracts from the sense of the state. There is an old saying in Italy that the family comes first, then the Church and then, a poor third, the State. It reduces the credibility of the Communists because they recognised the political power of the Church – as Mussolini had done – and not only supported the writing of his agreements with the Church into the Constitution but constantly sought to avoid conflict with the Papacy: they are the least anti-clerical of the lay parties.

But against this abstract verdict one has to estimate how an alternative would fare. Would the lay parties, more or less anti-clerical as they are, manage matters better? Would a cooler approach, spared the constant crucifixion of intense personal ambition within the discipline of dogmatic and ecclesiastical rigour, draw off the unnatural emotions which penetrate Italian politics?

The essential problem is that there is no genuinely democratic, left-wing, sturdily lay alternative to Christian Democratic rule and, that being the case, the Christian Democrats have the duty as well as the right to rule the country which was united a century ago against the anathemas of the Papacy whose territories were annexed. The core of the problem was too obviously revealed on 20 September 1970, the anniversary of the taking of Rome from the popes by Italian forces. President Saragat delivered a speech to the two houses of Parliament which was a reasoned interpretation of the event in the light of Italian history. At the Porta Pia, where the breach was made by the Italian forces in the walls of papal Rome, with the result that the royal house was excommunicated and Italian political life boycotted by Catholics, the Pope's Cardinal-Vicar celebrated mass.

The Christian Democrats are united by the mixture of piety and interest which binds them to the Church; the result is that they may fight each other with frenzy but, unlike the lay parties, do not split. Even the Communists have had their costly defections. The Socialists, the third largest party, have split half a dozen times since the Party was founded in 1892 (one of the splits being that in January 1921 which produced the Italian Communist Party). The Socialists have a natural vocation to fall apart and do so earnestly over differences of opinion of a magnitude which would not unduly perturb a Christian Democrat.

The effect of Christian Democracy's solidarity is that it can include within its ranks an astonishing range of opinions, from reactionaries far to the right of the Conservative right in Britain, really benighted men of the black right, and at the same time men of the left who are in many ways more radical in their thinking than the Communist opposition. The following comment on anti-Communism came from one of the old Christian Democrat leaders who had an uncommonly dry wit: 'I am not frightened by the Communists,' he said, 'but by our own left.'

This diversity within its ranks means that the Party can attract its mass vote by showing a variety of faces to the electorate. Each different section of society votes for a different sort of Christian Democracy. And the Party itself can fly the colours required at any particular moment. De Gasperi's definition was that Christian Democracy was a party of the centre moving towards the left. After his death it moved more towards the right, a shift which reached a climax in Tambroni's experiment in 1960 of governing with the Neo-Fascists and was again evident in the reinforcement of the Neo-Fascists in the summer of 1971 and the formation of a distinctly conservative coalition after the May 1972 election.

Theoretically it could be said that such a system assured the presence of the appropriate Christian Democrat at the head of any government that the country might require. In practice it is not quite like that. Leading Christian Democrat personalities tend to trim their sails to unfamiliar breezes rather than permit a compartmentalised system in which a certain personality represents the right and becomes prime minister when a more reactionary approach is required, while someone else consistently represents the left. This is because they all lead factions within the Party, which are highly organised on party lines, and the leadership must come to terms with the factions. Take any day, take 20 September 1970, when the Vatican and the Italian Government were celebrating the taking of Rome, and look at the Christian Democrat leadership. The left wing was led by Signor Aldo Moro, then Foreign Minister, who as Prime Minister had been known for his moderation, his efforts at gaining a consensus of opinion, his sense of the balance of forces within the Party and for his vulnerability to attacks launched on him by the Christian Democrat left for alleged lack of reforming zeal. The pioneer among left-wing leaders, Signor Amintore Fanfani, then Presiding Officer of the Senate, had moved well to the right, which was one of the reasons why Moro, as a part of their personal rivalry, had taken over the left. Giulio Andreotti, known in the past as one of the most conservative of all Christian Democrat leaders, was chairman of the parliamentary party in the Chamber, after two decades in ministerial posts, and had been the favourite of the Socialists for the prime ministership after Mariano Rumor had resigned in the summer. A lack of principles? No, not according to Italian judgement as to political standards. These men were being realistic and professional. They knew the requirements of power. Anyone who asked Andreotti at about that date where he felt he stood in the Christian Democrat phalanx – left, right or centre? – would have the reply that he did not feel any of these things; he had always regarded himself as a democrat and that was as far as labelling could or need go for him.

Of course, he was correct. No figure would last long in Italian public life if he insisted on standing on the dignity of closely defined principles. He would be looked on as inexperienced or not the type of man to make a politician, just as a man with a severe shake in the right hand would be best advised against taking up surgery.

Successive members of the British Embassy in Rome have been heard to complain that the Italians are difficult to deal with because you never know where you are with them or, worse, where they are at any particular moment with each other. The temptation has been to make light of them, in the way that an uncertain viewer of a difficult piece of abstract art will laugh at it because it is beyond his experience. The result over the years has been a series of meetings ending with statements that nothing could be better than Anglo-Italian relations without a serious effort to define them with accuracy, like those constant protestations that everything is fine with a marriage that has long lost piquancy and lustre. The European policies of both were weakened as a result. This is no place to give an account of British relations with the Italians but one other unpardonable mistake might be pointed out. It is astonishing that throughout the years in which the Italian Communist Party, the largest in Western Europe, was led by a figure of international stature – Palmiro Togliatti – the Foreign Office chose officially to ignore him and his whole party.

Which is more centaur-like? A Catholic party with ministries and patronage at its fingertips and its nose amidst the incense, or a Communist party looking frequently like a liberal opposition but remaining faithfully allied to the Soviet Union despite Prague and Budapest and Prague again?

The Italian Communists feel their own dual character more than do the Christian Democrats. The Christian Democrat duality is a binding force. Even when the mutual hatreds are at a hectic pitch, and the factions at their most intensely antagonistic, unity for them is somewhere there in the dark recesses of the baroque mother of churches. To the Communists this double personality is a cause of dissension. It gives them a deeper problem of identity and raises the question of whether they might have gone still further ahead had Palmiro Togliatti been a less clever man.

Togliatti set the pattern of all future behaviour by the Party with one stroke on his arrival in Italy from the Soviet Union in March 1944, when he immediately agreed to join the Government and, like every other minister, took his oath of loyalty to the King. Arguably any Communist would know that the oath to the King taken by a leader of the Party would be in no way binding. Even so, men now in eminent positions in the Party have recalled their shock as earnest young revolutionaries when they heard the news. The decision meant only one thing: the Communist leadership was reconciled already to the idea that the way to power would be through the proper channels, not by revolution. They had discarded violence without so much as trying it. The situation must have seemed reasonably favourable towards revolution. The war was still in progress and the Communist partisans were armed. The example of Yugoslavia was promising (as indeed it was to be for them in a different way ever since) because there the Allies had backed Communist guerrillas once they had shown their strength. What better than to replace Fascism by Communism imposed along the proper lines of an armed uprising? It must have seemed a marvellous moment to many ordinary Communists. Italy would pluck its long-postponed revolution, its rejection of the past which had led to Fascism, from the tooth of war and from the foreign invaders who would be made use of to support the revolutionary process. The result would be a perfect combination of violence and finesse, a historical consummation as much as a triumph.

But the uprising did not take place. And, as far as 'never' can be used in political affairs, it never will. The division of Europe had already been agreed between East and West. Togliatti would have embarrassed the Russians by attempting to take power. Italy was full of British and American troops, and the Communists believed that they would have been used against a Communist *coup*. His only course was to organise his forces so that power could be achieved by impeccably democratic methods; legitimately, in a manner that even the Americans would have to admit was the expression of the will of the majority and therefore sacrosanct even if Marxist. This outlook required as a corollary that the democratic parties would make their contribution by keeping democracy going. In early 1971, Giorgio Amendola, the Party's leading advocate of a place for the Communists in government, ruefully admitted in an interview that time was on the side of the Communists but wondered how long the governmental parties could keep things going without open Communist support. Looking back from the standpoint of how Communist affairs were to develop after April 1944, it seems as if Togliatti took the course, however far in its general lines it was imposed by

Stalin, most agreeable to his own temperament. It is difficult not to feel that he had an advantage here over De Gasperi who was, one suspects, not altogether happy with the nature of his own confessional party (he always insisted where possible on bringing in the lay parties to share responsibility even when he had his absolute majority) and not without doubts, in the early stages, about Atlantic policy in the way that Togliatti, after so many years in Moscow, was without doubts about the attachment to the Russians. One of the problems of Italian life has been the interference of foreigners in Italian affairs. After the Second World War, the Italians might have hoped to be free of it, to be left after the disaster of Fascism to try to set their own house in order with no more than some economic help from their friends. Instead the international feud between East and West meant that Italy not only had to choose one of two seeming irreconcilables (they were to become less so later) but saw the Western Allies, the Russians and the Vatican all taking a direct hand in Italian internal politics.

Togliatti was a cold-blooded little man with a sharp wit and an amiable chuckle in private which could be turned into biting sarcasm when speaking in public. He was a superb politician at a time when there were few in Italy, with absolute control over his own party which a humane person such as was De Gasperi, with a more humane and varied party to lead, could not rival; indeed, De Gasperi had lost control of his own party before he actually died. Togliatti was the undisputed master until the day of his death. While both men were alive, it was said with some frequency that after De Gasperi Togliatti was Italy's most brilliant politician. After De Gasperi's death in 1954 this judgement ceased to be uttered by the *cliché*-mongers: not everyone can look unpleasant logic in the face.

These brandishers of *clichés*, with which the landscape of writings on Italy abounds, used to say that they could well have envisaged Togliatti as a cardinal if he had gone into a seminary instead of the Communist Party. It is the type of remark which along with quotations from *Private Angelo* (which Macmillan himself was not above using – the lack of the *dono di coraggio* – about his hosts) is frequent from people who take a Don Camillo attitude to Italian affairs (what damage Guareschi did to his country's reputation for seriousness!). It reduces the whole problem to innocuous and seemingly cosy terms.

Togliatti could have been a priest, to judge from his superficial appearance. He certainly would not have become more than a bishop. There was something inescapably middle-class about him. He had committed the most dreadful acts as a functionary of the Comintern, things which De Gasperi would never for a second have dreamed of doing. But it was Togliatti who looked the *bourgeois*. His metal-framed spectacles and double-breasted grey suits would have gone well with some academic: in Britain he might have made a name as a caustic television-don. He had charm, but it was an intellectual charm. He could not be visualised high in the ranks of the Catholic Church. The Church normally draws its cardinals from the ranks of men emerged from the simple classes or gentlemen with noble or princely demeanour, inherited or acquired. Togliatti was not princely and not working-class.

He gave his party three basic lines of policy. The first was that it was to be a mass party backed by an even more massive parliamentary vote. When he died the membership of the Party was about 1,500,000 and one Italian in three voted for it or its immediate allies. The second was that it should come to power by constitutional means. The third that it should seek its own way of applying Communism in Italy while remaining loyal in spirit to the Soviet Union. The strain of maintaining this policy was considerable – even more so for his successors, who lacked his personal authority.

The search for votes was not difficult. The Communists came out of the war with the prestige of their preponderant part in the Resistance movement, and to this they promptly added leadership of organised labour. The Italian trade union movement has been predominantly Communist since the end of the war. A shift to the far left was natural in the minds of many people, particularly the workers, as a reaction to Fascism. To the more conservative-minded the Communists had behaved correctly first by joining the royal government and then by helping to write the republican constitution. To Catholics, though the Communists took full advantage of the traditional anti-clericalism in Emilia-Romagna to build their base there, the Party showed surprising respect for Catholic sensibilities by adopting the Catholic requirement of writing the Concordat into the Constitution. Once they were forced out of government in May 1947, the Communists became the one powerful party in opposition with an organisation formidable enough to attract the protest vote. And De Gasperi assured them their flow of protests by taking so markedly lax a view of the excessive self-enrichment of some of his colleagues and their clients and by making little progress with administrative reforms.

The geographical distribution of party membership shows how dependent they are on the two central regions of Emilia-Romagna and Tuscany. Their voters are six times the party membership.

Region	Members 31 Dec 1971	Voters 1972 Election	% of votes	Votes per member
VALLE D'AOSTA	2,871	28,878*	42·2	10·05
PIEDMONT	76,549	776,429	26·8	10·14
LIGURIA	70,609	404,388	31·6	5·72
LOMBARDY	171,756	1,304,864	23·8	7·59
VENETO	66,249	449,938	17·3	6·79
TRENTINO-ALTO ADIGE	4,108	38,820	7·6	9·44
FRIULI-VENEZIA GIULIA	21,317	167,959	20·2	7·87
EMILIA-ROMAGNA	406,868	1,179,463	44·0	2·89
TUSCANY	233,011	1,014,075	42·1	4·35
MARCHES	49,436	295,028	32·8	5·96
UMBRIA	36,228	222,000	41·7	6·12
ABRUZZO	25,870	192,495	26·9	7·44
LAZIO	76,363	784,900	27·1	10·27
MOLISE	3,113	32,422	17·3	10·41
CAMPANIA	61,713	618,148	22·8	10·01
APULIA	67,894	507,614	25·7	7·47
LUCANIA	12,418	81,864	24·9	6·59
CALABRIA	33,660	259,995	25·9	7·72
SICILY	62,263	537,824	21·3	8·63
SARDINIA	28,206	202,626	25·3	7·18
	1,510,502	9,099,740	27·2	6·02

* Left-wing list.

SOURCE: *L'Unità*, 25 June 1972

How near have the Communists been to power? This is the most crucial question in Italian politics after the question when they themselves envisage coming into government.

Italians have a marvellous gift for dramatising their own situation. The Communists never did better than in April 1948: the first post-war general election in which the world was encouraged to watch the battle for Italy's soul – as the picture was painted – has become the accepted gospel on which the temple of post-war Italian politics has been built. Italy's internal politics have been overshadowed by the notion, born fully grown in 1948, that politics for Italians means a choice between moderate conservatism and communism, a thoroughly dispiriting choice for intelligent people who genuinely wanted to make a better country, and a democratic country, out of the ruins of defeat. This approach may have been invaluable in obtaining the maximum of economic aid from the Americans but it was one of the basic factors in the gap between governments and electors. Years later it became fashionable to say that a left-wing, lay and democratic party was Italy's essential requirement. It was and it is, and the chances of having it were wrecked or at best indefinitely postponed by the theory that only two alternatives were available – perdition or reaction – and with this approach went the failure to make a clear break with the past.

For fear of upsetting conservative feeling, the Allies refused efforts at a wholesale purge of Fascists in office. And that is one of the reasons why the civil service, the police forces and judicial authorities have not been at the level of even the most moderate reforming spirit in the country. The Christian Democrats and their lay allies constantly turned to anti-Communist allies when the clear way to deal with the Communists was to keep quiet and govern reasonably well. One of the few prime ministers to adopt this view was Emilio Colombo, but he was faced with the heavy task of inheriting the centre–left idea, in mid-1970, when it was sadly weakened by quarrelling and years of slender achievement. The mirage of a crusade was always at hand to blight the politicians' concentration on real reform which would have been the effective, but not rhetorical, dramatic or sycophantic, form of anti-

Communism, and so fundamentally out of keeping with the times.

Undoing the dawn has no point, and the legend that Italy was only just saved from the Communist grasp was accepted and became the dominant factor in Italian political life. The object of taking a close look at Christian Democracy and the Communist Party is to show that they are not at all the mutually antipathetic forces in bitter conflict which is generally regarded as the main feature of the Italian political scene. Of course, Christian Democrats and Communists each behave as if the other is the principal enemy. There is at least that much genuine challenge in political life. Shortly after the end of the war, Pius XII prescribed the penalty of excommunication for Catholics who supported the Communists, and this ban was later extended to include parties which helped the Communists. A decade ago confession boxes had lists hanging in them of Communist and Socialist organisations, including Italy's biggest trade union federation; a man or woman would have to repent of having backed or joined them before being admitted to communion. The Italian hierarchy normally finds guarded but clear enough expressions before a general election to tell the faithful for whom they are to vote. All this should not mask the vital point that both the Catholic politicians and the Communists have their worst difficulties within their own ranks, not outside them, and the 'duel' with each other, though not entirely fabricated, is in the interests of both sides because it soothes their intimate problems. Each would have to invent the other if only one of them existed – the Christian Democrats because they are a federation of interests not a party, the Communists because of the constant spinal crack caused by the strain of dreaming simultaneously of constitutions and revolutions.

After the death of Togliatti in 1964 the Party was led with less brilliance but in a sense more effectively. Togliatti was too clever. He could intellectualise the emotional clashes of those who wanted revolution and he could give a satisfying emotional appeal to the constitutional road to Italy's form of Communism. With the result that he accumulated votes quite satisfactorily. He prevented quarrels and he could stand astride the factions. But he could not create, by Italian standards, a credible party of government. Of course, he collected the protest votes; but protest, as anybody in Italy knows, is not a basis for getting anything done. The only way is to join the system. And this Togliatti never did. He had much about him of the exile come back to the country which he did not fully understand. He seemed something of a foreigner. Once he had gone, his system was gradually but profoundly modified to suit Italian conditions.

The idea of the constitutional way to power was taken a step further. The Communists gradually made their own the concept of the party of law and order. From being the agitators whose skulls were the prime targets of the Government's riot-squads, they taught not only agitators but the riot-squads a lesson. This function to some extent went back to Togliatti's time; the crisis following the attempt on his life in 1948 was in part resolved because the Party called on its followers to abstain from violence. But the real change came after his death, long after, in the period of violence which was opened in the autumn of 1969 when the working-class movement became more militant that at any other time since the war. This militancy was due to three factors. The first was that the working classes, encouraged by the unions, and still more by the weakness of successive governments, took to the strike weapon not only to demand better wages and conditions but also to insist on such long-promised social reforms as a better housing policy, a rational health service and improved schooling as an integral part of their demands. The failure of governments to fulfil their promises in such fields brought the workers' organisations into the purely political arena. The second reason was that groups to the left of the official Communist Party, claiming inspiration from the Chinese example which the Italian Communist Party abhorred, turned to violence as a specific means of attacking the employers and the country's institutions in general. These far left-wing groups were active first among the students demanding university reform and then among discontented workers who had lost faith in the Communist Party as an effective rallying-point for protest. The third reason was that the police were hampered by their unpopularity after a series of clashes with striking workers had resulted in deaths. The result was that the Communist Party disowned its left wing, expelling a group known as the 'Manifesto', from the name of the periodical it published, and used its influence among students and the unions to curb violence. All this showed good sense. The Manifesto group had a high level of intellect in its ranks; its newspaper was for a time required reading for anyone wanting to know the background to left-wing affairs. They were extraordinarily well informed. But they did not have the means, or the wish, to build an organisation. Their fatal mistake was to challenge the official parties on their own ground by putting forward candidates for the May 1972 general election. They emerged without a seat, despite the fact that they had put at the top of their list of candidates Pietro Valpreda, an imprisoned anarchist whose case had become a *cause célèbre*. Young people now turned increasingly towards the larger parties, towards Christian Democrats and the Communists.

At much the same time the Communist Party took a vital decision about what the achieving of power by constitutional methods really meant. Togliatti's successors were more realistic than he. After his death the secretaryship passed to Luigi Longo, a dour Piedmontese with a record of fighting in Spain and in the Resistance movement, who had been a loyal but colourless deputy to Togliatti. He was deeply respected in the rank and file but he was certainly no intellectual. Longo's deputy was Enrico Berlinguer. He became the real power in the Party after Longo suffered a stroke and he was elected party secretary at the Milan Congress in March 1972. The Congress took place just before the general election in an atmosphere of some tension: two nights before it opened there was a pitched battle in the centre of Milan between police and far-left-wing demonstrators. But emotionally for the Communists the main attraction was the sight of the battle-scarred old Secretary handing over to the younger man on whose arm he was leaning for support.

It is worth pausing to look at Berlinguer who, while still under fifty, had become the undisputed head of Italian Communism. Indeed, he might be called the incarnation of it if he were not so slight in build, so inhumanly thin that to think of him as anything incarnate would be to go against nature. This was the impression I had of him while watching him take over the secretaryship at Milan.

His strength is not physical: it is in his intensity. His look of anguish, his sad eyes and furrowed forehead give him a perpetual air of suffering and overwork. He read his report intelligently but with no flourishes, as if content to pass over its often excellent phrasing in such a way as to conceal its quality rather than use it to stir the emotions. He knew that he would leave the Congress as Secretary, in the line of Gramsci and Togliatti. But, as he wearily moved away from the rostrum, a small, bent, seemingly overburdened figure, he looked as if he was trying to get away as fast as possible from the applause and the cheers so that he could go off somewhere alone and suffer in silence.

Like Gramsci he is Sardinian. He was born in Sassari on 25 May 1922, and as a child had a reputation for seriousness. The family is of Catalan origin and is regarded as noble, though a long participation in left-wing politics has removed any relevance from those aristocratic origins. His father was a Socialist member of Parliament until 1968, the year before he died. With this left-wing background goes a strong element of the Sardinian patriarch. He is in a real sense religiously attached to his family. His wife is a practising Roman Catholic. This family background goes some way to exonerate him from the charge of being guided purely by tactical motives when he talks of the need for an alliance between the left wing and the Catholic masses. He respects Catholicism, believes in the family and saw the introduction of divorce as necessary but only in so far as it provides the means for legally sanctioning the end of marriages which have long ceased to have meaning. He followed the same course as all Communist Party secretaries in being principally a party man rather than a parliamentarian: he did not enter Parliament until 1968. He officially joined the Party in 1944. He had earlier been in prison for organising a 'seditious' demonstration and after his release went to Salerno, then the seat of the royal government, in which his uncle was a minister. He met Benedetto Croce and also Palmiro Togliatti in whose presence, apparently, he was practically speechless. Berlinguer recalls, however, that as a young Communist he was shocked by Togliatti's decision to go into government.

Berlinguer then became one of the organisers of the youth movement, and at the fifth congress, in 1945, he was elected to the Central Committee. From 1949 to 1956 he was Secretary-General of the youth movement including a period, from 1950 to 1953, in which he was Chairman of the World Federation of Democratic Youth, which gave him his training in international relations. In 1957 he was appointed regional secretary in Sardinia. In the following year he was in charge of the party organisation, which is how he became master of the machine. He was hurt by the Prague invasion: he believes that every country should be allowed to develop a form of Communism suited to national requirements and thus he opposes direct interference in the affairs of other parties. He is a bureaucrat certainly: his physique shows clearly that he spends many hours at a desk. But he is not a soulless bureaucrat. He has retained his attraction for young people with whom he can still talk unaffectedly. He does not have all the power or all the answers. He has on more than one occasion shown himself to be eminently fallible in political tactics. He can give assurance to others. One night after supper in a Communist club in L'Aquila, in the Abruzzo, a group of young people came to him with their worries. They were having difficulty answering accusations about Prague and allegations that the party structure was cold and undemocratic. How could they reply? His answer was another question. Did they themselves believe that the Party was cold and undemocratic? No! No! came the reply. Well then, he said with a gesture of the hand and a sympathetic smile, what more did they need to convince others ... ? It was no answer but it was an effective encouragement.

This is the man responsible for taking over the inheritance left by Togliatti and not much changed by Longo. He has kept Togliatti's theory of 'an alternative majority' – to be constructed from Communists, Socialists and left-wing

Catholics. He has also carried forward, especially in the final months of Emilio Colombo's government, what might be called the alternative to the alternative majority, that of coming to power as partners in a coalition of the classic type led by the Christian Democrats. He may have been influenced in pressing this by his own knowledge of Catholicism. Togliatti's alternative majority was a splendid intellectual concept and logically sound, but it depended on attracting a large number of dissident Catholics who would join a Communist-led grouping of angry social reformers. Catholicism under three popes – Pius XII, John XXIII and Paul VI – has taken three different approaches to Communism, occasionally to the acute discomfort of the Christian Democrats. But a schoolchild in Apulia would know that if ever a real clash occurred, if ever the two sides had to stand up and be counted, dissident Catholics would, at a stern command from on high, return to their ecclesiastical allegiance and abandon Communists, social reform and anything else that Togliatti's mythical alternative would involve. And so the successors of Togliatti accepted the inevitable; if they wanted to go into government they would have to plan to do so on the terms laid down by the existing system. They would not then represent an alternative. They would become prospective supporters, or members, of a coalition on the lines grown familiar from the days of De Gasperi. The time for illusions might be over. The Party was offering itself as an instrument to re-establish a degree of industrial peace if the governmental parties, under pressure from the industrialists, cared to contemplate such an agreement and believed that the Communists could still take care of violence even when it came from the extreme left. The Communist Party appeared to have fallen from its pedestal but its price could still be high. And the Christian Democrats with their allies had to face the nasty truth that even with a large parliamentary majority they could somehow not make legislative ends meet and, with no reason except their own factiousness, were looking towards the wolf to help clothe the sheep. The clearest example of this drift came in May 1971 when Emilio Colombo's government was attempting to pass a housing bill through the Chamber. Nearly seventy of the Prime Minister's own party voted against him in the secret ballot. A hundred coalition deputies were absent. He and his government were saved by the Communist decision to abstain from voting.

The unspoken awareness of softness at the centre of political controversy increases the difficulties facing the smaller parties. The right wing has an easy time as do right wings anywhere when moderates fail to satisfy a country's demands. The Neo-Fascists know where they stand. In the past they were able to gain favours for their votes from several governments until Ferdinando Tambroni's experiment in 1960 revealed that the spirit of the Resistance was not so dead as to allow so soon a place for the extreme right in ruling the country. But they had begun to re-establish themselves seriously by mid-1971 as local-government elections showed in June of that year. Their reinforcement was due to three factors. They were effectively led by Giorgio Almirante, an energetic former journalist and an impressive if somewhat theatrical speaker. (His father had been an actor.) Secondly, the long series of strikes and the apparent incapacity of successive governments to deal with the problem of labour relations suggested in the minds of some of the electorate the benefit which might be expected from a benevolent but firm dictatorship. Workers would work, students would cut their hair and give up drugs, thieves would go to gaol and sex be something to be discussed among men, not brandished from every hoarding. And thirdly the Communist Party had become too obviously respectable and could no longer attract all those with a grudge against organised society. In no way was this true of the Monarchists for they, from the mid-sixties, were shown to be in such decline that they counted for less and less. Their strongholds were in the deep south. More than anywhere else in Naples where they were financed by Achille Lauro, the millionaire shipowner and, for many years, mayor of the city, whose semi-retirement from politics accounted largely for their decline. A sign that their times were past was the move in spring 1971 of General De Lorenzo from the Monarchist Party to the Neo-Fascists, and in 1972 the remaining Monarchists joined with the Neo-Fascists in what was termed 'the National Right'. The name was officially adopted at the extreme right's national congress in January 1973.

Still to the right of the Christian Democrats, the Liberals have had a broader experience and are the one party in the conservative opposition which is regarded as properly democratic. In De Gasperi's time they took office in his four-party coalitions and continued to have an active part in government until May 1957 when Antonio Segni's resignation from the prime ministership brought the end of the long series of centre coalitions. They returned to government after the May 1972 election. Their support comes largely from the north, and much of it from business interests. They are strongly anti-Communist, more intelligently so than the extreme right and more consistently so than the Christian Democrats. They have been determined opponents of Socialist participation in government. The Liberals gave outside support to Segni's administration but withdrew and brought the Government down, thus making way for Tambroni. They briefly supported a government of 'democratic restoration' led by Amintore Fanfani which was formed after the riots which marked Tambroni's end. They were then displaced as allies of the Christian Democrats by the Socialists whom they deeply distrusted as former allies of the Communists. The Liberal leader, Giovanni Malagodi, is one of the most gifted men in Italian politics. He is a brilliant linguist and was born and bred in London. His experience as a banker has given him a clear mind and one which, once it has arrived at a conclusion, does not easily change. All these gifts have been, in the Italian scene, disadvantages. He is one of the few Italian politicians who would have been at home in the House of Commons and it would not be difficult to imagine Malagodi as a Conservative minister in London. But under his leadership the Party in recent years has fared badly in elections, and circumstances rather than their own achievements brought them into Andreotti's second government after the 1972 election, and their contribution was a disappointment.

The nearest to the Liberals in spirit are the Social Democrats. More than anything else the Social Democrats have been the party of Giuseppe Saragat. The Party was formed in 1947 when Saragat left the Socialist Party because he objected to the close alliance of the Socialists with the Communists continued by the Socialist leader, Pietro Nenni. Understandably, with this origin, the Party is strongly anti-Communist; if it were not, it would have no reason for existing. More than any other party the Social Democrats insist on the importance of the Atlantic alliance. The Party's weight ought to have been greater after Saragat was elected President in December 1964. It fails, however, to be the rallying-point for a reunited socialist party and it was more from the Social Democrat side that the demand came for a break with the Socialists in July 1969. When Saragat left the presidency, he intervened to prevent his party from moving, as he thought, too far right. But, if anything were to show that the presidency does not possess real political power, it was the extremely limited hold which Saragat had on his own party after seven years in the Quirinale.

The Republicans have had an experience of government similar to that of the Social Democrats, but they have been the smallest party in the centre–left governmental coalitions which has managed to offset numerical weakness by their intellectual quality. Their leader, Ugo La Malfa, was one of the inspirers of the idea of bringing the Socialists into government. He envisaged this move as a means of isolating the Communists. Of all Italian politicians he is probably the most attuned to political thinking elsewhere in Western Europe, while retaining his unmistakably Italian character. He has best understood and expressed what belonging to Western Europe means to Italy. He believes that Italy's future must be as a part of the industrialised, advanced society of Western Europe. Though a Sicilian himself – or perhaps because he is a Sicilian – he feels a real fear of the pull upon Italy of the Mediterranean. He talks of scaling the Alps as if it were essential to Italy's salvation. He was the one politician in Italy who proposed, after the first French veto against Britain's entry into Europe, a bilateral agreement between Britain and Italy to offset the Franco-German understanding. There was much to said for his view: but it did not arouse British interest.

The art of politics is the art of simplification, and to this extent what La Malfa had to say about Italy's choice between the Mediterranean and Europe could be justified. He sees the confusion, the contradictions, the corruption as pulling Italy back from the essential trek beyond the Alps. But it is a difficult thesis to sustain when one looks at the map.

Finally, among what are called the parties of the 'democratic area', the most problematical of them all is the Socialist Party. It embodies Italy's ideological split rather than the geographical division. The Socialists are the third largest party in Parliament and the party with the longest history of continuous existence. They had an important role in Italian life before the First World War. In 1934 Socialists and Communists in exile signed a unity-of-action pact which was renewed after the war. Socialist splits have littered the Italian political scene; Communists, Socialists of Proletarian Unity, Social Democrats are or were all groups which originally belonged to the Socialist Party. In the first elections after the Second World War, the elections to the Constituent Assembly, the Socialists were a larger party than the Communists, the second largest in the country after the Christian Democrats.

Their essential problem has always been whether Socialism should be achieved by reform or revolution. They have passed on this duality to the Communists. Perpetual division meant in practice a problem of relations with the Communists; or, simply another way of putting the same problem, relations with the Christian Democrats because the Socialists saw, after a decade of alliance with the Communists, that revolution was out of the question and reform could only be achieved by joining the Christian Democrats against the Communist opposition. The general issue of alliances has always been crucial in Socialist history. Their inability to work with the Catholic politicians after the First World War was one of the main reasons why Mussolini, an ex-Socialist himself, could take power. This failure in the past and its disastrous consequences rested heavily on the minds of those Socialists who in the fifties worked for an alliance with the Christian Democrats.

They had had to make a long trek. It was no simple *renversement*; the Socialist move towards government, though helped by the Hungarian revolt and the Russian Communist Party's twentieth congress, was proof enough that all in Italian politics is not simply a matter of taking the side which is convenient and changing when immediate tactical advantage demands a switch. And they were then to face the disillusionment in the late sixties of their inability to have a decisive say in policy despite their membership of the series of centre–left coalitions. They were once more out of government by 1972. If the Socialists have not appeared to play such a dominating part in Italian politics as have the Christian Democrats and the Communists, it is fair to say that the Party's travails have told more about the true nature of Italian politics than have the activities of the two larger groups.

Nenni himself explains his post-war alliance with the Communists as a mistake but an understandable mistake. He had thought, he explains, that the Communists would have emerged from the war and from their successful battle with the Fascists more broad-minded and more liberal. He still felt the pull of working-class unity and of anti-Fascism. Communists and Socialists had been together in the Resistance, and this factor was of the greatest importance to Nenni. Of all Italian politicians he has the most human warmth. I never heard him speak ill in personal terms of other politicians – a remarkable feat given Italian habits. But I do remember the nearest he came to a personal reflection on another man's character. I was talking to him over lunch in the early days of centre–left co-operation, in a restaurant at Castelgandolfo overlooking the lake, about how he got on with Christian Democrats in general and Amintore Fanfani, then leading the centre–left forces, in particular. He replied that he had difficulties in dealing with people who not only had taken no part in the Resistance but had no concept of what the Resistance meant. He was expressing a gospel as well as a frame of mind because the Resistance movement was the crucible in which Italian democracy was remoulded. Ironically, the Christian Democrats had far less to do with the process than either Communists or Socialists but they have accepted the natural sequence of *Risorgimento* and Resistance, though having had comparatively little to do with the second and, as Catholics, would presumably in the preceding century have opposed the first.

Nenni's decision to ally with the Communists was made even more comprehensible by the nature of the choice of prospective friends and allies. He says himself that Christian Democracy and the allies were encouraging the worst of the forces of black reaction in the country. There was to be no break with the past. And so he chose the Communists and the prospect of a popular front. This prospect was remote at the beginning and was to become steadily remoter. And as time passed the Socialists were more obviously the junior partner. Nenni had condemned himself to the wilderness, brightened by a Stalin peace prize but a wilderness nevertheless. He came back from the wilderness, attempting to lead his people with him. Most of them came and, for the first time in the history of the Socialist Party in Italy, its members entered government. In 1963 Nenni became deputy prime minister in the first full-scale centre–left coalition. And he was ten years too late.

This is the broad outline of Socialist peregrinations. It is worth recounting because the Socialists did not fit the pattern imposed by events and external forces on Italian politics, a pattern natural enough for Christian Democrats and Communists. De Gasperi had solved his problem by taking one side – the Western alliance – and accepting the consequences as well as the benefits. He nevertheless did so with misgivings. He himself had to be persuaded and in order to make sure of the loyalty of his Christian Democrat followers he took the step, quite uncharacteristic of him and indicative of his state of mind, of convincing Pius XII of the wisdom of what he was doing so that objections within the Party would end. And Togliatti had to work within the framework of agreements between the Russians and the Americans. Nenni could not find his place. The monuments to his dilemma are the two Socialist parties born of his decision to ally first with the Communists and then with the Christian Democrats. The Social Democrats are one, the other was the Socialist Party of Proletarian Unity which sat to the left of the Communists in Parliament and was the most extreme of the parliamentary parties on the left until its defeat in the 1972 election, which put an end to its career as a separate party. It was less extreme and far less effective than the extra-parliamentary groups of the left, which are divided and inspired more than anything by their hatred of each other. But their hatred of the capitalist system is also obvious and this is an asset which the constitutional opposition cannot claim.

The logic of the situation is clear enough. All parties have over the years been shifting towards the right. The Socialists attempted to stop the process by bringing reforming zeal into the governmental ranks. They had not noticed that by stepping on to a revolving stage they, too, began to move at the same pace as the others. The promised decade of reforms never came, because neither the centre–left alliance of Catholics and Marxists nor the governmental machine itself were strong enough to bear it. For once it had seemed that external forces – Budapest, de-Stalinisation, the election of John XXIII to the Papacy – including a more liberal-minded president in the United States would influence the internal Italian scene to sound effect and not be, as was usually the case, restrictive. The frustrations felt by politicians sincerely wanting to introduce reform accounts for the longing looks which some of them threw in the direction of the Communists. Labour troubles which affected Italy seriously for the first time in late 1969 also gave some credit to the idea that industrial production – on which indirectly the whole cause of reform was based – could only be assured with some degree of Communist goodwill. The very question was divisive, just as the opposite side of the question – the Communist problem of whether or not to become more closely involved in government – strained the Party, though less publicly because Communists are better able to keep their differences away from the public eye. The natural course might seem to have been power at the national level. But there was the example of the Socialists to give the Communists pause. Nenni's policy had lost his party votes and the old leader himself had been displaced and humiliated by his former followers. And there was the point that government in Italy is a most difficult and unpopular pursuit. And so the two sides stand poised, the Communists with one eye on power and conducting an ineffectual opposition, and the Christian Democrats listless in government, each with less momentum than it used to have and each, as a result, with less and less to offer. And from about 1968 onwards the general tendency towards deterioration grew faster and faster.

CHAPTER SEVEN

Fact and Faction

THERE is a wonderful sketch of the Italian, drawn with the instinctive judgement of D. H. Lawrence, flashing with colour, with tension and earnest self-confidence that it is so, and only so, that the Italians behave:

> This is the soul of the Italian since the Renaissance. In the sunshine he basks asleep, gathering up a vintage into his veins which in the night-time he will distil into ecstatic sensual delight, the intense, white-cold ecstasy of darkness and moonlight, the raucous, cat-like, destructive enjoyment, the senses conscious and crying out in their consciousness in the pangs of enjoyment, which has consumed the southern nation, perhaps all the Latin races, since the Renaissance.

It is like saying that the pyramids are round or Pisa's tower straight so far is it off the mark. And it was never less true than in the two years from the summer of 1971 which saw the politicians forced to face a country suffering from nervous insufferance, tired of being harried by strikes, dissatisfied with the immobility of both government and opposition, anxious that more than the economy was running down, an edgy country too much taken up with that strange form of national pride which seeks to show that things have never gone as badly as this and could never have gone as badly as this anywhere but in Italy. A time, in other words, when Lawrence never seemed so out of joint. Wrong judgements can at times make excellent yardsticks.

The events can be told briefly but have to be told, because Italy's immediate political future depended on decisions taken, or pressures bowed to, in these two years. The period began with the efforts of Emilio Colombo to keep his centre–left coalition alive. He was unconvinced that its pattern was, for the time being, finished, that the end of a particular journey had been reached, not because the travellers had arrived any-where but because they could no longer go on together. Partial local-government elections in June 1971 showed sub-stantial Fascist gains, especially in Sicily. The great move-ments of population were now over. The northern industrial cities had reached such a point of congestion that immigration was directed more at the smaller towns and countryside around Milan and Turin. The year 1970 had brought the first minus statistic in industrial production since the period of recon-struction. Strikes were a part of life, as were political demon-strations. On Vietnam alone there were 145,300 demonstrations between February 1965, when the American escalation of bombing began, and February 1973. The lessons of political hooliganism taught by the Fascists, moreover, had not been forgotten.

The politicians had their own problems. The presidential election was due in December 1971 and no one doubted that it would lacerate the parties. Almost all parties were terrified at the impending referendum aimed at abrogating divorce. The Christian Democrats did not want to go to the country with only the Neo-Fascists for company. The Communists were worried that their own electorate would be split on the issue and had no wish to lead what would have amounted to an anti-clerical crusade. And so the idea emerged of a dissolution of Parliament by the new president. In effect this move cut a year off Parliament's natural life. There was no precedent in

Italy's post-war history: the last parliament to be dissolved early was in 1924 when the Fascists were returned with 403 out of 535 seats. In 1971 it had the attraction of bringing to an end the fifth and most unsatisfactory of all the post-war parliaments at a time when the country needed some gesture at least of resolution, and it would postpone for at least a year the dreaded referendum.

The presidential election was an unwholesome spectacle but the result effectively showed that a new period had begun in Italian politics. Senator Giovanni Leone, a conservative-minded Christian Democrat, firmly Catholic, from the prosperous Neapolitan middle class, differed physically, mentally and politically from his immediate predecessor. He was tiny after Saragat's bulk. He was following a man who, whatever his faults, was the embodiment of the centre–left idea, the advocate of the need for a lay, democratic party of the left able to provide an alternative government to the Christian Democrats. Saragat accepted the classic interpretation of Italian democracy as having drawn its lifeblood from the *Risorgimento* and the Resistance and now destined to prosper by remaining close to Europe and the West: in particular, to Britain for institutional experience and to America for security. The fact that the Socialists had opposed Leone and the Liberals had voted for him set the pattern for the next government. Logically enough, Emilio Colombo resigned on 15 January 1972, was invited by President Leone to try to put together a new centre–left coalition, failed, and reported his failure on 1 February. It was now the turn of Giulio Andreotti who, with relentlessness combined with great tactical skill, set himself to exploit fully the new circumstances. He was asked to form a government on 6 February. He went through the paces of trying to re-form the old coalition and then agreed to lead a minority administration of Christian Democrats destined to be beaten in Parliament and so open the way for the general election. Leone dissolved Parliament on 28 February and set the election for 7 May.

Though aged little more than fifty, Andreotti had had a ministerial career lasting two decades until, after the 1968 general election, he had taken over leadership of the parliamentary party in the Chamber. He is a Roman phenomenon. He was born and bred in Rome and Rome is his constituency. He could have appeared at any time in the city's public life: as an intimate of Augustus or a cardinal-nephew under the popes, and he is one of the few Christian Democrats with the gifts of irony and brevity. He has kept up his Latin studies and is a practising Catholic with firm and useful friendships at the Vatican, as well as a remarkable ability, proved unrivalled in the 1972 election, in gathering preferential votes. It was said of him that, when he accompanied De Gasperi to church, De Gasperi spoke to God and Andreotti to the priest. It was now his business to establish himself as a national figure rather than as an acute Roman politician. He knew his chance had come.

The election should have been a rout. The country was unruly, restive: nothing was going well and, as the principal governing party, the Christian Democrats were mainly to blame. They appeared destined to lose much ground to the far right. Instead, they emerged with a victory, gaining a little ground in highly adverse circumstances, not losing it, and holding the right within limits far closer than was expected; they somehow managed to pull off the supreme effort of correctly judging the general mood at a confused moment.

The Party was helped by the conservative habits of mind of the Italian electorate. This innate conservatism is never stronger than when the situation is bad. The Christian Democrats have learned by long experience of power how to apply the enveloping miasma of protection which attracts the waverers as much as the faithful, a sort of political *mammismo* which brings out in every Italian the little boy lost or the daughter anxious to follow in mother's footsteps. It is a remarkable party, one has to admit this. Logically it might have met the end of the Mouvement républicain populaire in France or been ousted, at least temporarily, from power like the Christian Democrats in Germany. Frequently it has appeared to be in great difficulties. Most of the time since De Gaspari's death it has seemed leaderless. Constantly it is told by the other parties, whether allies or opposition, that it must make up its mind on a clear policy and stick to it. It never does. Regularly it is said to be on the verge of splitting, but nothing, ever, seriously goes wrong; leading members boast that sometimes the situation looks serious but the Party never goes too far in its follies. If ever it were to go wrong, it would have gone wrong in May 1972. One of the secrets of its self-perpetuation as the governing party is this very ability to offer protection in times of troubles which are of its own creation. Did ever a political party reach such ultimate finesse in the self-perpetuation of power?

Of course there were other explanations for the success. Andreotti was a shrewd campaigner and so was the party secretary, Arnaldo Forlani, another Cassius-type but from the Marche not from Rome. And the ecclesiastical hierarchy rallied strongly to the Party. But there was a deeper feeling behind what amounted to a Catholic success.

For years before the calling of the election a growing feeling of resentment could be detected in the Catholic rank and file. Resentment that their sentiments were not respected; resentment that they were regarded as politically inferior to the lay parties; a genuine anger that the lack of consciousness of the state in Italy was laid firmly at their door. This feeling might seem puzzling to an outsider. The Catholics seemed to be having everything their own way and to have had it so since the end of the war. But, even after a quarter of a century of government, the old sensitivities remained. The divorce issue played on them more than any other. It is easy to be astonished at the sight of an issue such as divorce proving so controversial in a Western country in the latter years of the twentieth century. But, quite apart from doctrinal questions, which played a secondary part in the controversy, divorce saw the Catholic politicians divorced by their allies, past and present, and constantly attacked as representing the forces of obscurantism and ecclesiastical servitude. Posters such as 'Animals do not divorce but human beings do' caught the Catholics where it hurt most. One can sympathise with them or not, but the strength of this bitterness cannot be overlooked. Had they lost the 1971 presidential election, the Catholic reaction in the general election would have been even greater. And Andreotti was aware of this.

There were other troubles, this time in the foreign field. No country has conducted its foreign policy with a shrewder awareness of domestic interests. The strict American alliance gave security and, in the early days, massive economic aid. Membership of the European Community offered the prospect of political security and active membership in a prosperous collection of advanced nations with the means and the experience to help Italy in its efforts to raise standards in its depressed areas. A federated Europe would provide the proper framework for a decentralised Italy.

The Italians had had their disappointments, especially with Europe. The traditional outlook which formed part of what might be called the Saragat era was that British entry would help balance the danger of Franco-German hegemony in Europe. In the event, the situation did not develop in this way. The British spent far more time cultivating relations with the French and, to a lesser extent, the Germans than with Italy, on the assumption that there was little need to do more than raise a glass to their Italian guests, or hosts, accompanied by words of good will. The Italians had their disappointments in the Community itself. Their genuine belief in a united Europe had never really been thought out: the provincialism of Italian politicians was cruelly revealed when their turn came to preside over the Commission. This was clearly the moment to send one of their leading 'Europeans' of international standing. None of them wanted the post. The office was finally taken, with reluctance, by Franco Maria Malfatti, an Umbrian Christian Democrat and Minister of Posts at the time. He was not a success and gave up to fight the 1972 election campaign. The successor proposed by the Italians was regarded as inadequate and the rest of the Italian term was seen out by the Dutchman, Sicco Mansholt.

The reaction was a series of forays into the Mediterranean. Andreotti was the first prime minister to include in his programme a call for a Mediterranean conference. It would be wrong to over-simplify the Italian position. Preceding governments had paid a good deal of attention to the Mediterranean. Inevitably, given that the Italian seaboard is entirely Mediterranean. and two battle-fleets were confronting each other across its warm waters. But fascination with the Mediterranean is looked on with some suspicion. In part this is due to Mussolini's *mare nostrum* aspirations which gave a right wing tinge to a Mediterranean outlook. There was the suspicion that Italy was feeling more at home with Spanish and Greek dictators than with her Western allies and forgetting her aim to be part of a fully Western, industrialised community. The Mediterranean, moreover, has a different character in terms of policy: whereas the rest of Italian foreign policy could be seen as a natural projection of domestic requirements, the Mediterranean is traditionally a field for power politics. Arguably, Italy could be regarded as having to look after vital security interests in the Mediterranean but it is difficult to see how, when the presence of the Sixth Fleet was supposed to assure just that security. These suspicions were increased in Andreotti's case because his government's complexion was undoubtedly more conservative than its centre–left predecessors, and he went out of his way to draw attention to his interest in the Mediterranean not only by his proposal for a conference, but also by inviting President Pompidou for talks as his first visitor from abroad, making clear that among other matters they talked about co-operation in the Mediterranean – Lawrence's 'southern nation' taking a specifically Latin look at the world.

It probably helped Andreotti's recuperation of votes on the right. For a time it did him no great harm elsewhere. His government, despite its conservative character and lack of flamboyance, was treated with respect by the opposition. For months they attacked it, but quite clearly with no intention of bringing it down. The real danger was from the prime minister's own Christian Democratic ranks. Leone had won the presidency, at the cost of Fanfani who had planned for years to reach this height of his formidable ambitions; Leone had been helped into office by Andreotti; hence, a man of Fanfani's restless temperament was unlikely to allow the man who had helped to defeat him to govern in peace. By the beginning of 1973 the differences between the cool-mannered Roman and the restless Tuscan were being fought in private and in public, one of a series of difficulties which faced Andreotti in his attempt to keep his government alive until in May 1973 the Republicans withdrew their support a matter of days before the Christian Democrat Party's national congress met to seek a return to the Socialist alliance. And if Fanfani got the better of Andreotti? The latter would gradually become the aggressor and faction would go on taking its toll of Italian political energies. 'This is the soul of the Italian since the Renaissance.' This is the 'cat-like, destructive enjoyment' as it really is practised, the enjoyment which has consumed the southern nation. If it is not Andreotti against Fanfani it is Moro against Fanfani or Rumor against Andreotti. They do not bask asleep in the sunshine because faction consumes their lives as well as the well-being of the nation. No doubt all politicians intrigue against each other. Pehaps it is true, as an eminent Italian ambassador who had served in Moscow, Paris, London and in Bonn maintained, that no politician lived beyond the next day and even the greatest functioned by constant improvisation. The Italian politician is simply an extreme case. The vintage in the veins sharpens defects as well as qualities, destroys vision, denies creation, quickens the reactions and quite evidently gives delight, of its own kind.

CHAPTER EIGHT

Laughter and Criticism

AN ABILITY to laugh at politicians and a stimulus to them to laugh occasionally at themselves might have had a healthily corrective function. With a few gusts of laughter in the wings the actors on the political stage know how far their performances should be taken seriously and at what point their efforts would have to be toned down to keep their audiences with them. But Italian humour does not have this element of constructive criticism, and public life is the poorer for it.

Travellers sometimes note that in the process of crossing the Alps the natural expression of the faces around them changes from northern seriousness to a smile. The muscles are made for laughing the more one moves south. This view is true because Italians accompany much of what they say with a smile. But their smiles and laughter are due to their habit of thinking pleasurably aloud about the pleasures of life. They have humanity rather than humour, and the real significance of the distinction is seldom understood. In the British meaning of the term they have no sense of humour despite the deep admiration which they constantly say they feel for the British sense of humour. They do not appreciate irony or self-depreciation as a form of wit, and satire is still something which makes them feel a little awkward.

British and Italian humour are at opposite poles. On the whole the British laugh with assurance when they laugh at the system and the people involved in it. They have boundless confidence in their way of life and can afford to be amused. Italians laugh from a deep sense of pessimism, of the hopelessness of the human condition. Life is basically difficult, sometimes dreadful, and one way to deal with it is to laugh. Laughing or crying will make no difference one way or the other. This is the opposite to confidence in their way of life.

The master of this outlook and most accomplished among Italian comic actors is Eduardo De Filippo, the Neapolitan playwright, director and actor. He seldom appears in any but his own plays but can occasionally be seen in Pirandello, whose views on reality have contributed to his own outlook, and in the Neapolitan farces of Scarpetta. Eduardo carries much of the weight of the *commedia dell'arte* tradition on his narrow shoulders. He seldom says anything funny in itself. It is what he says in given circumstances which is funny, and the way he says it. His world is full of impending disaster, to which he is generally oblivious. He is busily decorating the Christmas crib with absurd little fairy lights from the street-market while his family is falling to pieces around him. Or he cannot make himself believe that he has not really won a fortune, already spent, from the national lottery because he had been told in a dream the winning numbers by Dante himself. He is funny and pathetic because he is defenceless in life's jungle, despite his Neapolitan verve and fundamental humanity. His technique is magnificent. He has his audiences, especially when he is performing in Naples, cheering and clapping with delight at a fine piece of comic timing. But all this is a long way from humour: it is a brilliant portrayal of helpless humanity and a call for greater resolution.

On an August night in 1969, a huge audience faced the prospect of hearing in person a comedian called Franco Franchi, a Sicilian who had made a series of films which were very popular but notably lacking in sophistication. He had begun his career in the nearest surviving equivalent of the music-hall, the stage-show which formerly preceded, and occasionally in more remote cinemas still precedes, the main film. That night in August he appeared on a stage set up in the principal square of the little town of Ariccia, in the hills near Rome, and looked as he stepped on to the platform his usual, disconcertingly ugly and unsubtle self. But he gradually took command of this audience with a series of brilliantly performed, shockingly funny stories of Sicilian life: how to swindle the barber; the ghastly experiences of a honeymoon couple adrift in a Roman hotel; and a set of wicked impressions of Sicilian grief including that of a shawled old mother wailing by the coffin of her dead son. There could be no question of his marvellous technical ability. But, again, this was not an exhibition of humour: it was a bitingly accurate imitation of some of the darkest aspects of Sicilian life.

He kept well clear of politics, which is wisdom on the part of an Italian comedian facing a large public. The test-case of the difficulties of mixing politics with humour was that of Alighiero Noschese. He is a brilliant mimic and one of the finest performers of any kind that Italy possesses in the field of light entertainment. When he first began imitating politicians in his television programmes, he made a polite announcement of thanks to the great men whom he was imitating for their having given permission. This happened in 1969. In the following year regional elections were due and he was forbidden to imitate politicians on the grounds that he might influence the results.

Noschese is a mild-mannered man, and if his mimicry is devastating in its accuracy it is on the whole good-natured. It was arguably true that some of his personal preferences showed through his art. His portrayal, for instance, of Pietro Nenni, the old Socialist leader, was markedly affectionate. He was attractively correct in his portrayal of the mannerisms of Ugo La Malfa, the Republican leader, who had taken the trouble to ring him up and offer to coach the master-mimic in his impersonation. These portraits were at least as popular as Noschese's gallery of pop-singers, film-stars, radio-commentators, the former Persian Empress, the Onassises and other such personalities unlikely to affect the balance of

Italian political life. Without the domestic politicians – he was allowed to imitate foreign politicians – his show lost much of its interest.

Mild-mannered though he may be, he accepted the chance for revenge. A Rome dance-hall asked him to perform the banned imitations. He appeared at about midnight before a packed and expectant audience and explained that he would not be giving them the imitations censored by the television authorities but others which would never have been allowed on any television programme in Europe, let alone in Italy. He remained reasonably kind with Nenni and La Malfa. But he was merciless with his leading Christian Democrats: Emilio Colombo, then Minister of the Treasury, whom he portrayed as a priest, smiling beatifically above his red missal as he preached on the subject of the stability of the lira: 'You could buy little enough with it last year, and just as little this year ...'; Mariano Rumor, then the Prime Minister, who chanted on his knees the ecclesiastical-sounding responses: 'Vietnam, Amen, Vietnam ...'.

Noschese's difficulties were partly due to the monopoly which the State enjoys in broadcasting. The corporation is constantly under political fire. The right wing regards it as a nest of Communists and the left accuses it regularly of being solely intent on flattering ministers and following the authoritative suggestions of the Vatican. In these circumstances, even if it were a model of objectivity, it would not be accepted as such. Objectivity in criticising it is also rare: certain powerful private interests want to break its monopoly and introduce independent television.

Much more surprising was the experience which Noschese suffered later. He took his imitations around the country, and in provincial theatres, especially in the south, he met plenty of applause but also legal actions: from sober citizens appalled at the indignity to which he subjected the great politicians, and even from a local policeman who felt himself dishonoured by a reference in a sketch to the low pay of the police. The television corporation obviously knew, or had helped form, its audience: 'As soon as I go beyond the television code,' Noschese complained, 'the code of not touching this person or running up against the ideas of someone else, I meet spontaneous repression. The censors are the good fathers of families, pious spinsters, constables. . . .' His conclusion was simple: 'The Italian public will have changed when on my tours I no longer find people ready with a writ.'

Worse was to come. In June 1972 he was told by the Milan public prosecutor that a citizen who had seen his imitations on television of the Shah of Persia and of King Hussein, broadcast on 12 December 1971, wished to bring charges of offending the honour and prestige of two foreign heads of state. The prosecutor took the charge seriously – the crime does, indeed, exist in article 297 of the penal code – and told the entertainer to nominate defending counsel. In fact, the case did not reach the courts, but it could not be dismissed simply as the foolishness of an individual Milanese whose action was taken too seriously by the public prosecutor. Noschese reacted correctly when he pointed out that his business was satire not politics and that political satire was in any case an integral part of the democratic system. Though his remarks seemed simply common sense, he was stepping on delicate ground. A famous case which actually came to trial in 1948 involving two Milan journalists who mocked Farouk ended in their conviction. The Court of Cassation laid down that 'the intention to joke ... does not eliminate the penal responsibility', an icy judgement which quite clearly could be extended to cover far less laughable cases than Farouk. The dangerous aspect of such an outlook is that the penal code can be used to quieten objections to a particular course of foreign policy, and a condemnation of political satire – or just political laughter – comes close to creating another category of crime of opinion, a restraint which Italians ought not to have to bear. As it happened, the 1948 trial immediately preceded an important general election and the Government would not have welcomed criticisms of British policy. This excessive respect for the powerful, whether Italian or non-Italian, keeps making itself felt in small details. When Edward Heath was in Italy in October 1972 he took occasion to attack the Labour Party's European policy and give public assurances that Britain would not go back on the European treaties. Several British journalists asked him firmly but politely by what right he thought he could talk on behalf of the British people as a whole when he might very well be back in opposition and no longer in control of events. His reply was also polite and firm. But the interesting reaction was among the Italian journalists: an intelligent political weekly commented that it was unthinkable that a correspondent of ANSA, the Italian news-agency, would dare ask Giulio Andreotti, then Prime Minister, by what right he was acting as he did.

Italians sometimes seem to take life itself lightly. But that does not mean that they find it amusing. And the centuries have given an engrained respect for the authorities as such and none at all for humble people, which is why satire to many of them seems like a thorn under the skin, not a laughing matter. But the thought of the pleasure given by a good meal in good company with cool wine in the sun will bring a smile as broad as the Alban Hills themselves.

They do not, moreover, like their prejudices challenged and one of these prejudices is that the authorities should be left to go their own way. It was, after all, only in December 1972 that the Constitutional Court declared unconstitutional the article (112) of the penal code prohibiting 'writings, drawings, pictures or other objects of any kind opposing the established political, social and economic order or harmful to the prestige of the State or of the authorities or offending national sentiment'. The mark of Fascism on the code was still deep.

Life in Italy is clearly departmentalised. A comic has no place in the world of politics any more than a politician is expected to know anything at all about the realities of daily life. Where there are exceptions, they are usually on the far left. The Communists have always been better served than the governing Christian Democrats by that compartment of Italian life known as 'culture' or 'the intellectuals'. Intellectuals in Italy are also supposed to know their place. They are expected to sign petitions – calling for the end of war in Vietnam, against the trials of Basque nationalists or censorship – but the limits do not include a direct contact with public opinion. It is not expected of them. They talk to each other and about each other and occasionally give their views on the vaster issues of international affairs. But even in their own field the impression they make is not large. Few writers, for example, could expect to live from their personal creative work, because the demand for books remains small. There are practically no public libraries. According to the publisher Mondadori, in 1972 only twenty-four out of every hundred Italians read a book a year. Of the total number of books sold in Italy in 1971, thirty-eight per cent were school text-books. Sales increased markedly with the introduction of cheap editions in the early sixties but the rise has not been maintained: there is still a wide sector of the public which simply is not a reading public.

There is a final weakening element in the critical function of the Italian performer or intellectual. Cultural life remains provincial. It does so in the best sense of the term. Rome has its groups of intellectuals but in no sense is it the capital of intellectual life. Milan could claim to be, with its many publishing houses. Turin has always had a strong intellectual tradition. So have Naples and Bologna, to a less robust extent Florence. Writers write about their own provinces; Bassani sets his stories in Ferrara, Moravia in Rome, De Filippo exclusively in Naples; and many people would say that once an Italian poet abandoned the original source of his inspiration, like Quasimodo's abandoning of his native southern Sicily, his work becomes less interesting, unless like Montale he writes poetry which rises wholly from his private self. Place is of vital importance to the Italian mental world and if it offers strength in some ways it denies strength to the intellectual as a national force. If issues have to be faced at all, they are more real at a provincial than a national level.

Each of these forces – provincialism, respect, the exceptional difficulty of being objective in a country that thinks on ideological lines – is present in Italian journalism. There is no national press. The best newspapers are printed in the north – the *Corriere della Sera* in Milan and *La Stampa* in Turin – and Italy's eighty or so daily newspapers have some outstanding critical journalists. But they are working against powerful currents. Only twenty newspapers make a profit: journalists are intellectuals, and in the public mind they are expected to write for themselves and an *élite*, and would be regarded as rubbing shoulders with the authorities rather than with ordinary people. And so, largely, they do. Especially those working for official party newspapers: they are the true masters of political linguistics which are far beyond any ordinary reader. They suffer strongly from the delusion that they are active participants in the public scene, and so frequently waste their opportunities by trying to out-debate the person they are supposed to be interviewing. Their dispersal throughout the country rather than in a concentration of journalists in the capital ought theoretically to give them a fresher view of national affairs. It does, but they feel as a result less of an estate because there is no obvious cohesion among them which geographical closeness and personal familiarity give. Small circulations mean greater anxiety on the part of editors not to offend important people. The ideological problem is one which affects all of Italian life. The fact that something is said by a Communist will automatically make it less true or unworthy of consideration to a firm anti-Communist from the Catholic ranks or from the conservative lay liberal tradition. They all belong on their own genealogical tree and their feet are not expected to touch the same piece of ground. For the journalist this frequently means that he must be content with producing his evidence along fixed lines, knowing that his colleagues with a different ideological background will be doing the same, so that the reader will be left with the task of reading widely each day and bringing his own critical faculties to work on the evidence put in print. In the circumstances, the contribution made by the Press is less substantial than it should be to judge from the combined weight of brainpower and integrity employed by newspapers. Independence is increasing, but by mid-1973 the danger was recognised of a similarly increasing concentration of ownership in the hands of industrialists.

This point was well put by the writer Alberto Moravia in one of his occasional, pithy contributions to a public argument. He wrote a letter on the value of the Press to the editor of *Il Mondo*, an excellent political weekly, which was published on 21 September 1972. His subject was the 1969 bomb explosions in Milan and the attempt by the authorities to lay the blame at the door of the anarchists in the person of Valpreda and the part which the Press played, and was playing, in the affair. He described the nature of whoever or whatever was behind the murders as 'something old, provincial, backward, nineteenth century, agricultural, Mediterranean ... the organising mind was that of someone born and bred in the least industrialised Mediterranean belt; southern Italy, Greece, Spain ... the organising brain looked to the past'. In other words, the bombs were prepared by people not only murderous in their intentions but out of step with everything for which modern Italy was striving. Moravia added: 'One shudders to think of what would have happened if there had not been freedom of the Press in Italy: if the organisers of the attempt had been able to impose, let us say, their point of view ... if we are still free, we owe it to the Press, even to a press so divided and prudent as the Italian Press. For this reason it is necessary that the Press becomes aware of its great importance. That it takes another step along the road of truth.'

They will have their chance with the predicted decline in the massive sales of weekly magazines. If it is true that few Italians read books or newspapers, it must be said that their appetite is huge for the illustrated weeklies: they buy fifteen million a week though these are primarily designed for entertainment at various levels and even those that have excellent political commentators would not be regarded as pursuing in the first instance a critical function and many of them are purely escapist.

Surprisingly, the one place in which criticism and the public meet is the cinema. Italians still like going to the cinema. Television has not ruined the habit as it has in other countries. And the cinema has kept faith with its immediate post-war origins of films containing intelligent social comment. The giants of the industry, such as Fellini and De Sica and Visconti, served the Italian cinema well and the country was fortunate in producing a second generation of talented directors, mostly strongly left wing in political sympathies, who carried on the tradition that the cinema should have a message as well as entertain. International recognition was given to this fresh look by younger Italian directors at the problems of their country when the 1971 Oscar for the best foreign-language film went to Elio Petri's *Inchiesta su un cittadino sopra di ogni sospetto*, a profound essay in the use and effects of power with the activities of the Ministry of the Interior's police as its setting. The resilience of the cinema in Italy is unique in Europe. In the decade from 1961 Italian cinemas lost some 200 million spectators, falling from 741 million to 550 million, but in Germany during the same period audiences fell from 517 million to 180 million and in France from 350 million to 190 million. Going to the cinema is still regarded in Italy as worth while: in general it is.

CHAPTER NINE

Industry and the State

T H E prime mover in Italian social change has been industry, for better or for worse. About one-third of Italy's industrial and financial life is controlled by state companies. This third is more than it sounds because it includes some of the most vital components of Italian life, such as the steel industry. In fact, the power of the State goes far deeper even than holdings in vital industries. Smaller firms rely on credits from official sources and, during the difficult period from 1970 onward, many of them were dependent on these loans.

The basis of state participation in economic life is a body known by its initials (as many are in Italy), I.R.I., an abbreviation for Istituto per la Ricostruzione Industriale, the Industrial Reconstruction Institute established in 1933. I.R.I. has a fascination of its own, especially to Socialist planners in many other countries who are seeking an alternative to nationalised industries. The I.R.I. formula is that, as the state holding company, it takes a controlling interest of shares in companies which pay dividends and for all effects are normal joint-stock companies. Apart from the fact that the State has this controlling interest, these companies behave like any other company in a capitalist world.

Originally I.R.I. was an improvisation. Its purpose when it was founded in 1933 was to bring discipline to the banking and credit system. Its first aim in that period of financial confusion was to disentangle relations between commercial banks and industry, between the banks and Government, between the banks and the central bank and, finally, between the central bank and the Government. It took over bank assets and found that as a result it had on its hands something that nobody much wanted at the time: a sizeable interest in Italian industry, much of which, in those depression days, was in a critical condition. Like other famous Italian improvisations such as opera and, indeed, the banking system itself, I.R.I. became a permanent institution. In June 1937 legislation was passed formally ending the Institute's status as a permanent agency and recognising it as the Government's permanent management agency for the State's industrial holdings. In the immediate post-war period, I.R.I. did not look set to play a great part as an instrument of planned expansion. Its chance to assert itself came in 1952 when Italy joined the European Coal and Steel Community. Italy's steel industry was a long way behind European standards, and the Community gave Italy a period of five years to reach those standards. As so often happens in Italian affairs, a man of immense energy and brilliance happened to be present at the centre of affairs. I.R.I.'s steel holdings were managed by Oscar Sinigallia, who proved to have the vigour and capacity to achieve a difficult task. By 1957 Italy's steel industry was competitive and efficient.

Apart from the steel industry, I.R.I. controls Italy's highly successful airline, Alitalia, the national radio and television monopoly known as R.A.I., shipbuilding which is of vital importance particularly in Trieste and Genoa, the shipping company known as Finmare which includes in its fleet the *Rafaello* and the *Michelangelo*, the best part of the Autostrade, the Alfa Romeo factories and three of Italy's leading banks. Its part in Italian life will be increased. Plans published in September 1972 allowed for total investments up to 1975 of 5,564,000 million lira to be subdivided as follows: 2,330,000 million in telecommunications, air and sea transport and radio/television; 867,000 million in public utilities, and 2,367,000 million in manufacturing industries. These investments were expected to produce 84,000 new jobs within the I.R.I. network and 70,000 in business indirectly.

I.R.I. is naturally intended to carry out the purposes of government in the field of national economic planning. Its chairman and vice-chairman are appointed by the President of the Republic for three years. The board of directors includes representatives from a number of ministries. General directives are devised by a standing ministerial committee which is presided over by the Prime Minister or by the minister responsible for state participation in industry. The Institute has much freedom to conduct its own affairs once the directives have been handed down, but obviously a vigorously intelligent interest on the part of ministers is an advantage. The Institute is generally seen to have been efficiently run by a Christian Democrat deputy, Professor Giuseppe Petrilli, though there is frequent criticism of the I.R.I. system itself and allegations of too close a tie with the Christian Democrat Party. Petrilli has the great virtue of seeing Italy's two principle fields of obligatory development as its own south and the integration of Europe. He uses his influence and resources to advance both.

Italian life depends on delicate balances. The whole economy, even at the height of the post-war boom, had its fragile elements. Fears are sometimes expressed that I.R.I. could become too strong, as if ironically an idea meant to provide temporary relief would finally dominate a country inured to placing its faith in expedients. Even some Socialists have said that they are worried that the State's hand in industry might prove too strong and even be a danger to democracy. Such fears express the lack of faith in the State itself and in political democracy, and also suspicion that too vigorous a part of the whole social machine could wrench the rest out of joint. There is also the feeling that democratic controls operate more effectively over a fully nationalised industry than one in which, through its holding company, the State has a predominant interest.

A more independent line was followed in the past by the

State's other great industrial agency, the Ente Nazionale Idro-carburi or E.N.I., following the Italian love of initials. As a generalisation, I.R.I. forces the pace of accepted policy: E.N.I. from the beginning was a policy-maker but less so after its chairman, Enrico Mattei, died in a mysterious air-crash in 1962. Its special place in Italian life was due entirely to the personality of Mattei. He was in the great line of Italian *condottieri*, with one exception: he had his own private vision of the part which his country should play in international affairs as well as strong views on the conduct of internal policy. He was not, as non-Italian oil-companies liked to think, just a pirate. He sounded cynical as he sat and drank his morning coffee on Via Veneto. But he was not.

Mattei led the Christian Democrat partisan brigade and after the war was given the state holding company A.G.I.P. to wind up. In 1945 natural gas was discovered in the Po valley and Mattei set off on the career which was to make him one of the most powerful men in Italy and a force in international affairs, so much so that his death was variously ascribed to the O.A.S., the C.I.A. and the international oil-companies. The discovery of this gas was one of the elements in Italy's industrial advance because it solved the country's lack of basic fuels and raw materials. In 1953 E.N.I. was founded for Mattei, with a structure closely following that of I.R.I. It was a holding company controlling a group of companies concerned with hydrocarbons. Mattei tied the price of his methane to that of oil and made immense profits. He used part of them to make sure that he had his way with the politicians. He handled these funds much as an eighteenth-century prime minister would have done in England; indeed, the Pelhams or Shelburne and Fox would have found themselves very much at home in the political cabals of Rome. One big difference is that politics in Italy is not an aristocratic pursuit, but its aims and methods and limitations are similar.

Mattei despised private industrialists, who hated him in return. His contention was that state industries were normally slow, inefficient and unimaginative and private industrialists the adventurous and brilliant characters in a nation's economy. But not in Italy. In Italy it was the state industries that set the pace, opened up the south and concluded astounding agreements abroad which made Italy a greater power to be reckoned with in international trade. He was a tall, good-looking man with a cruel smile. He never looked so happy as when he was explaining, a heavy ruler in his hand, that he had not only discovered large reserves of methane in the deep south, near Ferrandina, but had made the discovery in an area prospected previously and given up as hopeless by private industry. He laughed like a self-contented tiger. Few men gave such an impression of steel beneath the skin combined with an infectious impudence. But he had his ideals. He had been poor as a boy – his father was in the *carabinieri* and had made a local name for himself by capturing a famous bandit. And once the son had become a great industrialist he thought of the comfort of his workers, of their need for dignity. It was a completely paternalistic outlook but at least he had their interests in mind.

Probably no one would be able to estimate Mattei's real power. But it would be safe to say that when he was at the height of his power no one in Italy carried greater weight than he. A close associate of President Gronchi was walking through the state-rooms of the Quirinale on the evening it was known that Gronchi's bid for re-election had just ended in humiliating defeat and the presidency was about to pass to Antonio Segni. Gronchi bitterly felt that one of the principal reasons for his poor showing in the election was Mattei's decision not to support him. 'And Mattei', the ex-President's friend was saying, as if he had in some way let down the family honour, 'was always made to feel at home here.' The rooms that night were gloomy with only an occasional glitter of a gilt mirror or a candlestick; but no longer home.

Outside Italy, Mattei's feud was not with private industrialists but with the international oil-companies. Another of his convictions was that Italy must play an important part in Middle East affairs. He had, though without success, proposed the marriage of one of the ex-King's daughters to the Shah of Persia. It was in fact Persian oil which marked the opening of the international feud. He was refused a share in the Iran oil consortium. He replied by making his own agreement with the Persian Government, by which seventy-five per cent of profits went to the Government and twenty-five per cent to the company in which the host government would also have a holding. Mattei had wrecked the traditional fifty-fifty division and placed Italy firmly on the map of international oil-policies. He extended his new arrangement to other countries including Egypt and Libya (and his Libyan agreement survived the Ghaddafy *coup*, although the Italian population in Libya was expelled and its property confiscated).

Mattei's ideas were shared by some Italian politicians such as Amintore Fanfani (who went to Cairo officially as Foreign Minister after Mattei had concluded his Egyptian agreement) and feared by others. He gave glamour to the adventure of close relations with the Arabs, if no great political substance.

Mattei's second *coup* was to become the first customer in the West for Russian crude oil. Again this was part of his struggle with the international oil-companies and, just as with his Mediterranean and Middle Eastern ventures, was backed by a political philosophy. Like Gronchi, he felt that tensions between East and West should and could be relaxed by trade agreements. In his time such an outlook was advanced. As an example, when President Gronchi decided to undertake an official visit to Russia he was publicly attacked by Cardinal Ottaviani, then one of the most powerful figures at the Vatican, on the grounds that he would shake the hands that had slapped Christ. Mattei positively relished criticism: in December 1960 he sent as Christmas presents twenty-three volumes of newspaper attacks, including his personal card and best wishes. In January 1959 an 'extraneous object' was found in the jet aircraft that he was about to use.

After his death in 1962, when his personal jet aircraft crashed, he left no successor in the state industries who could bear his mantle of bravado. This was to pass instead to private industry.

It is highly significant that the most glamorous personality in the field of Italian industry after Mattei's death was Gianni Agnelli, chairman of Fiat. His background was the opposite of that of Mattei; Mattei was born in humble circumstances and Agnelli to an exceedingly rich inheritance. Mattei was attractive to women and liked to enjoy himself, occasionally seeking solitude in his passion for fishing; but there was nothing about him of the leader of the international social set in the way that Agnelli would claim to be. There was an impression of steel about Mattei, never of chromium plate, which is exactly what Agnelli sometimes seems to glint with. Agnelli is as paternalistic as Mattei or more so. But from Agnelli it hurts more. And this is one of the reasons why Fiat became the prime target of labour disputes, and striking Fiat workers became the aristocracy of the Italian working world. Turin saw the worst troubles in the black autumn of 1969, and only in July 1971 was there a promise of improvement in relations between workers and management. Mattei had no setbacks comparable to that which Fiat suffered when the Government decided to allow I.R.I. to build a huge factory near Naples for the manufacture of a specially designed new Alfa Romeo model the Alfa Sud, which appeared on the roads in 1972. But both men had the same air of unquestionable authority. It has been said of Agnelli that he makes most people who go to see him feel like peasants bringing a basket of eggs. His influence is immense. It is exercised through his chairmanship of I.F.I. (Istituto Finanziario Industriale), a family holding company which handles the Agnelli family's twenty-five per cent controlling interest in Fiat and interests in cement, chemicals, shipping, insurance, finance, hotels and property. The born chieftains appear occasionally in Italian affairs. They seldom emerge in the higher levels of politics, though acknowledged tribal heads are frequently found at the lower levels of public life. Industry, as these two men have shown, can produce them at the highest level. Equally important, it has come to matter much less whether a leading industrialist is from the state camp or from private interest. The old rivalry which Mattei so happily exploited is now attenuated and big industrialists seem to be thinking on much the same lines, whether state or private industrialists, just as one of Agnelli's great preoccupations is, like Mattei, agreements with the Russians. Fiat provided technical assistance to the Russians to build a car factory to produce Fiat models adapted slightly for Russian conditions.

The Government's presence is naturally more direct in the state industries than in private concerns. But the real challenge to the country's rulers comes from the combined effect of private and state production. And, indeed, the two sometimes combine as in the I.R.I.–Fiat–Olivetti electronics company and the I.R.I.–Fiat company Aeritalia for building aircraft. It is as well to remember that two-thirds of Italian industry is made up of small and medium-sized factories, even if many of them were facing serious difficulties by late 1972, the year in which the confederation of private industrialists made its most serious efforts at bringing its own organisation in line with modern requirements. Between them they have provided the force which has changed Italy in a way that few other countries have been changed within so short a span of time. It is worth looking back briefly over the process. Broadly speaking there were three steps. The first was the post-war recovery and reconstruction which dominated the years from 1945 to 1950; the ensuing decade was one of development leading to the years of high prosperity in the early sixties until the recession of 1963. During the development years, investment increased at an annual rate of between nine and ten per cent. Industrial production almost doubled. Exports more than doubled. At the same time they changed to include finished manufactured goods rather than just the traditional food-products. From 1957 to 1962 the deficit in the balance of payments was eliminated. In 1959 industrial production advanced by 11·1 per cent; in 1960 by 14·9 per cent, and in 1961 and 1962 by 9·5 per cent. True, Italy began at a low level compared with other industrialised countries and its economy in 1971 was still only about half the size of West Germany's, and by that time slipping back: 1971 was the first year in which industrial production dropped back – by 1·3 per cent by comparison with the previous year. But its expansion had been the fastest in Europe and second in the world only to Japan's. The 1971 census showed the *per capita* income to be 1,064,000 lire ($1772), which marked an increase of 80·5 per cent over that of 1958.

. The boom was uncontrolled. Its by-products were inevitably much greater prosperity for some, frustrations for many, and a change in outlook for almost everyone. Often forgotten, moreover, is the fact that Italy in 1971 still had two million artisans whose work represented an annual turnover equivalent to one-tenth of the national income and came fourth in economic importance after industry, agriculture and tourism. Italy was still very much the country of the little man. The boom was geographically limited. Even in the thriving north it meant for many a change from unsatisfactory life on the land to settling in an urban industrial slum, which somehow the self-justifying character of human endeavour appears to regard as an improvement. For the southerner it meant a trek northward to another world and another civilisation. How many times a day must southern immigrants in Turin turn over in their shift-beds (this is the system by which shift-workers share a bed in a dormitory with those working different hours to themselves) to say to themselves in an effort of self-conviction: 'It is better to be a Fiat worker, it is better to be in a big city....'

There are scenes in Turin and Milan which would have inspired Blake to his most exquisite pessimism, Disraeli to a new discourse on the Two Nations and his rival Gladstone to find a new negation of God erected into a system. Agnelli compares the performance of the industrialists favourably with that of the politicians and blames the politicians for the lack of facilities for the new working classes. 'We compete with Detroit,' he is reported to have said, 'but Rome does not have to compete with Washington.' What he says is true. It is another of the complaints that the politicians are not doing their part in the rapid changes which have tormented the country. The industrialists are giving Italy a modern economy but they cannot be asked to provide the palliatives for social change at the same time and carry out what the politicians do no more than promise. The industrialists argue that they cannot be expected to conquer export markets where Italian exports have never been before, if at the same time they are expected to pay for the construction of a welfare state when already they claim to be paying a higher percentage of social-security charges than their competitors elsewhere in Europe. Fiat's estimate is that a man who takes home 100,000 lire

($173) a month costs Fiat in all 183,000 lire ($305) with social charges and social facilities offered at the factory. But arrogance is not enough. It is perfectly understandable to despise politicians if you think that they are not doing their job. But the price to be paid for this moral and paternalistic superiority is, of course, to do a part of the job for them. And then we are back at the argument of the necessity of keeping down costs in order to be competitive in the world's markets. And so industrialists cannot do more than provide jobs. There are still priests in Turin who follow the old Piedmontese path of practical sanctity. The constant cry of one of them whose work was among the poor immigrants was: 'We shall only find a solution when we stop thinking of exports.' It was the cry of humanity in another sort of jungle, new to most Italians. Another priest, Don Lorenzo Milani, now dead but one of a group of Tuscan priests who tried to bring back the spiritual elements of Catholicism, wrote: 'The fact is that there has been no government, and this has worked entirely to the disadvantage of the poor.' Between them they had said everything.

The problems are huge. A nation's mind is changing yet still does not know where finally its promptings will send it. Women in some of the country villages, especially in the north, will only marry a man who promises to take them to live in the city. The men who wish to stay on the land have to look to the deep south for wives and arrange to meet them through marriage-brokers. There are exceptions. A girl of twenty-seven from Asti, in Piedmont, put an advertisement in the Turin newspaper *La Stampa* for a husband, saying that she was seeking a man of the fields who loved his native soil, was modern-minded nevertheless, intelligent, tall and, preferably, not exactly ugly. She had thirty offers within three days. Cases of this kind reinforce one's faith in the common sense of the Italians. They may still at a given point draw the conclusion that the wild race to catch up with progress has brought them unhappiness as well as real advance. They are a realistic people and would grasp this point, if anyone would. They do, moreover, have a more beautiful country than most, that is being ruined, and a more ancient form of family life which is now threatened. They are consciously shattering a civilisation with the danger that they might become nothing more than mock-Americans. Their danger is everybody's danger but Italians, because they are more enthusiastic than other races, have accepted the new concepts of Western living with more energy than any other country. They are also capable of stopping because the price is too high. In the way they react to new ideas the Italians are drawing an exact chart of the values which have been put to them: the values of materialism, of scarcely governed invitations to acquisition; a new kind of paganism with smoke and pollution instead of the sun and incense; and a restlessness balanced by only a semi-conviction that what they are doing is right. Someone pointed out to an Italian friend, as they walked down the Corso in Rome alongside an endless line of cars hopelessly blocked, that many of the drivers did not look particularly exasperated. The Italian replied, 'No: they are not moving but they feel they are where they ought to be, behind a steering wheel and not walking.'

The idea of a strong government still worries many intelligent Italians. This anxiety is due in part to the heritage of Fascism. But it goes deeper than that. There is still a deep-seated mistrust of government. This feeling was very clear at the time of Mariano Rumor's resignation on 6 July 1970. Rumor had found himself in the impossible position of wanting to provide a series of well-intentioned reforms by means of a coalition in which he genuinely believed. But he could not make it work. He blamed his coalition partners and, in particular, what he felt to be the disruptive behaviour of the Socialists. He concluded that the country was approaching ungovernability. And so he decided to hand over to someone else or produce a situation in which everyone would have the chance of clarifying their motives, even to the point of going to the country in a general election. He made up his mind on the Friday. He talked to friends on Saturday without allowing the news to be published because his deputy prime minister, Signor Francesco De Martino, the leading Socialist in the Government, had a wedding in his family and Rumor did not want to disturb the ceremony. On Sunday he saw the leaders of his own Christian Democrat Party and after having explained his reasons to them he telephoned President Saragat. He then instructed his staff to collect his ministers together for a cabinet meeting at noon on 6 July, at which those not so privy to his secret were informed that he had decided to resign and that the Government was at an end. Rumor's resignation was one of the crucial moments in Italian affairs. Its significance warranted a detailed description of why a prime minister who was supported by a substantial parliamentary majority, and exactly a month previously had seen regional elections produce a result favourable to the coalition parties, should feel that he must go. The parliamentarians who saw him on the Saturday found him in a condition of nervous stress. His closest advisers maintained that he was tired and tried by a heavy week but in no sense ill. And, to back this view that reports of a collapse were false, he sounded calm and much more his old self on the Sunday after having informed the President of his decision.

One of the dispiriting factors was the refusal of the unions to respond to his appeal to revoke the general strike which they had called for 7 July. In fact, they cancelled it as a result of his resignation, but the behaviour of the unions was one of the reasons why affairs seemed to be getting out of hand. For the first time in Italy's post-war history the unions were seeking a part in the formulation of policy. The Italian labour world is split; the biggest group of unions consists of the Communist-led federation, the C.G.I.L. It is followed by the Christian Democrat federation (C.I.S.L.) and, much smaller, the Social Democrat group of unions (U.I.L.). Three things were happening in their internal affairs. The first was that they reflected the general feeling of lack of confidence in political parties as such; even the C.G.I.L. was demanding greater autonomy from the parties. The second development was that the three groups of unions were trying to achieve greater unity and, in fact, the difficult autumn of 1969 saw them operating with a wide degree of unity of action. The third development was their quite deliberate intention to fill the political vacuum by demanding a voice in the formulation of national policy. They had grasped the point that there was little to be gained in asking for more money for their members if workers could find no proper homes, suffered from an insufficient system of social security and could not obtain proper schooling for their children. They were worried as well by the success of far left-wing agitators outside the unions, who incited the workers of Turin and Milan, especially the under-privileged southerners, to violence. These new developments within the labour movement coincided with the first serious breakdown in labour relations experienced since Italy became an industrial power, and added to Rumor's anxieties.

There was a certain menace in the air; a menace that some-one might be tempted to take decisive action in pulling the country to the right. It was exactly ten years since Tambroni had tried to do exactly that. With considerable courage the Turin newspaper *La Stampa* published an article by Vittorio Gorresio re-evoking the events of ten years earlier with the clear intention of warning anyone with similar ideas to think again. There was a feeling that Western Europe as a whole was moving right. The Conservative victory in the British general election encouraged this idea. A reactionary minority within the governmental coalition favoured a quick general election because they felt that it would damage the Socialists and register a shift to the right throughout the country as a result of the strikes and uncertainties of the autumn. Other counsels won the day and no general election was called at that moment. Emilio Colombo managed to form a govern-ment, after the failure, which came near to success, of Giulio Andreotti. The country appeared to settle down again. One of the few witty remarks attributed to Mussolini was to the effect that governing Italy was not impossible but pointless, meaning that the Italians could manage perfectly well without a govern-ment. The opposite had been shown to be true. Yet many Italians seem perfectly willing to accept a country which is over-politicised and under-governed. This is no invented para-dox: the system is designed to produce this result. And so is the temperament of, probably, the majority who look on the mere phrase 'good government' as meaning something at worst dangerous and at best undesirable.

CHAPTER TEN

Sitting on a Volcano

A COLLEAGUE summed up the political situation in Italy by saying that she thought the politicians were sitting on a volcano but ignored the fact. She happened to make the remark when the town of Pozzuoli was demonstrating how people behave when they literally are sitting on a volcano and only too aware of doing so. The town was rising disconcertingly as a result of volcanic activity. And, to make the symbol perfect, Pozzuoli may now be a nondescript little town near Naples but it has a fine history. It was founded by Greeks from the island of Samos, fleeing from tyranny, who settled there and called it Dicearchia, meaning good government.

Under the Romans its only rival as a commercial centre was Alexandria. Its port was famous: its streets were full of merchants from all points of the Mediterranean. It is set in that marvellous, still volatile area known as the Flegraean Fields, which were regarded with good reasons by the ancients as the entry to the underworld (Lake Avernus is a few short miles away) because of the sulphurous exhalations from the earth. Aeneas paused there and St Paul, on his way to Rome, stayed a week, a visitor who would have written some famous execrations if by chance he had survived until February 1970 when a majority of the priests of the Pozzuoli area became the first priests in southern Italy to criticise obligatory celibacy in public.

And then there was its slow bradyseism, a natural phenomenon which was to make it more famous than Virgil's predilection for its thermal waters (he is honoured with a medieval miniature showing not only Aeneas but also Christ descending into the underworld at a point apparently about two minutes' walk from the baths).

This phenomenon of bradyseism is volcanic in origin, and means a movement of the earth involving a change in the relative level of land and sea. The complaint is as tiresome as it is rare. In 1538 the upward movement ended in the crescendo of a genuine volcanic eruption which left many deaths and a new mountain behind it, still called Monte Nuovo. The recent bradyseismic history of the town shows that in and around the tenth century Pozzuoli began a long period of sinking. In the space of a century the soil dropped by about thirty-six feet. During the following five centuries the town was on the whole going up and regained about twenty-four feet before it began to sink again. The movement can be erratic. The 1538 rise was sudden and violent. In 1913, severe damage was caused by a sudden drop which caused flooding of the main street. These changes in level are recorded on ancient marble. Three Roman columns stand in the centre of the town in what is known as the Temple of Serapis but was, in fact, the public market. The marble when submerged is attacked by a form of shellfish, the *lithodomus*, and the marks left by these attacks record the level of submergence.

It had attracted attention first in 1962 because the town was sinking and again in February 1970 because the direction had changed and Pozzuoli was rising. In 1962 it was dropping an average of fifteen millimetres a year. One of the most obvious inconveniences was that six sewer outlets passed below sea-level and, once the sea became a little agitated, the sewage was swept back into the houses and, with it, the sewer rats. Dozens of them sat in the warm sunshine, blinking and eating the refuse from the market. The first warnings in 1970 were issued when it was found that the town was rising at a rate of a centimetre a month. There were cracks in the walls of the town hall. Fear spread. Part of the town might, it was said, collapse or as bad a tragedy as 1538 happen again. People began to move away. The Government, worried because of constant attacks about its inability to deal with disasters, such as the great floods of November 1966 and the Sicilian earthquake of January 1968, sent hundreds of troops and *carabinieri* in army trucks to deal with the problems of a large-scale evacuation. The beach was growing wider and fishing-boats were reporting difficulties in tying up at the mole as the water-level fell. The troops had a difficult time. They were having to behave as if a disaster had happened, though it had not. They were ordered to evacuate what was regarded as the most dangerous area, the slums known as Rione Terra, the ancient acropolis overlooking the port, but they could point to no tangible reason why people in this one area were being forced to go and others allowed to stay. Rumours spread that the danger was exaggerated because vested interests wanted to lay their hands on this area for purposes of speculation. There was an ill-defined fear, nothing very much to see except the comparatively huge military forces. The inhabitants of Rione Terra were desperately reluctant in many cases to leave their slums, and much tact and patience and insistence were needed to make them abandon this intricate pattern of stone stairs and walls, sanctified by the spirits of the ancients, and by all appearance eternal. Until the Army, under the pressure of fear, arrived to empty them. The local authorities decided to try to find out what was really causing the trouble, so delicate instruments were set up throughout the area and experts asked to come – from as far away as Japan – to give advice; all to enhance, said the voices of suspicion, the exaggerated feeling of danger.

The handling of the situation was not perfect. It was generous and vigorous. In the wake of an exaggerated fear and in some ways too massive an intervention by the State, Pozzuoli could see two of its problems solved. An ancient area of slums was emptied: scientific knowledge about the area would be more exact with the hope that the nature of the phenomenon could be better defined. These advances will have cost a great deal, in human sadness and in economic terms. But something will have been accomplished and two lessons made clear. The first is that an accumulation of ancient problems means that a disproportionately greater effort must be made to deal simply with one of the most urgent issues. Panic and the soldiers were needed to remove inhabitants from the Rione Terra like sea-urchins from a rock. The other lesson was that simple reactions are often best, even if the immediate effects are to bring hardship. There was fear and confusion and sadness. There was also energy, compassion, determination, and as a result something was accomplished. It will all have proved in vain only if the evacuated area is really – as the cynics fear – given over to building speculation: in which case the powers of the underworld might well become angry and split Pozzuoli with a shattering sulphurous explosion.

It is hard to imagine that Italian politicians are sitting on a volcano. The country will not explode. But one might sometimes wish they would act as if they were. They might well go about their business differently if they were given the feeling that beneath their feet a slow movement of indignation might one day burst around them, relentless and dangerous like the bradyseism with its threats of sudden eruption.

CHAPTER ELEVEN

Reform

T H E heart of Italy's political problem is social reform. So much is true of any political society in a period of profound social change but, Italy being Italy, it is more acute in its Italian form. Socially, Italy has made no progress comparable to its industrial expansion and to its position in international affairs. That is why Italian politicians with international reputations can behave at home like medieval barons. Italians, moreover, have created an artificial dichotomy between revolution and reform, and this leads them to talk constantly in theoretical terms about reforms while achieving sadly little in the way of legislation. For more than two decades, too little social reform presented the Communists with the parliamentary votes of a large mass which had something to protest about and a grudge against society. Because the Communists were scarcely likely to erupt into volcanic violence, except for an occasional riot, this protest never reached dangerous proportions. The Communist interest was to use it but keep it under control. The very use which they made of the protest vote stultified the cause of reform, because in many Christian Democrat eyes the mere thought of applying what their opponents called for had a deadly taint of origin. Another difficulty was that reform itself has associations of an ideological kind. It is the alternative to revolution. Hence the whole principle of reform is regularly debated whenever the word is mentioned. Deep down there has always been the feeling that the left-wing opposition was not as serious as it sounded and was not single-mindedly intent on pulling down the Government and replacing it with an alternative policy: indeed, on some crucial issues the Communists have no detailed alternatives ready to be applied. This interlocking of government and the main party of opposition explains why the most advanced reforming voices have frequently been, not Marxists, but disgruntled unhappy Catholics with a social conscience.

Such a conscience is a difficult encumbrance in Italian political life. There is no place for the purist, the single-minded reformer of the Wilberforce type: as several leading Catholics with an unbearable conscience offended by poverty and reaction were to find, the choice was compromise or the cloister. One of the uncompromising voices was that of the Tuscan priest Don Lorenzo Milani, already quoted on the lack of government, who was silenced by an early death. He described, with the ruthlessness of spiritual fervour, the gap between profession and achievement in a political party calling itself Christian. He was outstanding in spiritual force and courage but typical in the sense that real, relentless, revolutionary grasp of the obligation to improve the country's social conditions comes more from advanced Catholics than from Marxists, the true combination of humanity and tirelessness in a good cause. Among Don Milani's writings was a letter to a fellow-priest, Don Piero, dealing with the subject of religion and politics. In it he gives a series of hypothetical questions about Christian Democracy which might be put to him by a young man who is suffering unfair treatment from his employer:

'How', he might say to me, 'can you tell me that grace makes man resemble God, and yet these men whom you support because they are Catholics, as men guaranteed by grace, have been unable to show a capacity to act against this system of injustice, have allowed themselves to be conditioned by things as they are, by a situation created by anti-clericals, but which your Catholics have accepted and preserved as reverently as the relics of a saint?

'Why then implicate yourself in their responsibility? I believe in God and I want to live in the Church, but can this mean that I must give up trying to change our condition of social inferiority and my belief that wealth should be spent in such a way as to insure free work for all men?

'Make up your mind. Either do not meddle in politics or, if you do, these should be your objectives and these the candidates you propose to us. After all these years the sentence you deserve is this: that you realise the ability of your faith – the faith which you preach – to illuminate men's minds, to make clarity flow freely, to liberate men's best forces on the practical level by sustaining his will. If your faith is useless for this, then what do I have to do with you, political priest?

'If the saints are not adapted to this world, keep them in the cloister and keep your own distance from the dirt of politics, and it may happen that some day I will join you, attracted by this total separation which makes you different from everything and everybody. But if you lower yourself to this world, point out to us men to whom we may trust our earthly lot, men who can make this glory shine in their every act, transfigure their laws, and make their government with a holy, unmistakable, and inimitable seal.

'Admit it, Piero: this is not the look of the government we have produced....'

Putting aside the claims of pristine Christianity, which few Italians are so unrealistic as to think practicable, what are the individual problems which a moderate reformer would regard as exceedingly urgent? The choice is wide. The first essential for any state, and particularly a state still trying to evoke the confidence of its citizens, is a reasonable assurance of justice. In Italy this is a huge subject which varies from trivial impressions of injustice to the occasional conviction that the system of justice as a whole has almost ceased to function.

Italy has a codified system of justice, like the canon law of the Church. Crimes are spelled out and the punishments prescribed. The last revision of the penal code was in 1931 and, although a modern revision is part of the programme of any self-respecting government, a fresh approach had not been attempted after a quarter of a century of democratic government: a period which saw great changes in the country but not in the methods of dispensing justice. The judges of the tribunals sit beneath a crucifix and a sign which reads: 'Justice is equal for all.' It is not, and if it were things would still be bad.

In Italy judges are a separate profession; a man studies to be a judge as a youth, not first to practise law and later after long experience in the courts to be appointed judge. Hence the attitude of the 6900 judges as a profession is important in the application of the codes, and in pressing for reform or opposing it. Like everything else in Italy, they are divided into factions and highly politicised. Those who challenge the present system are usually regarded as Marxists whether or not they happen to be. A magistrate in Florence stood up to attack the system on Marxist lines and found himself faced with formal charges of insulting the magistracy, which was a curious charge to bring against a magistrate. The majority are conservative, and this reactionary element appears determined to give a reading of the law which is conservative in all senses, almost as if they feel they are the guardians of the structure of society now being challenged by so many forces. It is not so much the cases which are frequently cited of monstrously cruel sentences: three months in prison for stealing a chicken, children condemned for stealing apples, the wife of an unemployed labourer sent to prison for 'attempted theft' with a sick baby in her arms. Such miscarriages certainly occur, but it would be wrong to give an impression of Italian justice as cruel and oppressive. The system is out of date, as are the mental processes of certain judges, but the element of mercy frequently arises in penal cases and tends to be overlooked because of the more scandalous aspects of judicial incompetence. The most menacing impression is that the codes are constantly becoming remoter from the requirements of real justice as is the outlook of the average judge, and that personal rights invariably count for less than the demands of property. An apple, as one commentator remarked, is better protected in Italy than a person.

The best-intentioned judges will find that the regulations enforce a slow pace. Take as an example the trial in Florence in 1969 of a young American arrested nine months earlier, and kept in prison awaiting trial on charges of possessing and peddling drugs. The young man was obviously going to be found guilty on convincing evidence. The pace was slowed by the need for interpreting. But the real brake on proceedings was the rule by which the presiding judge dictated what would amount to the court record to an official clerk of the court who wrote down what was dictated to him in longhand with pen and ink, slowly at that. The judge was not only doing most of the questioning but then summarising the answers to dictate to the scribe. The judge was exquisitely careful to see that the youth was given a fair hearing. There could be no complaint on that score. But the court sat all day to hear this single, simple case and the youth was found guilty in the early evening.

The backlog is immense. The average time for settling a civil case is now a decade. Penal cases come up sooner, but it may well be a matter of years before one's case is heard, and much of the time – there are limits according to the seriousness of the charge – will be spent in an overcrowded prison. The distribution of judges is uneven. In certain areas they are insufficient in numbers; usually in difficult posts such as Sardinia where there should be too many rather than too few. But the south in general and Sardinia in particular are regarded as punishment stations. Not only the south suffers in this respect. Turin is an example of an expanding city suffering from a growth in organised crime. About 3000 cases are dealt with each year by the Tribunal. Most of these cases have to be looked into by an investigating judge who decides whether or not an accused person should be sent for trial. This department for investigations, with about 3000 cases a year to handle, consisted in 1971 of 14 judges, 7 clerks, 4 policemen and 2 typists. The backlog in 1968 was 190: in 1971 about 2000. The lawyers combine mastery of delaying tactics with a florid and lengthy oratory. They frequently appear to suffer from an acute longing to avoid being deprived of a case in hand, as if they had learned to love it with the passing of the years and cannot think of doing without it. Naples in 1972 had 4000 lawyers, of whom 500 practised and 300 made their living from the profession.

Not only the lawyers love their law-suits. Italians are very quick to go to law and reluctant to let a case drop. They are helped by the system that appeals to a higher court are practically automatic and are virtually re-trials. It is quite normal to expect one's friends to appear in Rome from the provinces, to carry out their regular sessions with their lawyer on the family's law-suit. Few provincials would be without one: it provides an excuse for a visit to the capital with all the dignity of a principal dealing with his executant, and a wronged principal at that.

Occasionally the count is made to see which outstanding case can claim to be the oldest. The record in 1973 was held by the Cabras case. The series of trials involving fishing rights in the lagoon of Cabras in Sardinia date from 1858. The most recent hearing was in December 1972 when the judges acquitted 174 fishermen charged with fishing illegally in the lagoon. Private fishing rights at Cabras were made over by Philip IV of Spain to a Genoese banker in the seventeenth century as security for a loan and have remained in private hands ever since, in spite of regular efforts to break the old connexion. The 1972 hearings did not settle the question of ownership and the lagoon will undoubtedly be the subject of hearings for years to come. It is true enough that law-suits are handed down from generation to generation like heirlooms.

The second prize went to a case begun in 1862 to prevent the State from taking possession of properties including a convent near Salerno. These were left by a nobleman in 1542 to three families who administered them for centuries. The State claimed possession on the grounds that the properties amounted to a religious house, whereas the administrators claimed that the inheritance was not religious. There had been a series of conflicting judgements, the last of which went in the State's favour.

For its combination of delay and sheer numbers of persons involved, there were few rivals to the trial which opened in Arezzo in January 1973 involving a tax-farming agency. Officials of the agency were accused of having corrupted politicians and other public figures in order to be able to take over the collection of taxes from certain local authorities. The trial opened eighteen years and three months after the original enquiries. The accused numbered 515 and there were 572 witnesses. Members of almost all parliamentary parties were allegedly involved in the scandal.

One potentially vital advance in the conduct of justice came with promulgation of a decree-law establishing that an arrested man was entitled to have a lawyer present at all stages of the enquiry. This right stands clear and proud in the Constitution, but was not made part of penal procedure until January 1971 and even then not always followed. Its importance went beyond the elementary rights of an arrested man. Traditionally, Italian justice is based on the inquisitorial method of enquiry. The object of the method is to obtain the arrested man's confession – or proof of his innocence – by interrogation and the pressures of prison-life, and not infrequently the prisoner will be held for several days and questioned closely without knowing what precise charges have been brought against him. This secret system is open to a variety of abuses, including blatant cruelty and intentional humiliation. Long before the Government changed this part of the code of procedure (in itself a decision taken years after the Constitutional Court had declared the earlier practice illegal) public opinion was beginning to be aroused by open misuse of a system which had more in keeping with the Middle Ages than a modern country. The new law helped remove some of the sinister aspects of arrest. At least it meant that the first days in prison would be less fearsome than when the newcomer was left alone to fend for himself while being 'examined' by the investigating judge. But it did not affect the nature of the system itself. The man arrested for the bomb explosions in Milan in December 1969, Valpreda, was not brought to trial till February 1972 and then, after preliminary hearings, the Rome Assize Court decided it was not competent to hear the trial and sent the case back to Milan. An appeal to the Court of Cassation that Milan was 'too dangerous' a place for the trial, put forward by the Milan public prosecutor, was accepted and Catanzaro, in the deep south, was chosen (in October 1972) as the place for the hearings.

This case had the virtue not only of representing all that is worst in the Italian judicial system but also of suggesting a dangerous political undercurrent. The background is worth recording in some detail.

On 12 December 1969 a bomb exploded in the Banca Nazionale dell'Agricoltura in Piazza Fontana in Milan. An unexploded bomb was found in the Banca Commerciale Italiana in Piazza della Scala and at much the same time three bombs exploded in Rome, two on the Victor Emmanuel monument and another in a bank. There were no deaths in Rome. The Milan bomb claimed sixteen victims and over ninety injured. The explosions came at a time of extreme tension. Italy was in the midst of strikes, Milan had already had a policeman killed, presumably by extra-parliamentary extremists. Mariano Rumor's government was weak and he himself despairing of being able to steer the country through so difficult a period with only a minority administration.

On the morning after the explosions police officials were reported as saying that anarchists were responsible for the outrage and police enquiries appeared largely to be directed at the Milan anarchists, many of whom were brought in for questioning, along with known members of the extra-parliamentary groups. Among the anarchists arrested was Giuseppe Pinelli. The magistracy was informed, according to the defence, two days after the arrests took place and the men were held without charges. Arrests are supposed to be communicated immediately to the judicial authorities. On the morning of 15 December, the police arrested Pietro Valpreda, a professional dancer and anarchist. He was immediately taken to Rome, itself an illegal step according to his lawyers, though the object was obvious, and the same day a taxi-driver, Cornelio Rolandi, who claimed to have driven Valpreda to the bank in Piazza Fontana, was flown to Rome. He died before the Valpreda case came up for trial but he was reported as having said that before being asked to identify Valpreda he had been shown a photograph of him. The identity parade consisted of the anarchist, weary after seven hours of interrogation, and four plain-clothes policemen. The taxi-driver identified Valpreda with the phrase, still according to the defence, 'if that is not him, he is not here'. On the same day, around midnight, Pinelli fell in mysterious circumstances from a fourth-floor window of police headquarters in Milan. He died in hospital that night. The Chief of Police pronounced him a suicide and described Pinelli's death as an act of self-accusation.

The theory of suicide was questionable, to say the least. A far left-wing newspaper *Lotta Continua* first hinted and then boldly stated that Pinelli had been killed by the police, naming in particular an inspector in the political section of the Milan police, Luigi Calabresi. Calabresi sued *Lotta Continua* for libel. The widow of Pinelli in the meantime behaved with imposing dignity. She spoke frequently of Pinelli's conscientiousness, of his love for her and the two daughters, his serenity and his habit of ridiculing the bombastic manner of Valpreda for whom he did not appear to have much sympathy. Licia Pinelli asked for the exhumation of her husband's body so that a more thorough examination could be made of the cause of death and charged all those concerned with Pinelli's questioning, from Calabresi to his chief at the political office of the public security police, with homicide, violence, illegal arrest, abuse of authority. None of these charges has reached court. Valpreda was still in prison with, as far as the public was aware, no additional shred of genuine evidence against him, until December 1972 when he was granted provisional liberty pending trial. Valpreda from prison wrote a letter to a woman journalist, Camilla Cederna, who had followed the case closely. One of the most striking passages was: '... it is just that we know what their plans are and they can only put them into practice because there is general indifference, we are ... monsters of forgetfulness'.

Valpreda was understating the case. He was the victim,

whether or not he was guilty, of the most blatant example of judicial blundering in Italy's recent history. The Fascists had been cruder but there was never an instance in which a political prisoner (Valpreda was not charged with political offences but he was nonetheless a political prisoner) was subjected for years on end to a caricature of the processes of justice. By the time the Court of Cassation ruled in autumn 1972 that the case should be held in Catanzaro, Valpreda had been held for thirty-four months without trial. In the meantime two Neo-Fascists had been arrested and charged with responsibility for the same crime and the evidence brought against them appeared much stronger. Calabresi had been shot down by a gunman in May 1972 as he left his home. As the judges, belatedly, took up the track of right-wing extremism, they found that evidence which would have led them along that path years earlier had either been ignored or concealed from them, and efforts were made – but promptly stopped – to bring charges against three high-ranking police officials, all in the Ministry of the Interior's political branch, for concealing evidence.

Whatever the final outcome may be of the Valpreda case, it served one extremely useful purpose. Under the pressure of public opinion, which mounted suddenly and surprisingly – given the indifference which Valpreda himself condemned from his cell – the Government was forced to take action. The result was an improvement in the rigid code of penal procedure. The principal innovation was that judges could use discretion in granting provisional liberty to a prisoner awaiting trial even on charges for which compulsory detention was prescribed. That was how Valpreda was released, and the change can be regarded as a substantial improvement in Italy's judicial processes.

A country's prisons do not show it at its best. This is peculiarly true of Italy. They are repeatedly described as schools for all forms of crime and for sexual perversity. A social assistant in Rome's Regina Coeli prison was quoted as saying that most people who left its gates 'came back sooner or later'.

The length of time spent awaiting trial was one of the

reasons for the great convict-revolt in April 1969, when the inmates in all of Italy's principal prisons rose in a frenzy of frustration. In Turin alone 3000 heavily armed guards were called to re-establish 'order'. The complaints were of over-crowding, bad food and primitive sanitary arrangements. The average population in the prisons at any one time is 35,000 and the average turnover is 450,000 persons a year, of whom about five per cent are women. This turnover is high, so that a relatively large section of the population is directly or in-directly touched by prison life, however briefly. According to a study completed in early 1971 at the Department of Socio-logy of Trento University, official statistics were so uncertain that there had been cases of persons tried in contumacy who were sitting in their cells but had somewhere become lost in the bureaucratic labyrinth of the prison system. Prison gov-ernors are personally responsible for the accounts: according to the Trento report, to apply for the cheapest ballpoint from official stocks the prison administration requires three sig-natures from the governor, and the annual budget shows about 30,000 signatures.

The accepted manner for easing the pressure on space in the prisons is to grant an amnesty. In May 1970, Mariano Rumor's government passed Italy's two hundred and thirty-fourth amnesty in a century and the twenty-fifth since the end of the Second World War. This institution is sometimes attacked as casting discredit on the judicial process and under-mining the morale of the police, as well as freeing real delin-quents. The same is said of the time-limits imposed on how long a man can be held before a definitive sentence is passed. Justice being so slow, a number of known criminals gained at least provisional release under this measure: an example of partial reform in the sense that it was a step ahead of other aspects of the judicial system and so neither fitted the old system nor changed it radically. But such measures also, and here their attractiveness to the politicians can be seen, ease the pressure of the demand for reform. A count taken shortly before the twenty-fifth amnesty showed that the number of penal cases awaiting hearing had reached 1,315,000 and courts of first instance alone were faced with 1,024,000 cases of all kinds. Relief of some kind was essential and reform was a forlorn hope.

The trouble with the system is much the same, though in an exaggerated form, as the trouble common throughout the Italian administration: the rules were formulated, like the penal code and the code of penal procedure, in 1931. The rules are not just out of date; they began badly, in the full atmosphere of Fascist Italy. They have also grown less and less appropriate with the passing of time and only feeble attempts have been made to bring them into line with more modern conditions. A governmental measure for reform was introduced in 1968 but three years later it was no nearer approval; it was revived in August 1972 but in the words of one prison official was inadequate to meet the situation.

The prison governors have been in the forefront of demands for radical change. They wrote to the ministers of justice and of bureaucratic reform in early 1969, before the outbreak of rioting, with a warning about the situation. Their letter, dated 17 February 1969, pointed out that conditions were 'seriously alarming'. They met in conference after the revolt and several of them showed an acute and urgent understanding of the fact that the system was brutalising in its effects. One of them, with the rank of inspector-general, Dr Vincenzo Marolda, entered a plea for allowing human considerations, as laid down by the Constitution, to enter into prison administration. No democratic character had been given to prison-life:

> No move dictated by love or democracy could mean that the accused (still technically innocent) before any judge declared him guilty, was condemned to satisfy his bodily needs in the presence of other persons, to eat prison meals using the bed as a table, and a companion to satisfy his requirements as a brutish reminder of reality. No governor is able to protect him from having to live with persons he has not chosen, to sleep with the light constantly lit, to move for many hours a day in a few square yards of space, taking turns with other companions in misfortune.

The Inspector-General for Prisons of the Ministry of Justice,

Marcello Bonamano, was quoted in mid-1971 as saying: 'Article 27 of the Constitution gives assurances that the accused is presumed innocent until found guilty. Experience authorises me to say that a few days in prison while awaiting a verdict suffice for the presumed innocent to end in an inferno from which, if found guilty, he will emerge irremediably lost and if found innocent irremediably marked.'

The question of sexual perversion caused by prison-life was treated in a study published in January 1970 which stated that nearly one-half of the specimen of convicts questioned admitted to homosexual relationships. The real proportion was felt to be higher because of the reluctance to admit perversion. Some seventy-eight per cent took to homosexuality after entering prison. Some of the evidence contained in this study was pathetic. One example is of a young man aged twenty-two who was in prison for having shot a neighbour: this neighbour had revealed that the man was homosexual and that the woman to whom he was married was lesbian. He was sentenced to ten years' imprisonment and three years of hospital treatment. In the first prison to which he was sent he made friends with a young Venetian: 'He fell in love with me, almost as a man might fall in love with a woman. He received 20,000 lire ($33) a month from his family and a monthly parcel so that he lacked nothing. I worked in the carpentry shop as a polisher and earned 4000 lire ($6.60) a month and my family visited me once a fortnight. My friend, apart from refusing to allow me to work, would not let me speak to the others and did not want me to eat prison food. He wanted to give me everything himself. . . .' In its warped way, this relationship had a certain humanity. But the same witness spoke frankly about the extent of the problem. In another prison to which he was moved, 'out of 300 convicts I can guarantee that 200 had relations with each other'. Other testimony pointed out that, as the months pass, perversion is almost an adaptation to environment: the real difficulties begin when the convict is released and returns to normal conditions.

Prisons in some of the leading Italian cities were built for the purpose and in some places, such as Trani, Foggia, Nuoro and the Rebibbia prison in Rome, more modern prisons have been completed. But an improvement in physical conditions can mean little when the old prison mentality is unchanged. There were serious accusations at Rebibbia in the summer of 1972 of organised violence against prisoners who had staged a protest. In many of the smaller towns improvisation is still the rule. The habit dates from the unification of the country a century ago when the Government expropriated many ecclesiastical properties and the State found on its hand a collection of convents and castles which were put to use as prisons and are still being used as such. In the principal prisons, the average size of the cells is nine feet by twelve and they normally take three prisoners. They are lit by one heavily barred window. Sanitary arrangements are a bucket. In the summer of 1969 a group of eighty-five non-Italian prisoners in Rome's Regina Coeli gaol wrote to *The Times* to denounce the nightmarish conditions in which they lived. Florence and Viterbo are examples of a few of the larger prisons in which the general rule is one prisoner to a cell, but the cells are so small that there is room for little apart from the bed. They measure seven feet by four with ceilings a little more than six feet above the ground. The surroundings themselves, as one critic said, are sadistic. And Italy was the one country in the Western world until the summer of 1971 in which prisoners were required to pay a contribution to their own keep. The demand for payment normally arrives some time after the man has served his sentence and is probably struggling to find his place in society. If he could not settle the account, what possessions he had were liable to sequestration.

In this atmosphere of pointless tension, fights are frequent, suicides and attempted suicides by no means rare; intimidatory violence, especially in the southern prisons, is a constant factor. The Trento report estimates that the proportion of broken limbs and other injuries among Italian convicts is some ten times higher than the industrial-accident rate (which is twice the British industrial rate). Testimony given by prisoners was of fearsome physical violence committed by warders, including the breaking of limbs; the suggestion is not that such conduct is general. But it is said to be frequent and the authors of this study expressed willingness to furnish the names of their informants and the tape-recordings of conversations if called upon to do so. The punishment known to prisoners as the *Balilla*, or officially as the 'bed of contention', remains in use; a man is strapped by the wrists and ankles to a metal bed, on a mattress with a hole in the centre for obvious purposes, sometimes for days at a time. There is no death-penalty in Italy but life imprisonment meant exactly that: prison-life for the rest of one's days with the hope only of being freed in time to die outside the walls. In January 1971 the life-sentence was abolished as an inflexible rule which paid no regard to such considerations as a change in a convict's character which might conceivably make him fit once again to return to society. Whatever is said of prison-life, it is important to remember that for the innocent and the guilty it is much easier to enter prison than to leave. There is an Italian saying that once people are born, registered and baptised they enjoy provisional liberty.

There are three main groups of national police, frequently working in rivalry with each other. The first is the Ministry of the Interior's Public Security Police, a largely barracked force and, of course, armed. The second is the force of *carabinieri*, a semi-military body paid for from the Defence budget which becomes a fighting force in time of war. The third is the Guardia di Finanza whose duties include the investigation of tax offences, the combating of smuggling – particularly the smuggling, possession and use of drugs. Each town has its local, municipal, police force, the *vigili urbani*. Feelings towards the *finanzieri* are respectful but indifferent because no strong feelings are aroused by men whose job is largely to prevent robbery of the State. The public security police are unpopular and feared. The *carabinieri* are by far the most popular. When, for instance, two people died during clashes with police at Battipaglia in the riots of April 1969, the mayor of the town negotiated an agreement by which the public security forces were withdrawn from the town and law and order left entirely to the *carabinieri*, who still had the confidence of the people. In Reggio Calabria, which was the scene of intermittent and extremely ferocious rioting from July

1970, both *carabinieri* and the public security police had requisitioned schools as temporary barracks. When the *carabinieri* left, the schools were said by the municipal authorities to be cleaner than when they arrived; the public security police left behind them damage which it was said would cost 30 million lire (£20,000 or $50,000) to put right.

At times, as at Reggio, the dislike and distrust of the police reaches a form of blind hatred. By accident and a regrettable perpetration of the idea that the police are a repressive force at the command of the most reactionary elements in government, the chasm between police and most sections of the population is unbridgeable. There are still older people who recall how the state police behaved under the Fascists. The overwhelming majority of *questori*, the title of local police-chiefs commanding the public security forces, were trained during Fascism. Much of the repressive character remains. But, worse, democratic governments have not only failed to change the character of the forces of law and order in what was a return, in theory, to a state based on law, not tyranny; they acted in a way that could only widen the gap between police and people. In 1949 Mario Scelba, then Minister of the Interior, extended to cover the police the penal protection against 'insult' which was accorded to the fundamental institutions of the State. Hence, it is a risky business to criticise the police in public, which is one of the reasons why there is comparatively little written about the police in Italy. Scelba (he held the Ministry of the Interior from 1947 to 1953) was also responsible for forming the special riot-squads of the public security police. They are still looked on as the particular enemies of workers, students and demonstrators of most kinds. The reported case of a Rome student is eloquent enough: asked for a document by the police he said, 'If you know how to read, you can see from my driving licence who I am.' He was given four months for the remark.

This simplistic picture of hard-headed hard-hitting tools of the right is, in fact, grossly unfair to the average policeman. To say so can bring repercussions. In June 1968 the poet, novelist, film-director and generally left-wing intellectual, Pier Paolo Pasolini, published a poem shortly after a serious clash between police and students in Valle Giulia in Rome. The poem included the lines:

When yesterday at Valle Giulia you came to blows
With the police,
My sympathies were with the police.
Because the police are the sons of the poor....

Pasolini was trying to redress the balance by pointing out that the police were drawn from the humble classes and the rioting students were from prosperous families; in other words the class-struggle was the opposite of that which popular legend insisted on attributing to relations between police and public. At his next attempt to address a group of students – in Venice – he was shouted down. It is not allowed, in Italy, to challenge the settled mould. Pasolini is a left-wing intellectual (with an almost morbid regard for the memory of John XXIII) and should in the Italian way of life have kept on the rails prescribed for such as he; to give his signature to any manifesto calling for an end to the war in Vietnam, or the release of Angela Davis or any other cause which fell within what public opinion regards as the place in society of a left-wing intellectual. To say that the police were, in the class-struggle, on the right side and the students, with thoughts of Mao trailing from their long hair, on the wrong side, was a heresy; heresy as a word was removed in February 1971 from the Vatican's official vocabulary but it survives as a concept in Italy's conformist society.

The average policeman is poor; almost all students come from families rich enough to keep them during their studies, and the percentage of children of workers and peasants who go on to higher education is small. Even to say that the police are poor implies too much; they are principally the products of centuries of depression; the public security police has been described as the industry of the south. The south provides two-thirds of the force, the centre under a quarter and the remaining few come from the north. From 1961 to 1968, Piedmont produced 460 aspiring policemen as compared with 4996 from Campania. In the south, enrolment in the police is an alternative to emigration; Antonio Annarumma, the member of a riot squad who was killed in Milan during the strikes in the autumn of 1969, came from Monteforte Irpino, a town of 4000 inhabitants and 1200 emigrants. Two of his four sisters had emigrated to England.

This is obviously not the material for creating a police force capable of taking its place as a pillar of democratic society. Basically ignorant, the rank and file of the police have not just been influenced by right-wing politics; politically they never quite know where they stand. From Scelba's day on they might reasonably have seen their duties as hitting anything that looked vaguely red. Once the Socialists (who had been allied with the Communists and so in simplistic terms were, in fact, 'red') entered the governmental area, the pattern of duty changed but not the pattern of the average policeman's mind. They were now called on, especially during the 1969 strikes, to act with exemplary restraint. Undue violence and, in particular, casualties when police were involved in controlling political protests or striking workers, would be sure to bring heavy attacks on their conduct from Socialists inside the Government, Communists outside and some Christian Democrats, accompanied by the cry to take away their weapons. The result was logical and self-evident: extremely low morale, a near-mutinous situation in many barracks and an actual mutiny reported from Milan. No demand for reform of a system can be more eloquent and pressing than that from the people operating it and in their turn suffering from it, at least at the lower levels. The situation was sadder because from about 1969 onward the Italian public was becoming extremely crime-conscious. This was not because of a general increase in crime or of a law-and-order problem in any way comparable with that in the United States or Britain or Germany: crimes to which Italians were not accustomed, such as armed bank-robberies and organised burglaries, had become more common and notably more violent, as had political clashes. The public needed to feel that the police were an effective defence against criminals and not just agents in a political struggle.

The Italian police do indeed use highly modern methods for tracking criminals. But the old mentality has not been eradicated, nor the idea that the police are as much a political force as a crime-fighting body. They are numerous: if to the three main forms of police are added prison warders, foresters, port police and the Interior Ministry's firefighters the total was 236,400 for 1973 and in that year the estimated cost 1,037,461 million lire (about £708 million or $1770 million). The public security police including civilian personnel (the police are a semi-militarised body) numbered 83,000: the *carabinieri* 82,500 and the *finanzieri* some 41,500. Calls on their services are frequent. The police have a telephone number – 113 – to be used by the public in emergencies. In 1971 there was a call on an average every thirty-five seconds day and night. And it should be added that the police are normally extremely prompt in replying to these emergency calls.

Promotion beyond non-commissioned rank is difficult. Of the 78,826 public security policemen in 1971 some 14,850 were non-commissioned officers but only 1227 were officers, of whom fifteen were generals. A certificate of elementary-school education is required for a recruit to the ranks. Of those enrolled in the decade up to 1972 slightly less than half the recruits (47·9 per cent) had an elementary education only. The 30,589 enrolled in that period were nevertheless the pick of a large bunch: they were chosen from 210,465 candidates. For several years serious attempts have been made to raise the academic standards. Basic training is now supposed to include courses in civic education and studies of the Constitution. In 1968 a police centre for secondary and higher education was set up in Genoa four years after the establishment of a police academy for training an officer corps instead of drawing them from among the non-commissioned officers or from other services. Again, the man in the ranks would feel that his chances of advancement were small, which was true, given the basic material from which the average policeman was drawn.

Theoretically any government could have faced up to the fact that the State, for many citizens, is represented largely by the police; that the police system should be rethought and reformed on modern lines. But it is more than doubtful if any government would risk the consequences of a frontal assault on its own security forces – even after the De Lorenzo affair had revealed that military counter-intelligence, then in the hands of the *carabinieri*, was an instrument of internal politics.

After justice, second among the contenders for urgent reform in most Italian minds would be education. Educated Italians are highly educated, often in unpractical fields. But it is extremely difficult for the greater part of the working classes to reach higher education. At all levels the system is out of date and lacking in essential facilities.

Once again the problem is of an institution which has almost stood still while the country changed around it. The universities functioning before the Second World War were capable of accommodating about 60,000 students. By 1951 there were 140,722 university students; in 1972, 900,000. Reform and a building programme have been promised by a succession of governments. Practically nothing was done in the course of a quarter of a century to deal with an increasingly absurd situation, which could only last as long as it did without inciting violence because Italian youth is on the whole extremely conformist and anxious to keep out of trouble. Or it was. There have been many other complaints, one of the most relevant being the lack of facilities for scientific research. Suffocating conditions mean that many students give up trying for graduate honours before their course is finished. The average of those who do not finish their courses, counting all faculties, is around three-quarters of the total.

One of the leading aims of the students was for a full share in the administration of the universities – not only because they felt that their professors were insufficiently aware of the needs of young people in the modern world, but also that university affairs were too closely controlled by a small, self-perpetuating group of professors holding important chairs. The professors had originally been given great independence, like the judges, as a means of ensuring the independence of the universities themselves. This monopoly had become reactionary and repressive, and students saw it as the symbol of the way in which Italian society had degenerated.

The result of this intolerable situation was the revolt of the students and the beginning of the period in Italian affairs when violence became a more regular aspect of daily life and as a method attracted more and more support, because violence seemed the most likely means of achieving what was required and what the democratic method was either failing to do or was taking too long in doing. The students had a particular reason for fearing that the political powers would not be objective in judging the needs of the universities. A university-reform bill, which was before Parliament but not approved before the 1968 dissolution, included a clause heartily disliked by a strong group of parliamentarians, that professors should temporarily relinquish their chairs when elected to Parliament. Italian political life depends heavily for its recruits on school-masters and dons; at the time this bill was discussed in the chamber of deputies some seventy parliamentarians were professors. Hence, the university system was visibly and personally connected with political interests.

The student revolt in Italy began to mature in 1966. Its centres were Turin, Pisa, Venice and Trento. It flared up later in Rome. But Rome saw the most famous of the early battles with the police, that of Valle Giulia about which Pasolini wrote; this took place in March 1968 and was a crucial turning-point in Italian affairs. More attention was given to the student uprising in Paris in the following May but the Italian students were the first to rebel and for more pro-found reasons. The Paris riots stimulated another wave of violence in Italy, but the genuine protest was of Italian origin. There was a certain reformist element among the students, the majority of whom would have been satisfied with a reason-able undertaking on the Government's part to carry out its promised improvements. This element for a time gave the revolt a fairly wide popularity. Some of the students were more broadly discontented with the form of consumer society im-posed upon them by economic expansion. The tiny nucleus which directed the revolt was a mixture of Maoist left-wing Communism and old-fashioned Italian anarchy. Their method of making decisions was the assembly in which all took part, and if certain individuals won prominence and were listened to more than others it was not because they had rank or office, for neither was allowed within the movement. They opposed political parties, Parliament, courts of law – all forms of established institution – and their formula for improvement was to destroy what existed and see what evolved from the wreckage. In fact the winter of 1967-8 saw a full-scale rising and higher education came to a stop. Then pressures were applied which brought more confusion to a naturally splintered movement. The Communists had their first taste of being regarded by the students as just another pillar of established society. The Communists were at the same time worried that student violence would be blamed on them even if, as was often the case, they were not responsible. And so the Party carried out one of its intense actions aimed at calming the students and reasserting the Party's authority over left-wing youth. The Communists were not entirely successful but they managed to win over some of the first heroes of the Student Movement including Mario Capanna, the outstanding figure in Milan, who had earlier talked passionately, and with apparent conviction, about the need for armed violence as the one way of introducing change.

In practical terms the revolt did not bring the students nearer to their first goal, which was to force reforms. Nevertheless, they had by their efforts overturned a whole tradition of youthful conformity and the explosion was all the more resonant because successive governments had taken for granted that the care of youth was the responsibility of the family, and the Italian family, as everybody knows, is to the body politic what each grain of rice is to a *risotto*. The inevitable result is that no government has thought about a policy for young people. And there was every reason to do so.

Italian young people are attractive: they are bright-minded and physically more advanced and more conscious than their counterparts in northern and western Europe so that they are able to express the exuberance of youth without physical awkwardness. They are sometimes excessively pleased with themselves. But they are not wrong. They are just taking a justifiable sentiment too far. Their drawback in the past had been a deadly conformity of mind and behaviour imposed by the sameness of the family background and by the fear that an impression of being different, not thinking within the mould, seeking challenges for the mind would bring difficulties in finding a job. Their fears were not unreasonable. At the end of 1972, some 700,000 young people under the age of twenty-six were looking for a first job. Their conformity in the past had come dangerously near to backing the concept that a semi-permanent hold on power by the Christian Democrats and their allies would become a régime. The revolt changed all of that. Like so many Italian turmoils, it need never have happened if governments had given their attention earlier to the minimum requirements of reform; and it was the work of a small minority. They adopted a strange, disconcertingly formalistic behaviour, with their processions, their flags and their chants, and their seeming unawareness, apart from moments of violence, of the bourgeois world around them, an attitude of disdain. The appearance of one of these pro-cessions could suddenly transform a perfectly normal atmosphere and give it an edge of ingenuous malice.

The university students were joined in some of their demon-strations by pupils at the stage of higher secondary education. At still lower levels, both teachers and parents have become used to protesting about the shortage of classrooms and the shift-system.

Under the Constitution, education is 'open to all' and is free and compulsory to the age of fourteen. Pupils begin their education at six, in their black or dark-blue smocks and floppy bows, and hope that there will be a desk for them. In the school year beginning on 1 October 1970 there was a forty-per-cent shortage of classrooms. Elementary school covers the ages from six to eleven, and the lower secondary from eleven to fourteen completes the compulsory phase of education. Pupils can then go on to higher secondary education – the *liceo* – or to one of the teachers' training institutes or to technical school.

The problems are what might be expected in a rapidly changing country. The massive shift to the cities has over-whelmed the accommodation available in schools. No effective check is kept on school attendance, especially in the poorer areas, and because of the difficulties in reaching schools in country areas and the lack among the more backward families of belief in the value of schooling many young children do not even complete the compulsory period of elementary education.

Throughout the whole system, the disadvantage to which the poor are put is plain. Only a small proportion of the university students are from working-class families. Scarcely more than a quarter (26·2 per cent in 1969) of secondary-school pupils finish the diploma course. The children of poor families predominate among those who leave early. They cannot afford the private lessons required by a wide syllabus and overcrowded classes (and by underpaid teachers who live from private coaching); and they have other troubles due to a humble background, such as being expected to do their homework in the kitchen amidst the screaming of younger brothers and sisters. A disadvantage shared by all pupils is the tendency on the part of teachers to retain old-fashioned methods and ideas. The schoolmaster must after all be the most conservative member of society because it is his task to impose on young people the ideas of previous generations. A study of schoolteachers published in 1970 was entitled *The Vestals of the Middle Class*. As an indication of the effectiveness of the system and the issues facing it, Italy's total labour force in 1970 was 19,069,000; of whom, eleven million had completed elementary education only; three million had gone on to lower secondary education; 1,370,000 to higher secondary education and 555,000 had a degree; 3,323,000 were illiterate and had no academic qualifications of any kind. Between the years 1964 and 1970 the number of illiterates had been reduced by 1,361,000. According to figures issued by the Organisation for Co-operation and Economic Development, Italy will require by 1975 some 1,071,000 degree-holders in the professions, 14,000 in agriculture, 300,000 in industry and 757,000 in other fields. The Italian problem is not just to find holders of degrees – the unemployed lists have plenty of them – but to find young people with the right degrees, and this is a problem which will remain while the machine produces an immense excess of teachers and lawyers instead of technicians.

The irony of the 700,000 unemployed graduates is that about 500,000 children of school age were illegally employed at the same time. Italians mature at a more precocious rate than other Europeans, but a child's mental processes are damaged by the gradual awareness of his being exploited. In early 1971 there were indications that child-labour was increasing because of the rising costs in employing adults. The phenomenon might be a surprise to those who accept the legend that Italy is a country where song-birds may be ill-treated but never children; they are supposed to be spoiled from the moment of birth, especially if they are boys. Child-labour is now mainly concentrated in the south although originally the systematic exploitation of children began in the last century in the northern textile mills. Official figures show that in 1870 the number of child-labourers was 132,000 and by 1888 the figure had risen to 300,000. Most of the 500,000 or more employed in 1971 worked on farms in the depressed south, in shops, at artisan-trades or on building-sites. An unofficial estimate gave the average number of accidents on building-sites at 3000 a month of which a tenth involved children of school age. Thus, ten children were hurt, more or less seriously, every day.

The great obstacle to overcoming this tragic situation is the traditional mentality of the south and the sheer poverty which is the basic cause. A particularly nauseating scandal came to light in the autumn of 1970 when child-labourers were found living in conditions of appalling filth in a pigsty near the Apulian town of Altamura. A study conducted at Altamura itself showed that in this town of 46,000 inhabitants some 400 children were simply not attending school and sixty-five per cent of those who did failed to complete the course. Local opinion did not accept the cruelty, but reasons were forthcoming as to why child-labour should not simply be rejected out of hand as a wicked institution. Shortly after the Altamura scandal became public knowledge, the local southern newspaper *La Gazzetta del Mezzogiorno* printed irate letters from shopkeepers who were facing fines for employing children. Their main complaint was that they were being given the same punishment as cruel exploiters of child-labour though they treated their child-employees well enough and gave them only light work to do ('... delivering a bunch of flowers, brushing a client down after he has had his haircut, taking a cup of coffee to the *commendatore* in his office, or two *etti* of salame to the lady on the second floor ... the children whom we accept are almost always pressed on us by their parents ...').

The children learn a trade and have a feeling of security even if their parents decide to emigrate, and some of them are in fact the children of emigrant workers who leave them in the care of employers. This is obviously not an evil mentality but it is the type of mentality which maintains a social evil, and only a strong lead from the authorities in insisting on the application of the constitutional requirements of schooling for children can hope to overcome the habits of mind of centuries. And the problem is not simply of obliterating an old mentality; modern developments, in the unplanned, untamed, type of expansion which Italy has suffered, have increased the dangers in which children are placed. Cruelty towards children is an increasing vice. It is ascribed to the frustration of parents who see the growing prosperity of the consumer society, are encouraged to believe its values but fail to share in economic wellbeing. This feeling of humiliation and of disappointed hopes, combined with the innate need – not limited to politicians – to feel a sense of power is expressed in the ill-treatment of children. Again, it is social reform and a fairer distribution of prosperity which would solve this and other attendant problems.

Some people feel that there has been a deliberate intention on the part of conservative interests in Italy to hold back reforms, such as those of justice, the police, the universities and the schools, because fundamental reform would necessarily change the structure of Italian society. The Constitution was there to show what should be done, but constitutional principles are not volcanoes; they can be safely sat on without fear of an eruption of principles. But if once these principles were to be taken seriously in just one field of reform the whole system would fall to the ground.

The overriding impression that the State has been absent from the field of reform, has done nothing to facilitate the transformation of Italian society from a traditional, pre-dominantly agricultural, civilisation to an eager experimenter with modern life, would not altogether be fair. There were two periods in which reforming measures of some amplitude, though still insufficient, were introduced; during the five-year term of the first parliament, elected in 1948, and the early years of the centre–left governments. A third period promised reform – the re-established centre-left of Emilio Colombo, who took office in August 1970 – but disagreements within the coalition spoiled its effectiveness.

The first parliament dealt with two measures of outstanding social importance: agrarian reform and the establishment of the Development Fund for the south. Both could have been used to better effect than was the case because essentially they were both conservative measures; or at best lacking in constructive foresight. But at the time they were a fresh approach to ancient problems, with staffs recruited outside the normal bureaucratic machine.

Agrarian reform is a leading example of a change introduced by government which suffered a taint of origin. Because of this taint it could not make a real contribution to Italian social development. The object was to break up the large estates and give the landless labourers the chance to own their own smallholdings. The original intention was to apply it to the whole country but this ambitious – indeed, wild – idea was abandoned both because of fears of the opposition it might arouse and because even the most starry-eyed reformer would have had to admit that the big northern farms worked well. And so the reform was limited to the south and the islands, the Tuscan Maremma, the Po delta and the Fucino basin.

The political taint was due to the fact that the Communists preceded the introduction of the reform by organising symbolic occupations of the land, particularly in the south. They were thus able, with some justification, to claim that if it had not been for their efforts the Government would have postponed for as long as possible the breaking-up of the big estates. It was a reform done without grace. And with scant respect for the way in which Italian agriculture and Italian society were about to develop.

The individual holdings were small, up to ten acres. When the reform was concluded in 1962 some 430,000 hectares

(105,110,000 acres) had been distributed among 85,170 southern families. The holdings were to be paid for over thirty years at a rate of about £10 ($24) a month. For a landless labourer, a few acres bought at low mortgage-rates represented a certain improvement. But it was not sufficiently an improvement for him to feel that he had a stake in the land. The boom soon caught up with even this limited area of satisfaction and the predominant feeling among workers of the soil was that, rather than have a stake in the land, they wanted to leave it. The small white farm-houses of the reform looked attractive. They were spread about the countryside as the ancient Greek farms must have been before malaria, landlords and Saracens sent the farmers into their hill-top refuges. But this new sense of space was in itself a disadvantage. All Italians are gregarious. The price of a slendid, solitary villa rises as the view is spoilt by other villas built around it. A sense of insecurity partly accounts for this outlook; and partly the fact that Italian life, particularly in the south, is lived in public. Hence, many of the peasants felt cut off from the companionable squalor which they had known. Some went home to their villages and returned during the day to work the piece of land given them under the reform. Others sold their farms and went back to the familiar business of labouring. The left-wing opposition was given too easy a target: a reform which would not have come about without their prompting but had not been carried through in a sufficiently radical manner. The political object of reform was to cut the Communist vote and to provide the governing parties with a source of patronage. Most of the labourers chosen were known to vote solidly Christian Democrat – with some discontented examples among them in the hope that they too would find contentment as peasant-proprietors. This plan badly misfired. There was a swing to the left in the reform areas, especially in the early stages.

In agricultural terms, the reform had even less to be said for it. The creation of tiny farms made no sense when what was – and still is – required was to prepare Italy to hold its own in the European Community, with large, efficiently run holdings. In February 1971, only 40,000 out of 3,600,000 farms reached the minimum turnover of 12·5 million lire

(£8300; $20,750) fixed by the Community. And no Italian farm reached the minimum level of daily productivity fixed by the Community at 20,000 lire (£13; $34) for each worker. Owing to the exodus of young people from the land, Italian farmers are older than their European counterparts. Taking the average of the six countries belonging to the Community in 1971, fifty-seven per cent of their farmers were aged fifty or more; in Italy the proportion was seventy-five per cent. The average age of the Italian farm-labourer was sixty.

Statistics give only a part of the picture: agriculture in Italy is a more complex affair than figures can explain. The flight from the land and such attempts as there have been to make Italian farming more modern amount to nothing less than a dash by farmers, and especially the young men, out of the medieval dark into the glare of modern living. That having been said, there is the point that many farmers in Italy have other jobs and many ex-farmers who have moved into factories keep up their contact with the land by working in the evening as labourers or by cultivating a small piece of ground for the needs of their families. They vary from the building labourers of Reggio Calabria who seek work at night in the olive-groves (literally 'moonlighting') to the Alfa Romeo worker who lives outside Milan and digs a large allotment. This is a large section of Italian farming for which the planners can find no place, especially the European planners, because there is nothing on a comparable scale in the countries of Western Europe. Italy remains the country of 'arranging oneself' as comfortably as possible in any given circumstances and this adaptability applies in agriculture as elsewhere. Yet the farmer remains at a clear disadvantage in that he is low in public esteem and is forced to manage with even fewer public services than the urban citizen. A report issued in mid-1971 showed that thirty per cent of farm labourers' children and twenty-eight per cent of those of peasant farmers did not complete the course of elementary education. As a result some forty per cent were illiterate or semi-literate. To a substantial extent this basic ignorance in terms of lack of schooling accounted for the disappointments suffered by politicians in attempting to deal with the problems of the soil, particularly in the south where the reform was concentrated.

The Communists met the greatest difficulties in organising political life in the south. Their evangelists fared badly for very clear reasons. Italian Communism is a sophisticated political doctrine. The Communists teach the constitutional application of Marxism, which presupposes a certain level of political understanding. Southerners were faced with the impossible task of absorbing a northern doctrine, devised by northerners for northern conditions. Had Italian Communism after the war been a form of peasant revolution on Maoist lines, it might have been able to take the south, but not the north or centre. Anybody who has visited the peasant towns of the south, where the landless labourers live, will have seen that life has been too basic for too long for the inhabitants to have produced a culture, a folklore, a sufficiently reasoned outlook on life to make a proselytising appeal possible. Every man's mental digestion needs a lining, however thin, of sophistication. The lack of it among the landless labourers was one of the great complaints of the Communist missionaries.

The democratic parties on the other hand had what the south understood: power, which meant the ability to grant immediate help or make the vote worth something to the voter in terms of money or favours. Christian Democracy had the bishops behind it. There was popular support in the decade after the war for the Monarchists and the Neo-Fascists. The south was under Allied military government while the war moved slowly northward and knew nothing of the Resistance movement except for sporadic outbreaks against the German invader such as the popular uprising in Naples. The traditionalist politicians knew what democracy meant to people devoid of political sophistication: one shoe before the vote and the other after. And they saw where power lay.

Christian Democracy had patronage, power and religion. It fell in easily with the southern client system. But there was a danger of seeking short-term benefits. Antonio Gramsci, the first leader of the Italian Communist Party and a Sardinian himself, regarded Christian Democracy as a useful stage for the south on the way towards Communism because it would give the people an elementary education in politics. He wrote in 1922:

> Christian Democracy is a necessary phase in the process of adhesion of the entire Italian proletariat to Communism. Christian Democracy creates forms of associated life outside the industrial factory, that is, in areas where socialism cannot operate because of lack of the objective conditions of a capitalistic economy. They are furnishing an initial orientation to the still confused working masses who know that they are part of a great historical process but who do not understand it because they do not live within the walls of a modern industrial plant.

He felt that Christian Democracy would ultimately collapse because the masses, having acquired through collective action a sense of their own power, would reject a leadership invoking transcendental values in political and economic life, particularly if the politicians fell consistently short of the values which they professed. Christian Democrat handling of the southern problem will in the end be judged in political terms on whether Gramsci was right. He was an instinctive genius, rare among Communist leaders, who could be just as wrong as he might be correct. Events at first suggested that he was right. In the 1953 election, the first after the introduction of the agrarian reform, the areas in which the Christian Democrats had done most showed Communist gains. But in more recent years the political danger has been the increase of the extreme right.

The south would never have been lost or won by the effects of the agrarian reform; far profounder influences were at work. But agrarian reform had the important effect of showing for the first time that the central government was trying to do something for the south. This in itself for the southerner was hopeful and comforting (and to the local landowners horrifying); or at least to those southerners who were not nullified politically by the inheritance of centuries of bad government. The setting-up of the Southern Development Fund was even more important. To a large degree, the question of whether the south will be moved from its ancient Mediterranean heritage to take its place as part of the technological West depends on the ultimate success of this fund. An official publication of the Fund put its national significance in these words:

It is true to say that Italy can become integrated into the European economic system provided that the southern problem is radically resolved, since the economic unification of the country is a condition of that integration. And this requires that absolute priority should be given, and is continued to be given, to the effective solution of the problem of southern Italy. Any slackening of the national effort, any manifestation of relaxation at any level, would harm the interests of the south, bringing incalculable consequences for the entire nation.

The effort has not been at the level of engaged tension prescribed by this text. But uncharitable carping ought not to obscure what the Fund has done. The situation to be faced in 1950 can be expressed simply. The south had more than a third of the total population of the country but accounted for little more than a fifth of the gross national product. More than half the active population – fifty-three per cent – was dependent on agriculture. The amount of land that could be cultivated was estimated at about 0·45 hectares (1¼ acres) *per capita*, the lowest of any southern European country except for Greece. People were outrunning resources and the traditional palliative, apart from resignation to poverty, was emigration.

The Fund was intended to prepare the way for the arrival of industry; at the same time it financed more fundamental improvements such as reafforestation and irrigation. It can be attacked on four principal grounds: that there was a lack of over-all planning; that much of the money sent through it to the south went back to the north; that a substantial amount went into private pockets and, still more, its resources were used as an instrument of political power. These criticisms are true. But in two decades the Fund built 1500 miles of dykes, 8400 miles of canals, 18,000 miles of roads and 7500 miles of aqueducts which bring water to eight million people. The proportion of the labour force employed on the land was about halved. Personal income and gross income increased at a rate of five per cent between 1964 and 1967. Its work has encouraged some private firms to take the risk of using the extensive tax-reductions and other incentives offered by the Government to move south. The Fund's work has been accompanied by growing efforts on the part of the great state corporations and leading northern industrial concerns such as Fiat and Montecatini-Edison to place more of their investments in the south, a movement favoured by the congestion of the northern cities which inevitably followed the indiscriminate immigration from the south and the northern countryside.

When originally established, the Fund had an endowment of £60 million ($144 million) a year for ten years. This period was later prolonged to fifteen years and in 1965 was renewed for a further fifteen years. It is now envisaged as a semipermanent instrument until, and if, the south should no longer have need of special governmental help. In its first two decades, it had certainly not reached the point at which the problem of the south could be said to be approaching solution. Public proof was provided in its most dramatic form by the Calabrian revolt of 1970 and 1971. Political questions were involved but behind it the predominating feelings of the people were that the average income of the two million inhabitants of Calabria was about £220 ($528) a year, a third of that of Milan and half the national average. Life expectancy was three years less than in Lombardy, and infant mortality double; agricultural yields were between one-half and a third less, and emigration was running at about 30,000 a year. The central government was hated. Young people – the generation hearing of the horrors of industrial life in the north from returning emigrants – had nothing to do, but were determined to reject emigration as the answer to the problems of the south.

The south has progressed but much more slowly than the north so that the economic gap tends to increase. The somewhat sporadic methods of the early years were replaced by a concentration of effort in particular areas, mainly the Naples –Salerno area, the Bari–Brindisi–Taranto triangle and the east coast of Sicily. This decision meant more than an attempt at avoiding the creation in the south of even greater 'cemeteries of public works' than in the past. It suggested that the blind faith in the ability of industry to solve all problems anywhere was at last coming under intelligent criticism. Some parts of the south have little to gain and much to lose by the arbitrary placing of industry amidst the olives. This truth – unmentionable a few years ago – is now being recognised *sotto voce* for at least three principal reasons. The first is that a generation of emigrants has witnessed what undisciplined industrial expansion has done in the north to reduce men to the level of miserable units for exploitation, especially men from the south. The second reason is that modern planners have not solved the problem of how in industrial terms to create a herbaceous border; they can produce a huge petro-chemical works or a steel mill but not the tapestry of interconnected industries, which is what a true industrialisation means in the sense in which the south thinks of it. Southerners are beginning to reject as a solution the huge, highly automated factories which produce goods for export. The southerner, moreover, is particularly sensitive to pollution by industrial processes because it is peculiarly damaging to the traditional life of the south, where the freshness of the food, the clarity of the sky and the cleanliness of the sea are essential to life: they are not luxuries. Pollution is simply an adjunct to life in Western Europe; in southern Italy it poisons life itself, though no government has yet admitted as much.

Whatever the economic future of the south as a whole, access and the ability to move about in areas where roads were notoriously bad is having a deep effect. This was the meaning of the governmental decision to place much of the country's resources in the marvellous system of motor-highways which has brilliantly confirmed the Italian reputation as road-builders. By the end of 1973 the total length of motorways completed will be more than 5000 kilometres. The *autostrade* are beautifully set into the landscape. They have transformed the task of driving the length and breadth of the peninsula. It has become immeasurably easier but at the same time exhilarating; essential because Italy is an inordinately long country. The motorcar is the mortal enemy of Italian towns and cities, most of which were constructed around a centre with narrow streets opening into broad squares. The idea of turning the squares into car-parks and choking the roads between them with motorcars is one of the most destructive abuses of traditional urban living. Once out of the city centres, the motorcar comes into its natural element on the motor-highways and once again becomes an asset. To prove it, and to prove the rightness of it, Italians drive with respect for nothing in the towns but once on the highways they are, by comparison with the British, Americans, French and German drivers, very disciplined and orderly, hardly qualities one would expect to find in Italian drivers anywhere.

The highways arguably are not a reform, but in fact they are part of the basic structure of reform and were deliberately decided on as worth the huge investment when the money might well have been spent on schools or hospitals. They were moreover a reassuring symbol at a time when Italy was about to face the adventure of decentralisation. Potentially by far the most important internal measure adopted by the centre–left coalitions was the establishment of the regions. More than a reform, this measure offered the instrument by which reform could be achieved. Parliament approved legislation for setting up the regions in 1969. In effect all that was being done was to apply the Constitution, which lays down the division of the country into regions with a wide degree of administrative autonomy. The object was to break down the excessive centralisation of the Italian state and to meet local separatist demands. Five regions as laid down in the Constitution were to have a special status: Sicily, Sardinia, Valle d'Aosta, Trentino-Alto Adige and Friuli-Venezia Giulia. These special regions were duly established; the last in 1963. But the remaining fifteen ordinary regions (which under the Constitution ought to have been established by the end of 1948) were held up because of fears of a disintegration of the State. These fears were felt mainly on the right. Specifically conservative opinion was fearful of the effect of handing local government in most of central Italy (the regions of Emilia-Romagna, Tuscany and Umbria) to Communist rule.

The Socialists once in government insisted on pushing through this issue despite the reluctance of their coalition partners. Pietro Nenni was particularly eloquent in explaining the importance of the reform. He and the leading regionalists looked on the regions as the means by which the mortmain of the centralised civil service would be broken; a new generation of young civil servants would emerge and, with them, a new political class trained in facing real, not rhetorical problems, knowing the feelings and the needs of the people and eventually bringing these shining, invaluable and generally unheard-of qualities to the national political scene. The regions were also regarded as the natural level at which to deal with such matters as urban development, tourism, agriculture, public works, pollution and as many of the outstanding social problems as could be wrested from the incompetent hands of the central government.

The gospel of decentralisation begins with the assumption that Italy gave itself the wrong form of administration and the wrong idea of the state when it became a united nation in 1870. The Napoleonic style of administration inherited from France through Piedmont, which was the organising centre of the movement for national unity, was too rigid for Italian requirements. It functioned even worse in practice because, although a northern invention, it was applied in Italy by southerners; the Piedmontese could manage it in their painstaking, incorruptible way, but once the system began to be applied on the national level, largely by Sicilians and Neapolitans, its shortcomings were obvious. The Fascists did little more than increase the degree of centralisation, and the habit of corruption. The nineteenth century gave Italy its unity, but on the century's own terms: the centralised nation-state. And so Italians found themselves dressed in the modish but inappropriate constitutional trappings of the moment in historical fashion that coincided with unification. Italy has been free of the great centralisers, and Cavour himself was in favour of regionalism. The dream now is to undo the mistakes of the past and at the same time offer regional Italy as an example for an integrated Europe.

Not if the bureaucrats have their way. The hunt for places

in the rich regions began as soon as the legislation was passed. By the early autumn of 1970, Lombardy, the richest region, had received more than a thousand applications from civil servants for jobs. The requests came from all levels: judges, municipal secretaries, janitors, vice-prefects, provincial veterinary officers, every type and class which the mention of the term 'civil servant' brings reluctantly to mind. Some wrote with the backing of their bishops; one could give an assurance that an archbishop who normally did nothing of the kind would speak in his favour; others gave modest descriptions of themselves such as 'unusually active and of exemplary life' or, in the case of a policeman, as having already 'shed my blood for the administration and would now like a minimum of tranquillity'. The immediate danger facing the regions was that the fresh spirit desperately needed to justify the experiment might be spoiled by the old spirit of the bureaucracy and that the change would simply mean the duplication at regional level of the official mentality which has been the State's most effective scourge.

This mentality is one of the most difficult elements to understand in Italian life. It has no relationship to the Italian genius for spontaneity, for the sweeping gesture, for the humane action. The bureaucratic world is something quite different. It anchors Italy in a sea of documents to be signed, countersigned, legalised, lost, found and issued with a brief time-limit of validity, so that the whole transaction will have to be repeated once the validity of one of the documents has expired before its usefulness. This mentality was faithfully reflected in answers to a circular sent from the Prime Minister's office asking for ideas on the future civil service once the regions were in operation; at least four ministries proposed increasing the number of officials at the centre, or asked for the definitive confirmation of departments hitherto temporary. A good friend who knows much about Italy once said that there would be no improvement in the administration until angry citizens had taken a few civil servants and hanged them from the nearest tree.

Cases are frequent of bureaucratic mistakes which bother a citizen throughout the years: girls called up for the army because Paola has become Paolo in the registry; people have been officially declared dead when they are very obviously alive – a Turin woman had this trouble after her husband declared her bureaucratically dead before going off with another woman. She discovered her official death when applying for a pension. After consulting lawyers, she was last heard of stating in terms of resignation that only nature would eventually settle the matter – though in the meantime she would not draw a pension. In August 1969 the Naples tribunal dealt with a case involving a bureaucratic slip which made two men one. The trouble arose in January 1935 when two boys were born on the same day in the maternity ward of a Messina hospital. Both were foundlings and at a jointly celebrated baptism they were given the same names. These names were inscribed in the registry of births at Messina. But a conscientious official who saw two identical birth-certificates thought that his colleague had made a mistake and, with an extraordinary act of initiative, destroyed what appeared to be the superfluous set of papers. And so two newly born boys went out into the world bearing the same impressive list of names: Santi Mario Leonti Bisignano Nerviani – the last three being the name of the family which had adopted one, or both, who knows? In 1969 one of them was living in Tremestiere Etneo near Catania and the other in Naples. The Neapolitan Santi decided to get married and after asking for the necessary documents from Messina found that he was married already. The Catania Santi – the married one – had earlier been prevented from doing his military service because the documents showed him to be already under arms, though of course it was the Neapolitan Santi who was serving in the forces. The solution of their problem in 1969 looked several light-years away and the one hopeful element was that the two men made bureaucratically one met and liked each other.

The real problem caused by the bureaucrats is not just a matter of personal inconvenience to individual citizens, though this in itself is enough. The real problem is that they have the power and influence to slow down or remove the life from any attempt at reform. Most of what has been done in Italy since the war in the way of progress has been done by bodies set up outside the State's civil service; this applies to agrarian reform, the Southern Development Fund, the motor-highways; all were taken out of the hands of the State's administrators. The formula does not always work well; special agencies become moribund in their turn or are distorted to serve political interests. And the problems themselves grow out of hand with neglect, like a gothic garden of unkempt trees, weeds, a ruin or so and a statue, once a man, standing dilapidated in the midst of the undergrowth.

Emilio Colombo's government, formed in August 1970, picked out two problems for special attention. As prime minister, Colombo urgently wanted to show that the essential reforms could be carried out by a centre–left coalition following the normal constitutional practices. He decided to concentrate much of his attention on housing and the health services.

The problem with housing was never that there was too little of it but there was not enough housing available at a low enough rent for the workers. This is why in all the big cities blocks of luxury flats stand empty while strikes and processions of protest are organised to draw attention to the housing problem. People able to pay high rents have a wide choice; elsewhere there are the shanty-towns, the spreading industrial slums and overcrowding. A report issued at the end of 1970 by the National Institute of Statistics stated that nearly one-half of the Italian population – twenty-six million people – were badly housed. About 1,500,000 people lived in conditions of more than one person in each room; 13,300,000 lived in conditions varying between 1·2 and 2 people to a room and 1,300,000 lived in what were described as the 'tragic' conditions of more than two persons to a room.

The situation is gloomier the further one moves southward. About half the municipalities of north-west Italy, the richest area, have an average of less that one person to every room (the figure given was 0·80) while the north-east and the centre showed averages of between 30 and 35 per cent. Yet in the south and the islands the municipalities with this reasonably satisfactory level are scarcely 5 per cent of the total. About 85 per cent of the northern municipalities are listed as having either satisfactory or normal housing conditions; for central

Italy the figure is 73 per cent, in the islands – Sardinia and Sicily – 26 per cent and on the southern mainland 17 per cent. The total number of municipalities with unsatisfactory housing conditions was about 3000. Some 111 have an average of more than two inhabitants to a room and, of these 111, 97 are in southern Italy. The principal fault – not stated in the report – is that the main object of new building since the first period of reconstruction was speculation. According to the unions, who have made a rational housing policy one of their main political demands, about 3 per cent of building in Italy is accounted for by official subsidised projects for providing cheap housing. Greed was not the only cause; one of the obstacles to a sound housing policy has been the failure to introduce legislation on powers of expropriation. The idea of housing as a public service barely exists.

Much the same could be said of the health services. There are too many of them and they cost too much. Few people have penetrated the luxuriant undergrowth of the systems of social insurance in Italy. Those who do so are equipped to join another controversy which appears unending: what should be done about them.

Social insurance in Italy is in the hands of State-controlled companies. Contributions must by law be paid by employer, worker and the State, with much the largest share coming from the employer. The system was founded early in the century and covers practically all dependent workers, pays pensions, unemployment assistance and family allowances. All medical services and medicines are free. The branch most urgently in need of reform is the health service.

Because the health service works badly the whole field of medicine, including the hospitals and the doctors, is infected by the disorder. The health services provide about three-quarters of the income of the hospitals. The remainder comes from private patients, endowments and gifts. Estimates vary as to how many health-insurance funds exist in Italy; in mid-1970 when the public was feeling the crisis in the system most strongly there were no less than 2000. Of these by far the largest was the Istituto Nazionale Assicurazione Malattia, known as INAM. It had thirty million contributors and 24,000 employees and in three years, from 1968 to 1970, had accumulated debts of 680,000 million lire (£428,500,000; $1,333,000,000). The principal victims, apart from the public, were the hospitals. The 1080 public hospitals had a deficit in 1970 of about 500,000 million lire ($833 million). They could not pay their bills and at times their personnel. Their weakness was that they were the one element among INAM's creditors which had no immediate weapon to enforce payment. If benefits to sick workers were not paid, there would be a strike; the same would be true if the doctors were not paid their admittedly low fees of 1170 lire (about $1·80) a visit and 585 lire (less than $1·00) for each patient coming to the surgery. The healthservice doctors had begun a series of strikes for better pay and conditions in 1967. If reimbursement for medicines was not forthcoming the wholesale chemists would stop their supplies. And that left the hospitals.

The second largest of the health-insurance schemes, that dealing with state employees, with a membership of 4,894,000, had a deficit at the end of 1970 of 160,000 million lire ($233 million). An item in its 1969 budget showed one of the reasons for this indebtedness; the positive and increasing mania of Italians for expensive medicines – 370,000 million ($616 million) was stated to have gone in paying for medicines, an average of 12,000 lire ($20) and 15 prescriptions for every member, three times the British figure and five times the Swedish average.

This huge inflation was not entirely due to honest purchases. The method by which the INAM pays compensation for medicines bought is to reimburse the chemist who sends in the prescription with attached to it the price-label of the medicine. According to Paolo Turchetti, chairman of INAM, in a newspaper interview given in September 1970, these price-tags could be bought by the kilo at Porta Portese, Rome's fleamarket. He also remarked that the double standard of morality existing in Italy meant that robbing the State was not regarded as infamous.

This last remark could have been turned against the speaker. The bigger social-insurance companies in Italy, particularly the two giants, are under fairly constant criticism for two reasons: first, lavish spending on themselves in the form of luxurious offices, immense sums in retirement gifts to officials, and overstaffing; second, they are attacked for allegedly being the political tools of the Christian Democrat Party. This explains why, in the inevitable quarrels within the governmental coalitions, the Socialists argue in favour of a single health service on strictly British lines to replace the existing labyrinth while Christian Democrat opinion is more for a reform which would improve rather than do away with the existing state of affairs. And, quite apart from the health services themselves, there are practical problems such as finding the means to build more hospitals instead of sinking money into repayment of the debts of the social-insurance companies. In 1970 Italy had about 300,000 hospital beds, half of the total Britain had with much the same population. Overcrowding gives Rome hospitals a Crimean aspect. And the usual geographical discrimination made the problem worse; the general shortage of hospital beds was much worse in the south than in the north; of the national total of 300,000 beds, Lombardy alone had 78,000. To which must be added another division: the idea that hospitals are charitable institutions, with nuns as nurses and pious ladies to leave them endowments, will be a long time dying, and until that idea is dead the right to hospital treatment will not be regarded as an essential public service.

Everybody, or nearly everybody, made the same mistake in November 1966 of thinking that the colossal floods of that month were somehow a watershed in Italy's administrative history. Italy is familiar with natural disasters, from earthquakes to avalanches to cloudbursts. But the calamity which struck on 4 November was of immense proportions. A third of the country suffered the effects of gales and storms. One hundred and twelve people died; 12,000 farms and homes in the countryside were damaged, and 10,000 in the towns; 50,000 animals and 16,000 tractors and other pieces of farm machinery were destroyed. Hundreds of bridges, aqueducts and roads were damaged or destroyed. In Florence and Venice not only was grave damage done to homes and shops and businesses but also to famous monuments, collections and works of art.

The onslaught once more revealed Italy's weakest points: among them the Po delta, which suffers the double danger of high seas liable to break the dykes and a breaking of its banks by the river, and the low-lying plains of the Veneto and the Maremma, which is another area reclaimed from swamp and intensely cultivated under the agrarian reform. The Dolomites, particularly around the town of Belluno, suffered unimaginable affronts from the weather; twenty-four hours before the full disaster struck the country, more rain had fallen than usually falls in six months; this rain was accompanied by warm winds which melted the first snows, and the resulting inundation swept through the valleys with such force that whole forests were removed and river-beds left so full of wreckage that the level was raised well above the level of the banks. Huge boulders were left in the centre of villages, and squares were packed tight with rubble.

Throughout the country, individual Italians showed immense resilience, a quick recovery from the shock and a capacity for spontaneous organisation. Florentines behaved as one would expect them to do: by working to clear their stricken city and cursing the lack of help from Rome. Young people surprised their parents, who by that time were beginning to feel the first simmering of the revolt of youth, by taking a leading part in clearing wreckage and leaving the comforts of undamaged cities and homes to help in the worst-hit areas. Local leaders emerged: in some places it was the mayor, in others the priest. There was resentment at the slow and clumsy reaction of the State. In some ways this was not altogether fair. No government, however efficient, could have handled without difficulties a disaster of this magnitude. Indeed, one of the reasons why the Government was so slow to begin its work appears to have been that the full extent of the blow was not immediately grasped. The Communists made some political capital out of the administration's failure to treat as an emergency Italy's worst natural catastrophe by putting large party-placards on the lorries which they improvised for sending supplies. They would have done better to have limited themselves to pointing out the examples of some of the Communist municipalities – Grosseto in the Maremma was an outstanding example – which showed excellent powers of organisation and recuperation. The administration showed that it neither had the habit of initiative nor the flexibility to deal with such a situation. The narcissistic element in government was at last fully revealed: politicians inured to a life of detailed intrigue could not draw themselves away and take decisive action. Its intimate affairs were its life-blood. While the country was angry, there were demands for change, assertions that reform was now essential and could no longer be postponed. Never again would commentators be allowed to reach such bitter conclusions as that 'a state worthy of the name does not exist ...'. But anger fell away as quickly as the flood-waters themselves, quicker in some cases. And two years later there was the Sicilian earthquake, and three years after that no start had been made on permanently rehousing the earthquake victims despite appeals, marches and the refusal by some of the young people to undergo their compulsory military service on the grounds that the State had not carried out its own obligations. The watershed showed that the old positions were even more deeply entrenched than was supposed.

CHAPTER TWELVE

Family and Friends

THE accredited masterpiece of Italian society over the centuries, the bulwark, the natural unit, the provider of all that the State denies, the semi-sacred group, the avenger and the rewarder, the means by which injustice and incompetence and indifference can be met, is the family. In its traditional form, it has been badly damaged by social change and would be struck a mortal wound if it were not for one factor. Italy has not yet reached the point where it is safe to attempt to live one's life without the family close at hand.

Until hospitals are adequate and efficiently managed; until the guarantees for personal liberties are given more serious meaning, and justice made speedier and less expensive, the prisons tolerable without help from outside, the need no longer present for a wide circle of acquaintances in order to feel one's way through the bureaucracy or make use of the *sottogoverno*, the solidarity of the family will have its importance. Too much, in one way. The readiness of the family to help any of its members in trouble is one of the reasons why governments have done comparatively little governing and why there is less pressure than should be on the politicians to introduce social reform.

An institution which took its strength from the lack of government or from misgovernment in the past is apt to foil efforts at bringing about reforms now. So much is clear enough from the sight in public hospitals of members of a patient's family arriving with clean sheets, warm food, soap and towels and gossip. Or a feeling given an old woman in the midst of a large brood of grandchildren that she is performing a useful function; as, indeed, she is in a country in which nursery schools are seriously inadequate. Most of those that exist, like the majority of orphanages and homes for handicapped children, are run by nuns who also provide a high proportion of the nurses in public hospitals. The Church and the family between them have taken most of the social load from the back of Italian governments.

This partnership, now greatly weakened, has been the best that could be offered but it was never efficient. Infant mortality, as one example, is extremely high in Italy by comparison with other European countries. At 32·7 in 1971 for every 1000 live births it is followed in Europe only by Greece, Hungary, Romania and Portugal. Even with advancing medical science, the figure remained stubbornly high. In 1970, out of 920,000 children born in Italy, 27,000 died before reaching the age of one year. Six years earlier the situation was much the same; 36,600 died out of 1,000,016 births. There was a sharp difference between regions: in the north, the average was 21 out of every 1000; the centre 23 (27 in Rome) and the south 48. The large southern cities reach alarming figures; in Naples in 1970, out of 36,465 live births, 2370 lived less than a year. Infant mortality is inevitable where there is poverty, but a country of Italy's position in the world ought to be able to take over such responsibilities from old-fashioned mothers and old-fashioned nuns. The State's corporation for dealing with mothers and children, the O.M.N.I. (Opera Nazionale Maternità e Infanzia), a highly centralised remnant of the Fascist system, has long been discredited. The full extent of its incapacity was revealed in investigations following a series of scandals in 1969 and 1970 involving orphanages and homes for handicapped children over which the O.M.N.I. was supposed to be exercising supervision. Before that it had come to public attention after a former Mayor of Rome, the Christian Democrat Amerigo Petrucci, was charged with having made use of funds of the Rome O.M.N.I. federation for electoral purposes. He was acquitted shortly before the 1972 general election. The cry for the organisation's immediate demise and its replacement by offices under regional responsibility followed and is a reasonable approach to what is a shocking mixture of three Italian social ills; bureaucratic over-centralisation and inefficiency; the distortion for political ends of bodies originally intended to carry out social tasks, and the difficulties met in attempting to wind up ineffectual organisations even when public indignation combines with reason to demand their demise.

The cases of cruelty to orphans and handicapped children mainly involved institutions run either by ecclesiastics or by people making much of their good relations with the hierarchy and their pious spirit. The worst cases brought to light were in Prato, Cagliari and the Rome area. They included straight-forward cruelty and also a certain level of financial acumen on the part of the persons involved because there is money to be made out of charity by taking the official subsidies payable for the upkeep of these children and saving on the sum by producing false receipts or simply spending less than was paid. The cases caused much repugnance and the Press was full of demands that something be done, the recurrent point being that there might well be many more cases as yet undiscovered displaying the same mixture of piety and sadism.

This was one point. The fundamental issue remains that a modern country such as Italy cannot go on improvising its social welfare. The State can hardly be accused of falling short in the provision of facilities for helping the halt and the lame; no one could give an accurate figure of how many organisations were responsible for welfare in Italy but it was about 40,000 dealing with seven million old people, orphans, illegitimate children, the handicapped, the insane. What was lacking was the clear conviction that reform was necessary in order that available resources should not be wasted and the will to carry it out while public opinion still had child-cruelty on the mind as an issue of importance. But it did not remain long on the front pages.

The anti-clerical element in much of the protesting was understandably resented by the Vatican. Though bishops had been photographed with the principals and inmates of institutions accused of cruelty, the Church was on reasonable ground. It had made available a rudimentary social service over the centuries and was trying to continue, despite the changes in Italian society which made its own work more difficult and which successive Italian governments made little attempt to meet. The Church as the friend of the family can be better sustained than the Church as the friend of the Italian state.

Relations between Church and State are a product of the peninsula's history. Relations between Church and family are a by-product which draws some of its character from the primary condition. The Church would not have been able to exercise its authority so powerfully over the family if it had not learnt to rule in the political field and, more important for Italy, learnt to provide a governing class. To many Italians the idea may be unwelcome but it is true that the hierarchy in Italy, often down to the level of the parish priest, has the habit of authority which the Italian ruling class cannot rival. In later centuries to prevent the growth of a lay ruling class in the papal states was a part of policy, but the aura surrounding the clerical official goes back to the days immediately after the fall of the western empire when the Church was left as the one surviving element in the old relationship of Empire and Christianity.

This habit of authority made the priest the natural advisor and interlocutor of the family. In times of need it was, and frequently still is, the priest who talks to the civil authorities about an individual's troubles. Spend any day in the waiting-rooms of the Rome municipality and one sees the coming and going of the priests, who arrive with their soft smiles and tone of gentle insistence on behalf of some parishioner who needs a certificate or a job or a helpful word from an official. They seem to be constantly on the move, these unpretentious black-garbed visitors to the offices of the State in one of its forms;

they feel they have the right to expect respectful treatment and thus be of use to their own followers. They are as relentless about their requirements as is any Italian. But their training as much as their faith gives a different flavour to their persistence. It is seemingly softer and more sentimentalised. The priests are the one estate in Italy which has adopted sentimentality as part of its personality and as a point of distinction from other Italians. They have understood the dangers in the harshness of the Italian character and adopted the tender smile, the hands clasped delicately over the protruding cassock and the slightly coy way of expressing great truths or commonplace morality, as a form of antidote. The Christian message has been a soothing one as far as the majority of Italians are concerned, an attempt to keep the wheels of society turning by applying unction to the places where friction may become dangerous. There is a certain ingenuousness. In a village near Rome, for instance, the priest placed posters along the main street with the words: 'You have an appointment at 8.30 every evening with the Madonna. Could it be that you have forgotten?' And, to make the reminder appear rather more naïve, a printer's error giving the time as eight o'clock for the appointment with the Madonna had been put back half an hour in ink.

This relationship varies throughout the country. Like everything else in Italy, it bears the mark of a sense of place. The priest is still held in highest respect in the countryside around Venice, which as a result is the great Christian Democrat stronghold. In Lombardy and Piedmont and Tuscany, clerical prestige is lower but still high by comparison with the Naples area and much of the south with, as its nadir, Emilia and Romagna, which are the geographical base of the Communist Party. As a general rule respect for the priest is highest where the governments of the past were powerful. The Venetian Republic governed strongly and in particular brooked no interference from the priests and indeed hung them in cages in the hot sun if they were found to be truculent. And after the fall of the Republic the Austrian occupiers were honest administrators, firmly opposed to ecclesiastical pretensions. Lombardy had much the same experience as Venice; Piedmont had the distinctly lay hand of the house of Savoy and Tuscany its traditions of enlightened rule. The southern kingdom was weak and the priests felt that they could, or should, take a hand in civil affairs. In Emilia and Romagna there was direct rule by the priests because these regions formed part of the papal states. This rough guide is illuminating from the point of view both of Italian officialdom and priestly responsibilities. The constitutional dictum that each is sovereign and independent in its own sphere is properly rooted in Italy's history, and the advantage to both sides would be great if it were followed faithfully.

There is no such easy rule to apply to the changing relationship of priest and family as modern developments diminish respect for both. The priest over the centuries taught a comparatively simple message of the fundamental importance of the family, the usefulness of children, the sinfulness of artificially preventing birth, the superiority of the man but at the same time the woman's claim not to be abused. What he said was sanctioned in Italian law and built, especially in the south, into a system of customs, such as the virginity cult and the family vendetta which turned law into popular belief and remains strong despite the onslaught of sexuality and the lessening of male authority.

But the challenge to both is daunting and, as far as one can see, inexorable. Before the challenge came the system was not functioning well. It was an expedient which had gathered immense virtues and strength. But it depended on a view of right and wrong which had become surrounded by superstition, on the inequality of the sexes which presupposes a level of ignorance, as did the lack of sex education, and it depended on such practices as abortion. It is estimated that there are as many abortions in Italy as live births each year – about a million – though reliable figures are unobtainable. The internal migrations of the post-war period tore away at the foundations of the family, though many of the immigrants made a point of going back to their original homes for holidays and such occasions evocative of their youth as the feast day of the local patron saint. Statistics for a decade show that, while fewer Italians were marrying, more asked for legal separations each year. In 1961 there were 391,000 marriages and 9940 requests for separations: in 1970 the respective figures were 370,000 and over 17,000. City life in particular was taking its toll: 53 per cent of all separations occurred in the four cities of Rome, Milan, Turin and Bologna. One in six marriages in a big city ended in separation. The basic weakness of the system was its inflexibility. Children increasingly found that they were faced with acceptance or rejection because the intermediate way could not be found. And Italians suddenly began to realise that they had a youth problem on their hands. In 1970, 8537 minors were officially known to have run away from home and about 1000 were not traced. The situation is worse in the large cities with Rome and Naples worst in this respect. In Rome, one minor vanishes and is not heard of again each week. The average age at which Italians marry has been falling. In the decade from 1960 it fell for men from 29 to 27 and for women from 25 to 23. One of the reasons why the average is low is because children could still marry in Italy without great difficulty so long as the boy was 14 and the girl 12, though this was to be changed in the new family legislation to 18 for both unless permission was obtained from a judge. Another reason is that hire-purchase has reduced the need for the customary long engagement. And, finally, there is a growing tendency to marry in order to escape from the oppression of traditional family life. The city diluted the family. There could no longer be a self-contained family unit. Italian life had been based on a general conformity but a variety of individual cells within the monotonous pattern. Monotony is now imposed, not chosen; imposed by the television, by advertising, by how they think more socially advanced nations behave and what they feel they must do in the name of Western values.

They had no priest to turn to because he had troubles of his own. The Italian Church failed to give a lead to a flock which was trying desperately to know what was meant by living in a modern world. It would be absurd to suppose that many Italians looked to the Church for moral guidance when facing the prospect of prosperity. The majority simply wanted to know how best to enjoy what could be had from the new prosperity. But there could have been a greater degree of sharing between Church and people of their experiences and difficulties. Elements of the lower clergy were willing to do so. And those who tried did so from a serious sense of their vocation and from the feeling that the Second Vatican Council and John XXIII's teaching had changed the situation in Italy.

There should be no doubt that the great figure in Italian Catholicism since the war was John XXIII. His reputation suffered almost immediately after his death. This is a normal development. Pius XII, after all, was never thought so badly of as during the early stages of John's reign because the new pope seemed to be everything that Pius was not and yet was what a pope should have been. In this case the comparison was also unfair but understandable in that John was a far more popular figure than his withdrawn, ascetic predecessor and, although Pius tended to be underestimated, he was a far less effective Pope than John. But John's particular gift was optimism. His old-fashioned belief that God still intervened benevolently in the affairs of men was exactly attuned to the modern world. His rejection of pessimism (his speech at the opening of the Vatican Council contained an attack on 'prophets of gloom') was where his real strength lay and why he was able to capture the hearts of otherwise cynical men. This optimism died with him. Pope Paul VI has many qualities, but a cheerful disposition is not among them. His constant theme is that the world is going from bad to worse and until men grasp this they will go on becoming more technologically efficient, more challenging to all the old precepts, less moral, more hedonistic, and further from God, and so doomed to dissatisfaction if not self-destruction.

The personality of a pope naturally impinges on Italian life more than on any other part of the Catholic world. The Pope lives in the heart of Italy, is Italian and officially not only Bishop of Rome but the country's primate. Pope Paul VI's declared policy has been from the beginning to bring the Church more in touch with the modern world. But application of this policy has been stamped with doubts and diffidence at a time when what Italy required was a firm but innovating hand on its spiritual life. Instead, the Italian bishops have, with about half a dozen exceptions, remained firm but reactionary and the lower clergy has been bewildered. They have also seen their number diminish; in 1966 there were 47,000 diocesan clergy in Italy and 43,000 in 1970, with at the same time a disturbing fall in new vocations. Italian priests have the same difficulties as priests in most parts of the Western Catholic world of establishing a clear identity in an industrialised society, in living a lonely life in a world of growing conglomeration, accepting the disciplines of celibacy and the preaching on sexual matters of doctrine regarded by much of the world as having little relevance to modern life. Enquiries have shown that almost half of the Italian clergy would have liked to see priestly celibacy made a voluntary matter. Acceptance of the papal ruling on birth-control was easier in Italy than elsewhere in the West. Italians are used to rules which they cannot keep and regard the lot of the faithful to be either that of a saint or of a sinner: nearly everybody is in the second classification. It came before the interest of Italian womanhood as a whole had been aroused by new methods of contraception. All forms of contraception were at that time against the law and so was the distribution of information or the advocating of birth-control, measures which, like the firm laws against abortion, belonged to the Fascist ideas of protection of the race as much as to ecclesiastical teaching. But interest inevitably grew, especially and as a direct result of the papal ban. This was followed by the Constitutional Court's ruling which lifted the ban in the penal code on contraception. The position of the priest then became much more difficult. Practical arguments for and against birth-control, leaving aside those of morality and natural law, come down in Italy to the conclusion that an economic case can be made for large families in a stable, agricultural, poor society but the opposite is the case in an industrialised, urban society. The priests were forced to run against the current of social change while at the same time suffering its effects themselves.

The climax to this process of alienation was, in the eyes of practising Catholics of traditional stamp the passing by Parliament of a bill introducing divorce. Italians awoke on

2 December 1970 to find that at about dawn the Chamber had approved the bill by 319 votes to 286 and that, for the first time since Italy was united, divorce was possible. (Before unity there was a brief period in which the French revolutionary forces introduced divorce and divorce was possible in some of the colonies.) The principal grounds for divorce were to be a period of separation. The minimum was five years when both members of a legally separated couple were agreed on divorce. This period rose to six years where the legal separation was mutual but one of the two opposed divorce, and to seven years when the innocent party to the separation opposed divorce. Other specified instances were when one party was condemned to a long prison-sentence or had committed acts of immorality against members of the family. Politically the measure was of immense importance and potentially dangerous. Its social significance was much less. The Italian sense of drama, however, seized on two principal ideas: on the Catholic side, the ruin of the family, and on the lay side the black hand of the Church, which was trying to prevent the Italians from being able to divorce like any other enlightened people.

The introduction of divorce had no direct effect on the Italian concept of the family. At the time the bill was passed there was probably a small majority in the country against divorce. Many Italian women would have been expected to vote against it, especially southern women who would have had no future and a great deal of shame once divorced. Even women whose husbands had emigrated and set up new families abroad, the women known as 'white widows', apparently preferred this fate to divorce. Most Italian women would find life difficult if divorced because their training from girlhood aimed at teaching them to be wives and mothers. But fears that divorce was about to stride through the land leaving behind it a pitiful army of abandoned women and children were out of place. Estimates at the time the bill was passed of those likely to make use of it varied from one to two million. But few indeed took advantage of the measure for which they had supposedly been waiting with high hopes set on liberation. Two months after the bill became law some

7000 people had applied for divorce and most of these put in their applications almost immediately, so that, as time passed, the figures fell off. By August 1972 there had been 71,678 requests for divorce, of which 40,830 had been granted. Supporters of divorce had always argued that they were offering a normal facility to the citizen and were not attacking the idea of the family; they were more right than they knew. Italian common sense is a great national asset and is a far more weighty part of the Italian character than the voluble passion which non-Italians are inclined to think is typical of the race. The Church, moreover, had made the granting of annulments simpler and cheaper. Many people living in irregular unions felt that the worst was already over once the Constitutional Court had struck out the crime of adultery from the penal codes and did not see the point of going further; others were worried that the Constitutional Court would declare against the divorce law (in fact the law was pronounced perfectly constitutional by the court in June 1971, but impugned a second time, with a verdict expected in 1973). Perhaps some of the men who had left their wives and were living with other women felt that living with a woman was more masculine than marrying her, and certainly it would be regarded as more prestigious; those who went to the court for a divorce were mainly those who wanted to give the social respect of marriage to a long-standing relationship and have legitimate children by the person with whom they shared their life. In other words, the traditionalist view of the family was amply proved by the way in which use was made of the divorce law. Four-fifths of the divorces granted by the end of 1971 were asked for on grounds of an existing legal separation by mutual agreement.

The political importance of the law was that for the first time the Italian Parliament had approved a measure which the Pope himself had publicly attacked on numerous occasions. He was in Australia when the bill was finally approved, and from those distant parts, on what was supposed to be a demonstration of the Papacy's world-wide interests, he issued a statement expressing his 'great sorrow' at what the Italian Chamber of Deputies had done. Defeating the Pope on his home ground is not in itself a virtue. But there should be no harm in it if the Italian Parliament chooses to exert its sovereign authority in a direction distasteful to the Papacy. That was why lay interests were so enthusiastic at what they had done. The Rome newspaper *Il Messaggero* expressed this feeling: 'For a country like ours which did not experience the Reformation but has suffered all the negative effects of the Counter Reformation, the approval of divorce means above all that the Italian Parliament has been able to carry out its deliberations in full liberty and affirm, against absurd interpretations of the Lateran Pacts, the autonomy of the Italian State.' And, indeed, it gave direct stimulus to other measures. Communists and Christian Democrats almost immediately sat down in committee with their drafts for a radical reform of family law, now made essential as a result of the introduction of divorce, above all to defend the rights of divorced women. The drafts were prepared on both sides by women: the Communist Leonilda Jotti, widow of Palmiro Togliatti, and for the Christian Democrats Maria Eletta Martini. Their ideas on many points were close; for instance, private property at the time of marriage would remain the property of the individual partner, but anything bought after marriage would be regarded as owned jointly, and both agreed on the highly important innovation that a value should be attached to a woman's domestic work. The equality of the two sexes was boldly stated in a way which both these formidable ladies found acceptable: 'The two spouses decide the unitary course of the family by joint agreement.' This draft legislation was obviously of the highest importance. The man would no longer be the one head of the family: he and his wife would be joint heads. In Italian conditions, the changes brought by this legislation were sweeping. In the words of Oronzo Reale, the Republican parliamentarian who fought for years to see family law reformed: 'The supremacy of the man is finished.' The only flaw in the draft was that it had not been completed and applied years before. The Communists blamed the Christian Democrats for this, pointing out that if past governments had found the time to revise the existing family law – a reform costing nothing – the bitterness of the dispute over divorce could have been avoided. The lay parties would still have wanted divorce but it would, so the Communists argued, have become a less-contested issue: with the rights of both spouses so clearly laid out, the likelihood of unexpected disagreements would have been so much less.

There was room for some surprise that Communists and Christian Democrats could agree with reasonable ease on a subject of such fundamental social importance. But the Communists had been careful since the war to avoid as far as possible any direct onslaught on Catholic beliefs and any attitude that would appear to be aimed at revolutionising Italian society, of which they increasingly claimed to be the defenders against corruption, poverty and repression. The divorce bill caused them some annoyance. They certainly could not have voted against it but they would probably have preferred that the issue had not been raised at all. From their point of view, the voting on the bill brought one great advantage; it isolated the Christian Democrats together with the Neo-Fascists because all the other parties in the Chamber voted in favour of divorce. The Christian Democrats were in the strange position for an Italian governing party of having to watch the passage of a bill which they detested but were unable to stop. They could only hope that the Constitutional Court or the referendum would come to their rescue. The measure was a combination of two private members' bills, one drawn up by a Socialist and one by a Liberal, and although the Christian Democrats led the opposition, and their coalition allies voted in favour of divorce, the Government as such was officially neutral. But this isolation was dangerous. Catholic groups with the support of the majority of the bishops began a campaign immediately the bill was passed for a referendum aimed at abrogating the divorce law. Under the Constitution they had a perfect right to do so and the Christian Democrats had seen to it that the necessary legislation for calling a referendum had been approved before the divorce bill came finally before Parliament. The supporters of the referendum based their appeal on the argument that the family must be saved from the threat of divorce. They easily produced more than twice the number of signatures required (1,300,000 instead of 500,000) within the time-limit to call for a referendum. From being a symbol of a new-found freedom on the part of Italian democracy, divorce appeared to be gathering serious clouds around it because democracy might well, it was thought, not survive a clash between the lay groups on one side and the Catholics allied with the extreme right on the other. Friends of the family were capable of bringing down the temple.

CHAPTER THIRTEEN

Regions and Reality

ITALIANS have an unnerving habit of talking in dates: it is a kind of code. 'While far from expecting an 18 April, but in the spirit of 20 September, renewed by 21 April, we offer progress without adventure in 1972.' This man is talking a political jargon (a dictionary of political phrases was published in 1971 to help the public do their own deciphering) in which he is saying that he expects something less than the Christian Democrat absolute majority in Parliament won in 1948 and, while remaining true to the spirit of the taking of Rome from the popes in 1870, sees this final act of the *Risorgimento* as strengthened by the uprising of the Resistance forces in support of the Allies. Streets are named after dates. Rome has streets called '20 September', '24 May' (the day Italy entered the First World War) and '21 April'. It is unlikely that 7 June will take its place in the highest galaxy of the commemorative calendar but it should do: on 7 June 1971 Italians went for the first time throughout most of the country to vote for regional councils, the local parliaments which according to the Constitution should wield semi-autonomy. The fact that the Italian legislators waited nearly a quarter of a century before applying this fundamental constitutional requirement and that it began rather badly does not detract from the importance of what, by 1971, had become known as a reform though in fact it was simply a matter of giving the country what the Republic's founding fathers thought was appropriate.

The Constitution is full and explicit about the regions. It explains in some detail their functions and attributes. They are meant to complete the trilogy of organs of local government which are the municipality, the province and the region. Italy's administrative structure consists of about 8000 municipalities, 94 provinces, 15 regions of normal character and 5 regions of special character.

The five special regions were all established long before 7 June 1971. The first were Sicily, Sardinia and Valle d'Aosta. Their special status had already been recognised by the time the republican constitution came into force on 1 January 1948. In this same year, the two Tirolese provinces of Trent and Alto Adige became a region and in 1963 the special region of Friuli-Venezia Giulia was added. All of them were in border or peripheral country with particular problems. The feeling of separatism was strong at the end of the war in Sicily and Sardinia. Valle d'Aosta has strong French affinities. Trentino-Alto Adige (in particular Alto Adige) had large German-speaking populations. The area was made a region as part of an international agreement with Austria though the Austrians claimed that the Italians had been less than straight-forward by putting the two provinces together as a region, thus assuring an Italian-speaking majority, instead of giving Alto Adige regional status on its own. In Friuli-Venezia Giulia the local problem concerned relations with a Slav minority and with Belgrade after the settlement in 1954 of the Trieste dispute with Yugoslavia.

Municipalities and provinces already existed and the remaining problem was to establish the fifteen ordinary regions. The ruling Christian Democrats had been in favour of regionalism until their own overwhelming electoral victory in 1948. They then saw no further point in subdividing the country and thus handing over to the Communists a substantial part of the administration. The Communists were at any time certain to predominate in much of central Italy. Except for an effort in 1954 to legislate for the functions of the ordinary regions, the question was left dormant until the Socialists entered government as partners in the series of centre–left coalitions. They forced the reluctant Christian Democrats into calling regional elections. The best of the Socialists did so for the best of intentions. Pietro Nenni, when leader of the Party, pleaded for use of the regions as a means not only of decentralising the State but of reforming the state bureaucracy, which would have its functions diminished. The less admirable among them saw in regionalism the opening of a new and luxurious enchanted garden of patronage. Regionalists of strict profession, such as Piero Bassetti, the first head of the Lombard region, who refused to stand for Parliament because of the value he placed on the regions, saw in the new administrative structure the means by which the slowness, the incompetence and the corruption of the State could at last be overcome. The Constitution gave the regions wide powers in the fields of agriculture, town-planning, tourism, communications, hospitals and health services, local police forces and professional training. Each has its own statute, approved by Parliament, and a representative of the central government – the prefect in the regional capital – is supposed to act as a kind of custodian of the interests of the State. In the event of a serious dispute between a region and the State or between two regions, the power of adjudication lies with the Constitutional Court.

From Italy's point of view, the idea of the regions was originally put forward as a theoretical solution to the fact of the country's great diversity and its strong feelings of local patriotism. The theory was then put into practice because a quarter of a century of centralised rule proved the case for the regions. There was strong opposition from the right – best put by the Liberals – on the grounds that a central belt would be handed over to the Communists and that the country was too young to be able to handle so great a dismantling of the State's apparatus. There were also objections on the grounds of expense. The debates introducing the necessary legislation were the longest in the republic's history. Then came the elections in 1970 at a difficult moment during Mariano Rumor's third administration. A good part of central Italy went to the extreme left as was expected. The rest of the country had majorities based on Christian Democrat leadership. There were immediate riots in the Abruzzo region because of the rivalry between the cities of Pescara and L'Aquila, both wanting to be the capital. In Calabria there was open revolt for five months and spasmodic outbreaks later because Reggio Calabria refused lightly to give up its claims to being capital. It was promised instead the next steel mill – Italy's fifth – to be placed by I.R.I. in the south. This offer did not appease Reggio Calabria and annoyed the Sicilians, where the regional administration and regional secretary of the Christian Democrat Party resigned because they had understood that the steel mill was coming to Sicily.

The Socialists performed their balancing act between government and opposition. Though members of the coalition in Rome, they allied with the Communists in Tuscany and Umbria while in Emilia, where the Communists and Proletarian Socialists had an over-all majority, the Socialists agreed to stay in opposition. The result on the whole was pleasantly surprising to the centre–left government; the parties comprising it were successful with the electorate. The fact that the Government resigned within a month of the result was neither here nor there. The elections were not in the first instance applicable to the Government, and Italian voters are used to seeing their efforts treated as if they have little to do – which is true – with the business of running the country. There were some suggestions from the left that the office of the prefect could now be abolished. The prefect is the representative of the central government, dependent on the Ministry of the Interior; a prefect is present in every province. They are regarded not only as representatives of the State but, unofficially, of the Christian Democrat régime. Requests for the abolition of prefectures comes naturally enough from the opposition, though with little expectation of success. Prefects have lost some of their powers to the regional authorities but they will not be removed. To do so would be like disbanding Cesare

Borgia's army and expecting the Borgia pope to maintain his authority with only his spiritual attributes. He could still have announced the division of the world between Spain and Portugal but he could not have kept order in the Romagna.

The regions make a curiously unbalanced collection. Lombardy is the richest and alone accounts for one-third of all Italian exports. Lazio has Rome and almost nothing else. Calabria will need help for generations before its poverty and resentment have been overcome. And Sicily will require even longer to raise itself from the crippling condition of instability, corruption and waste to which its quarter of a century of semi-autonomy has brought the island. But they fulfil the requirements of strong local patriotism and offer an example for the future development of a united Europe. Italians are proud of being able to offer a vision of a united Europe but a Europe decentralised into regions, a contribution that they can make because of their own lack of a centralised tradition. Of course, the danger is clear enough that in effect the regions will simply become yet another administrative structure that does not function. The lists of members of the first regional councils were not encouraging: 763 out of the total of 912 were over forty years of age and a mere two dozen were women. No women sat in the assemblies of Campania, Lucania, Molise, Calabria, Sicily and Sardinia, and even in Lombardy there were only two women out of eighty councillors. And a high proportion were professional or semi-professional politicians.

The full diversity of Italy can only be appreciated by looking at each region in turn. In doing so it is essential not to forget that Italy has long historical memories of a loose unity subdivided administratively into regions. The term 'Italy' itself took centuries before achieving much identification with the whole peninsula. The Greek explorers knew it as 'Oenotria', referring to the number of its vines. 'Italy' was used in the centuries leading to the birth of Christ to mean the southern part of the peninsula. As Rome's annexations continued, the name was applied to the north as well and later still to Sicily and Sardinia. Under the Romans the name came to mean a large area within the Empire though not a closely defined unit. Roman predominance managed to keep this unity in being for some 500 years as part of the administrative whole of Rome's dominions. A look at the regional maps of Augustus's time show that some of the names have continued in use or been revived, such as Calabria, Apulia, Lucania (still used as an alternative to Basilicata), Campania, Aenilia, Venetia, Liguria and Latium (now Lazio) and that Calabria has somehow managed to shift to its present position from having been what is now southern Apulia. Under Augustus, Italy consisted of eleven regions, which did not include either Sardinia or Sicily, both being treated apart.

It is still in Rome that a beginning must be made. The unity which Rome imposed has never quite been lost and now it is, after all, the capital; and a very strange capital at that. There is little point in reopening the debate on whether it should or should not have been the capital of Italy. Nobody who has lived in it could be in doubt; it should not. A seat of government ought in some way to be exemplary, or simply designed to house the government. London is a great port, an international business-centre and an emporium of culture which has always been at the centre of the nation's affairs; Washington is designed as a political capital; Bonn is provincial in the pejorative sense of the term, small-minded and resentful as befits a place chosen in part as a non-capital, a temporary convenience until Berlin is usable again; Paris is what is left of France if provincialism is taken away. Rome is simply Rome. It is only the administrative capital in the sense that parliamentarians and bureaucrats have their offices there. To the south it personifies the heartless concentration of power which the southerner regards as constantly working against his due interests; to the north it is an intolerable burden which is holding back the development of enterprise and modern society, like some elderly, overdressed, self-centred old mistress who refuses to give way to the new young wife. But government forms only one part of life in the city which is made up of a series of segmented, self-contained communities: the ecclesiastics, the intellectuals, the film world, the local aristocracy the diplomatic corps (there are two: those accredited to Italy and the separate corps accredited to the Vatican), the various international communities, the industrialists who are few and the artisans who are still numerous. It is possible to live in one of these communities and have no contact with any of the others; many people prefer to do so. This is one of the reasons why the population of Rome is neither a community nor a heartless metropolis; it is a series of villages. It can safely be described as the worst-administered city on the mainland and yet has an unfortunate power to attract new residents from its surroundings and beyond, who come in the hope of finding work. It has little industry apart from building, and after the great and aesthetically horrifying boom of the 1950s and 1960s the building industry has been in a highly uncertain condition.

Southern Italy is littered with factories in the desert, huge concerns such as E.N.I.'s petro-chemical works at Gela, which stand loftily amidst Greek remains or olive groves but lonely because they have so far failed to attract other industry around them. Rome for centuries, and particularly in the last half-century, has doubled this performance because it not only stands like a giant in the midst of the ailing Lazio but is con-stantly drawing away fresh energies from the surrounding countryside. Lazio has an area of 17,200 square kilometres and a population of 4,500,000 of whom about 3,000,000 are crowded into Rome. According to Communist estimates during the regional election campaign, eighty per cent of the popula-tion of the region will be concentrated in the area of metro-politan Rome within a decade if present tendencies continue. The principal victims of this spoliation of Rome's hinterland are the two northern provinces of Lazio, the provinces of Rieti and Viterbo. Rieti has been struck in particular by the flight from the land; Viterbo less so, but still its medieval splendour, dating from the time when it was a papal residence, constantly loses its remaining contact with reality. In the south of Lazio, the province of Latina, in the middle of the plain which was once the Pontine marshes, is the richest after Rome because of a fairly widespread development of light industry, in which electronics and pharmaceutical products are important. The other southern province – Frosinone – is poor. This is the zone known as the Ciociaria and, although much of it is still depressed and emigration continues, a more promising future is before it. The Southern Development Fund and the Autostrade del Sole, which touches Frosinone, have stimulated local industry and Fiat have chosen a site near Cassino for a factory. Development is taking place or planned around Frosinone itself, the valley of the Sacco, Sora and Isola Liri. Among the most famous emigrants from this area, but by no means typical in the extent of his success, is Charles Forte. The development will only touch a small proportion in geographical terms of the province. But at least there is something tangible to be expected which is denied the two provinces of the north. In the province of Rieti, it was estimated in autumn 1970 that forty per cent of the buildings were uninhabited; the school at Forano Sabina had seven classrooms and eleven pupils. Rieti is the capital of the Sabine area and what Rome's attraction has done in robbing it of its population has been described as the Sabines' second rape. This depopulation is the continuation in modern terms of Lazio's social history. To the popes, Rome was the centre of the universe (as a matter of fact, Rieti lies exactly at the centre of the Italian peninsula, but this is another matter) and there could be no room for a rival. This neglect is why towns and villages of Lazio, some of them close to Rome, carry on archaic rites of a primitive kind. A character in the carnival at Ronciglione for instance, called Naso Rosso, is dressed in a woman's night-cap and night-shirt and carries a chamber-pot full of *rigatoni* with a tomato sauce; on Good Friday at Capranica trumpeters play funeral marches outside the hospitals and at Sutri, famous for its Etruscan amphitheatre and Mithraeum, before Christmas supper is eaten the head of the family is supposed to throw spaghetti on the fire as some ancient form of exorcism or propitiation.

It is tragic that the principles of modern planning have scarcely been applied to Lazio. The problem of employment is growing worse; in six years up to 1970 unemployment rose from 44,000 to 71,000 and only 33 per cent of the inhabitants were employed. The national average is 36·8 per cent, which is lower than any other country belonging to the European Economic Community. And the problem of Rome does not end with its process of absorbing the energies of its region. It makes of the whole region an economic anomaly in another way; over a half (50·6 per cent) of income in Lazio comes from secondary activities, such as transport and communications, banking, business and shops, and over 20 per cent from the public administration; industry contributes only 22 per cent and agriculture 6·7 per cent. Sheep still graze in the limestone highlands, and spring lamb from the Lazio countryside is still one of the turning-points in the shape of one's year. They are killed very young and roasted over a very hot fire with rosemary and garlic, and if the time comes when the supply ceases Lazio's loss will not be Rome's gain.

To the east of Lazio is Abruzzo, which in many ways is the most surprising of the regions. It looks on the map as if it belongs to central Italy but in fact must be considered as part of the south – of the deep south when that term means remoteness and poverty. Until the opening in December 1970 of the Autostrada from Rome to L'Aquila, Abruzzo's regional capital, the drive was not easy and took one among people who were traditionalist in their ways and clung to old mysteries. The reason why they seemed so different was an accident of geography. The old route from Rome could only be used in the summer and the natural run of communications was north and south rather than to the west with the southern connexion predominating. This is why the mountainous Abruzzo looked to the south and why it has been compared to Sardinia in its remoteness. Rome's traditional connexion was the sight and sound of shepherds who came down to the city with their bagpipes at Christmas. And still do.

If Abruzzo lost any vocation that it might have had as a link between central and southern Italy, it is southern in its economic problems and in the way that they have so far been faced. With a population of little more than a million, it has lost 214,000 people by emigration in fifteen years and its total population is slowly diminishing. Its deserted villages, or houses lived in only by women and old people, are a sign of this distress. It has practically no industry: agriculture was distorted from its natural form of pasturage to the cultivation of wheat by the ill-considered 'Battle of the Grain' insisted on by Mussolini. The region has its own resources; methane has been found in rich deposits at Cellino Attanasio, the Sangro valley and at San Salvo, but it is pumped elsewhere, and similarly the output of its power-stations is swept away without regard to the requirements of Abruzzo's economic needs. Help from the Southern Development Fund has tended to be directed towards a variety of projects without regard for overall planning, a phenomenon undoubtedly encouraged by the feuding among local Christian Democrat politicians whose party dominates the region. This feuding was one of the reasons for the outbreak of violence on 27 June 1970, immediately after L'Aquila had been declared the regional capital. Civic committees were formed in L'Aquila to defend the title against the claims of Pescara, a city which had grown much faster in recent years and regarded itself not only as much larger than L'Aquila but destined to continue its development. L'Aquila, locked among its mountains while Pescara stood on the Adriatic coast, appeared to be in decline. But now, with the breaking of its isolation and its new purpose as regional capital, it may revive. Its future, like that of the whole region, depends on whether the optimists are correct in assuming that Abruzzo has its rational possibility of economic development. They base their theories on the expanding net of excellent highways which are quite new in Abruzzo's history, the supplies of methane and electricity, the possibility of re-establishing pasture as the basis for agriculture and introducing re-afforestation on a large scale to help attract tourists as mush as the farmers. A new generation of politicians would be required to apply fresh solutions to the region's ancient problems. If the Christian Democrats remain predominant they could do worse than take stimulus from the Communist jibe that wherever they have an over-all or very large majority, as is the case in Abruzzo, Veneto, Lucania and Molise, poverty and backwardness and emigration follow naturally.

Molise used to be regarded as attached to Abruzzo but was granted independent status in 1963 and became a fully fledged region after the 1970 elections. It falls well short of the constitutional requirement of at least one million inhabitants and its population is falling. In 1961 it was 358,000: in 1965 351,000 and in 1970 330,000 officially although about 30,000 were thought to have left the area without having taken their names off the lists of the local registry offices. The principal reason for allowing semi-autonomy was the geographical difficulty of crossing the mountains to L'Aquila and Pescara, the administrative centres of the Abruzzo region, for the constant bureaucratic details essential to Italian administration. Over half of Molise (55 per cent) consists of mountains and 45 per cent of hills. Geography has imposed a scattering of the towns and villages; Molise has 136 municipalities with an average of 1600 inhabitants each. Of these 56 are designated 'particularly depressed'. As a region it has the lowest income per inhabitant of the whole country: 300,000 lire ($500) a year by comparison with 450,000 lire ($750) for the south as a whole and 750,000 lire ($1250) which is the national average, rising to 900,000 lire ($1500) in the industrial triangle. And, predictably, it voted strongly Christian Democrat in the first regional elections. With Veneto, Molise shared the distinction of giving an absolute majority to the Christian Democrats. Abruzzo was not far off an absolute majority, while in Lazio the two leading contenders were closer. These three regions are mixed and Rome, in a special way, is unique. But they form a natural hinterland to the capital which certainly does not belong to central Italy, though it borders on Tuscany and Umbria, or genuinely to the south which is first felt with its fullest impact in a region touching all three: Campania with its centre in Naples, the former capital of the southern kingdom.

Campania has one of the difficulties experienced by Lazio: its principal city overbalances the rest of the region. Naples is a city which seems almost visibly to be declining, minute by minute as one watches its chaotic, exuberant life: the decay of its old buildings, the desperate liveliness of its famous slums which, without this especially strong life-force, could suddenly turn into the still, decorous void of a pagan necropolis, and the dreadful new buildings which have ruined the face of what must have been one of the most beautiful cities in the world. Its vivacity comes from two sources. It is the centre of a highly fertile, overpopulated plain which, from ancient times, has sustained a bustling life as volatile as the volcanic activities which continue beneath its surface. The second source is that economically it has too many people to support and tries to do so in an atmosphere of confusion and drama. More than any other people in Italy, Neapolitans get through the day by the quickness of their wits.

In organisational terms, Naples is in a dreadful condition. Infant mortality is not only the highest in Italy (51 per thousand for the Naples province compared with the national average of 32 per thousand; and this rises to 70 per thousand for the municipal area of Naples) but is actually rising. Building speculation has not only ruined the city's appearance but has reduced the ratio between inhabitants and green spaces to a ludicrously low level, about half a square metre for each person. Unemployment proportionately is higher than in Campania as a whole, which has the highest rate of any region. The politicians have treated Naples as a feud to be fought over. The worst depredations were committed during the long rule as mayor of the Monarchist shipowner, Achille Lauro: they were able to continue because of the constant fighting for local predominance among factions of the Christian Democrat Party. These feuds took some symbolic meaning in the later sixties when they turned around the rivalry between the Gava family and Ciriaco De Mita, who comes from Avellino and could thus be seen as struggling to break the grip of Naples on Campanian political life. The inland provinces present a completely different impression to the heavily over-populated coast and its plain. The province of Avellino, for instance, has lost 150,000 people, nearly a third of its population, in fifteen years. Avellino itself has grown substantially because it was the gathering-point of the provincial middle class, unwilling or under no immediate pressure to go north and abroad like the working class. And their arrival brought the local boom for building speculators. The lack of planning or of any constructive political hand brought such results as an entire district – San Tommaso – of 7000 inhabitants with not so much as a shop among them. Much the same pattern is found in the province of Benevento; an artificially expanded provincial capital, an exodus from the countryside, a disastrous mixture of old and new problems. Benevento still suffers from the ancient problem of water which does not reach the homes of the high part of the town for five months in the year, and at the same time is searching amidst its debt-ridden finances for the means to build sewers in the new quarters. These inland provinces lack roads and public services of every kind. They claim, with justice, that Naples, for all its continuing squalor and congestion, has been unduly favoured in the amount of industry placed there. With the great new Alfa Sud works completed near Naples, no start had been made in the inland provinces to supply basic services. A redistribution of industry was in fact included in the development plan for Campania for the four years from 1966 to 1970. The aim was not reached. Salerno and Caserta have done better than the mountainous, inland provinces and have a certain air of prosperity about them unlike Benevento and Avellino, with a more solid impression than Naples itself provides. But it is a fragile touch of wellbeing. The town of Battipaglia is in the province of Salerno and was one of the first centres to rise in revolt against a failing economic situation, and Caserta itself revealed its profound weaknesses and psychological tensions in the serious riots there in 1968.

Campania is one of the most famous areas in the world: it has the entry into the underworld, Capri, Vesuvius, the greatest archaeological sites in Europe, the tarnished splendours of the Bay of Naples. And is one of the worst cases of confusion as a way of life. It has been described as Eden which produces poverty. And the figures bear out this description. Campania is Italy's second region in terms of population (5,159,000, of whom about two million live in the Naples metropolitan area and rather more than one million in the city itself) but it is the seventeenth in terms of average income of the inhabitants (536,000 lire – about $900 – almost exactly half that of Lombardy). The region, in order to be a success, will have to provide more work, a future for the neglected areas, which means regional planning and, above all, a political class which is not engaged in the spider's web of intrigue and corruption so long the main concern of Neapolitan politicians. The new regional administration began badly; disagreements among Christian Democrats were the main reason why Campania had to wait six months before a regional government could be formed and even then it was unconvincingly based on a compromise between the two main groups.

The road from Campania into Lucania – the old Via Appia, in fact, which runs from Rome to Brindisi – used to be a tormenting drive. It was asphalted, but few main roads were so full of curves as the stretch from the coast across the mountains to Potenza. Potenza is now the regional capital (and at 823 metres – 2700 feet – above sea-level the second highest seat of a provincial administration) and is the one large city in the region apart from Matera, which is the capital of Lucania's second province. The provinces are dissimilar. Almost two-thirds of the province of Potenza is classified as mountain and the remainder hills. Matera is mostly hills with some plain. Though to talk of prosperity would be a mockery, Matera is relatively better off than Potenza. It is less rugged and the coastal plain provides reasonably rationalised agriculture. In 1959 deposits of methane were found in the Basento valley. Matera, moreover, achieved some fame beyond the borders of Italy because of the special efforts made by the Italian Government to rid the city of its cave-dwellings, the *sassi* of Matera which can still be seen though most are empty. In the past, Matera tended to look towards Bari and Apulia while Potenza was attracted towards Campania and Naples despite the barrier of the mountains. In December 1970 that barrier fell. A super-highway connected Potenza with the Autostrada del Sole in Campania and, from Potenza, improved communications bring the Ionian coast within an hour of driving, including the developing areas of Apulia around Taranto, Bari and Brindisi.

Lucania offers a challenge to its regional authorities because, although much of it is impoverished, there are unused resources. Manpower is there in such abundance that once again emigration has been a traditional palliative: one of the constant points made by the Communists in the 1970 election campaign was that an average of 330 inhabitants were abandoning Lucania every day, to seek their fortunes elsewhere. This is one of the few regions in which the total population is diminishing; from 645,000 in 1961 to 629,000 in 1970. Rainfall is high and there are five rivers of some size (Bradano, Basento, Agri, Cavone and Sinni) which deposit into the sea a generally accepted total of 2,500,000 million cubic metres of water a year, a waste that could be put to good use in extending irrigation for agriculture. Experience has already been gained in the highly developed farming in the Metaponte area. The mountains and hills are unsuitable for farming but could, by re-afforestation and a revival of their use as pastures, be given an economic life of their own and saved from total abandon. The methane deposits in the Basento valley have disappointed hopes of attracting a variety of industries to Lucania but they remain an asset to be exploited.

Politically, like most depressed areas, Lucania is largely Christian Democrat. The Party did less well in the 1970 regional elections than it might have hoped but still retained 42·4 per cent of the vote. The future will turn less on the question of party politics and more on the emergence of local politicians willing to break away from two sets of traditional behaviour: the client system which ruins any form of economic planning because it depends on the ability of one politician to obtain more for his own clan and followers than another; and the more recent shibboleth that industry will put everything right, like a rain of gold from the clouds. Hope that a new governing class will appear is one of the basic articles of faith of those who believe that the south has a future. This is also an article of faith of the convinced regionalists and one wishes them well with a whole heart, which for the moment is the best one can do.

All these problems are present, but to a more disastrous extent, in Calabria. This region is the most dramatic both geographically and in the character of its inhabitants, at times a cauldron of resentment and gradually nosing its way ahead of its neighbour Sicily in the amount of violence associated with its name, which is a pity because Calabrians fundamentally are more upright people than Sicilians (a broad generalisation but only offered as such). Superficially this is not the impression they give. Calabria has a dark air about it. The inhabitants appear involved in a perpetual conspiracy. Like the Syrians in relation to other forms of Arabs, the Calabrians are more conspiratorial than any other type of Italian. Yet when they open their hearts they reveal a surprising naïveté and honesty of intentions. This fundamental honesty is accompanied by a haunted feeling, like the prioress with the monkey on her back.

Nature is at its cruellest in Calabria. The region is a long, narrow peninsula dividing the Ionian Sea from the Tyrrhenian, 250 kilometres (155 miles) in length and between 30 and 90 kilometres (between 20 and 60 miles) in width. Mountains and hills account for 92 per cent of the surface area and so break up the countryside that individual towns and villages glower at each other across valleys from one hill-top to another and each community has for centuries been turned in on itself, lacking contact with others and distrusting the people and the life outside. The narrowness of the peninsula and the height of the mountains mean that its dozens of short rivers become rushing torrents in the winter which cause floods and erosion of the soil. Only the Crati, which flows northward between the Sila and the Catena Costiera, has a broad valley and does not descend sharply into the sea. It flows through Cosenza where, according to legend, its course was temporarily changed while the tomb of Attila was dug, and now it flows over the remains of the great barbarian and his treasure. Such a colourful legend is not typical of Calabria. The past from which it is trying to escape is the poor, self-contained, patriarchal tribes set high above the malaria of the swampy lowlands. Malaria has not been a problem since the Americans eradicated it at the end of the war. But still about one-half of the population of 2,067,000 live in their isolated villages. There are now roads between them but much of the old mentality remains.

The escape in the past was emigration. 'Flight', Corrado Alvaro wrote, 'is the theme of Calabrian life. In some ways it has always been so but today one has the impression of a primitive tribe abandoning an inhospitable territory. Physically and mentally Calabria is in flight from itself.' There are as many Calabrians living outside its borders as emigrants than the two million still inside the region. In the two decades since 1950 about 60,000 left in the search for work. There is almost no industry in Calabria and Calabrians have given up believing in promises of industrialisation. Their one windfall was that a Calabrian, the Socialist Giacomo Mancini, was Minister for Public Works in the late sixties and stimulated or concluded a mass of public works beyond anything seen in any other region of the south. The blessing was a mixed one. His insistence brought about the ill-fated choice of Catanzaro as regional capital and he himself, in November 1971, found himself charged with corruption.

Despite the massive emigration and the public works of which by far the most important was the continuation of the Autostrada del Sole to Reggio Calabria, the average income of the Calabrians is near the bottom of the national scale. At 330,000 lire ($550) a year it is about forty per cent of that of Lombardy and half the national average. Economically the region still depends on an ailing agriculture, public works and administrative offices. There was hope that tourism would provide a substantial source of income. Calabria has the most striking scenery of any part of Italy with its 700 kilometres (430 miles) of indented coastline and the forests and lakes of the Sila. So far the efforts at exploiting the very nature which has caused so much suffering to Calabrians in the past has been disappointing. There has been neither grasp of the requirements nor the evolution of a style recognisably Calabrian in the buildings or other elements of hospitality. And quite extraordinary decisions are made concerning crucial steps in Calabria's economic development. One of the most beautiful parts of the region is the plain of Gioia. It is also one of the most fertile and the Southern Development Fund has contributed to its agriculture. Yet it was chosen as the site for the new steel works.

Regional development will have to begin from the most basic premises. The first is that an area split into three provinces (Reggio Calabria, Catanzaro and Cosenza) and subdivided into traditionally closed communities must somehow gain a regional consciousness. The tragic consequences of the choice of Catanzaro as capital set back the process immeasurably. Much is expected of the new university. It is planned to have 12,000 resident students and to concentrate on technology. In the meantime, unrest and frustration in Calabria have become one of the new bases of right-wing violence, despite the fact that the extreme right has had no great political success in elections in Calabria. Its other southern bases are Catania and Messina across the strait.

As if to belie the idea that the south in Italy is the south and that is that, Apulia could scarcely be more different from Calabria. The Apennines scarcely touch it and hence much of the region – 53·3 per cent – is plain, an extraordinary amount by Italian standards as the national average is about 23 per cent. The low-lying areas around Lecce, Taranto and Brindisi are very fertile. The olives and the vines seem to stretch to the horizon and owe their luxuriance to a combination of porous soils and underlying limestone with very low summer rainfall but very high summer temperatures. Free entry of wine into other Common Market countries was of great value to Apulia, which annually produces 11 million hectolitres, much of it of high alcoholic content, about a tenth of the consumption of the whole European Economic Community.

The principal cities have in the past found their own characters and, if now the natural centre and regional capital is Bari, the others do not suffer from such bitter rivalries as are found in Calabria nor from the overwhelming importance of the capital as is the case in Lazio with Rome, and in Campania with Naples. The total population of Bari is 350,000, which is slightly less than one-tenth of the region's total population. Bari was already given a modern function in Mussolini's day as the main port for the African colonies. Taranto was Italy's principal naval base. Brindisi early had the official seal placed on its usefulness as the port for Greece and the east by being the terminus of the Via Appia. Lecce was an intellectual centre and produced an extraordinary marriage of the artistic fashions favoured by its Spanish masters in the seventeenth and eighteenth centuries and the fine-grained yellow stone of the area to produce its magnificent baroque. Lecce now is a surprisingly sophisticated market-city with an active university: a visit to the local law-courts proves that it remains the repository of the finest, florid oratory of the old-style southern barrister which fits well with the tortuous brilliance of the architecture. Taranto now has Italy's largest steel-mill and is destined to be the centre of even greater industrial development financed by I.R.I. Brindisi has a huge petro-chemical works belonging to Montedison. Bari has its own industrial zones and a new port.

Because there is more bustle in the Apulian cities than elsewhere in the south and the people have a briskness which contrasts so strongly with the resentments of Calabria and the sinister elements of Lucania, the impression can be that at least one southern region knows where it is going. It does, to some extent, but it has problems both of development and of underdevelopment. The rapid expansion of Taranto has brought building speculation and a sharp rise in the cost of living as well as pollution, which is particularly resented by southerners and was almost unknown in Apulia. One sad industrial by-product in Taranto is the destruction of the shellfish beds. A splendid old craft has been washed away by the polluted waters. And men of no great age can recall that the fishermen's society had its own social rules as well as its skills: the daughter of a cultivator of mussels could not realistically have aspired to marry the son of an oyster-grower. Class was class, even among the crustaceans.

The porous soil and the long, hot summer brings the problem of a water-supply which has still to be finally resolved, despite the work on the Apulia aqueduct which began almost with the century itself. The hill-country in the province of Foggia is poor and the biggest towns in the area, apart from Foggia itself (San Severo, Cerignola and Lucera) are little more than inflated settlements for farm-labourers. They have lived in this way rather than on the land because of the dangers in the past from the Saracens and from malaria and because, as farm-labourers without land of their own, they needed to be at hand for the parades in the main square where the administrators of the large estates took on labour for the day and might send the men to work in different parts of the estates on different days. These humiliating markets in manpower are now supposed to be illegal and employers are required by law to go through the local labour-exchange and to indicate with some precision what their requirements for the season will be. But, in fact, they continue if in a less obvious and so less undignified fashion. Conditions are shocking in these peasant communities. Because of the large number of inhabitants and the impossibility of producing in such conditions a form of popular culture, there is little feeling of belonging to a civic body or self-contained tribe which is so strong, even if distorted, in the Calabrian countryside. The limestone plateau of the Murge, which is good for little more than grazing, is a pale reflection of the rich red soil, the *terra rossa*, of the plains around Bari and Taranto and Brindisi and Lecce. From 1951 to 1970 some 600,000 Apulians left the region for the industrialised north or to seek their fortunes abroad. At the same time as this exodus from the region, there has been a constant descent from the unfruitful areas of the Murge and the Gargano to the plains and to the coast, which is not only why the principal cities and towns have expanded but why new building is a feature of smaller places such as Gallipoli, which has spread beyond its ancient island site across the causeway, Otranto, Monopoli, Trani and Barletta.

Parts of Apulia are an enchanted garden; the almond blossoms in the spring; the two seas meeting around the cape at Santa Maria di Leuca: the tree-less splendour of the coast to the south of Otranto. Others are poor, like the inland villages. Still others have some of the most inhuman urban slums to be found in Italy: the backstreets of Barletta or Trani offer some prime examples and the majesty of their Romanesque cathedrals, which are among the finest buildings in Italy, is not a sufficient counter-balance any more than is Frederick II's hunting-lodge at Castel del Monte for the barren infertility of much of the Murge. Cerignola is another case. These slums are inhuman not because they are particularly shocking but because they show no hint of an awareness which elsewhere lightens the effect of misery, the brightness of mind, for instance, found throughout the slums of Naples, or the dour but time-honoured sense of belonging to an ancient form of life which used to emerge from the cave-dwellings of

Matera with their brass bedsteads and chickens running about the stone floors.

Apulia will clearly be the best organised of the southern regions. It appears to suffer far less than the others in facing relations with the world outside its borders. Its pride in its Greek origins (Idomeneo, no less, is traditionally said to have settled there after marrying the daughter of a local king), its long struggle with the Saracens and the degree of self-assertion which its inhabitants maintained under the Spaniards and the Neapolitan Bourbons probably account for this openminded-ness. With the presence of the Franciscan friar known as Padre Pio in the Gargano, Apulia was the centre of a revival of traditional religion in the south in the post-war years before Pio's cult became too heavily compromised. And in more recent years this region provided the diocese – Conversano – in which the faithful stoned their bishop because they objected to his decision to send away a young priest who was trying to introduce fresher approaches to religion in the post-conciliar period. Apulia sent to the United States a poor emigrant who was to achieve fame with a different type of devotion under the assumed name of Rudolf Valentino, one of the arch-founders of the myth of the Latin lover.

Politically, Apulia is somewhat more to the right than Cala-bria. This is explainable both because the Fascists had helped develop Bari and because the Neo-Fascists after the war had an effective leader called Crollalanza whose name, curiously enough, is an exact translation of Shakespeare.

The traditional border country between north and south is – as its name implies – the Marche, which follows the Adriatic coast from Emilia-Romagna to Abruzzo. The left wing has lately begun to take offence if the Marche are regarded as inter-mediate territory between depression in the south and un-disciplined industrial development in the north. Historically, however, the frontier between the Papal States and the King-dom of the Two Sicilies was along the Tronto, which now marks the southern extremity of the Marche, or Marches as the region can be simply translated into English.

In a more subtle way, the Marches are a social border-country. They have felt the effect of the massive changes in

Italian society. Indeed, one of the region's principal problems is to undo the damage caused by the flight from the inland farms to the proliferating cities of the coastal strip. There is little industry. The farmers who abandon the hills can expect to find work in hotels and restaurants which have added their disastrous contribution of concrete structures to the coastal road and railway, or they can attempt to find a living by opening little shops in the new suburbs. But there is no choice of civilisations in the sense, for instance, of a choice between poverty in Lucania and a regular job in Turin. The Marches are not poverty-stricken and, for this among other reasons, do not qualify for receiving massive state investments like the south: nor are they industrialised. Artisan trades still survive. The region is the centre, for instance, for the making of musical instruments, notably piano accordions, guitars and electric organs. But such concerns employ few people and keep going by faith as much as by good works.

The region might well have become a charming city-state. Its total population of 1,363,000 is smaller than that of Milan and historically has never been concentrated around a particular centre or area. Ancona is now the capital but Pesaro, Urbino, Ascoli Piceno and Macerata have strong feelings of local patriotism. Ancona, moreover, throughout much of 1972 suffered the torture of seemingly unending earth-tremors: more than a thousand in six months. The coast was beautiful and still is in the parts where hideous resort-development has not ruined its appearance, and tourism could have been both valuable economically and reasonably unobtrusive had there been some intelligent planning. The people of the Marche have one blot to their name: they were well known as papal tax-officials. There is an old Roman saying: 'Better a dead man in the house than a live *marchigiano* on the doorstep.' But in general the human qualities of these people are valued. Before the exodus from the countryside which in the last ten years has halved the agricultural population, the patriarchal conduct of family life was highly esteemed. So much so that the tightness of the clan leaves little loyalty for other social conveniences, such as co-operatives or collaboration among smallholders to make their little farms more productive. This family feeling will break down amidst the ill-planned concrete suburbs of the coastal plain, but for the present generation it still has force, as does local patriotism among the towns. The electors of Fermo, when faced in 1968 with the dilemma of voting for a Christian Democrat candidate for the Senate who did not come from Fermo, solved their problem by handing in blank ballot-papers. The flight from the hill-farms has reduced a village such as Astorara in the province of Ascoli Piceno from 300 people to 14 old folk by late 1971. It is said that the church-bells ring softly if a passing jet aircraft breaks the sound barrier. Of the 246 municipalities in the four provinces of the Marches, only 27 have more than 10,000 inhabitants. The average age is rising because of emigration: from 1951 to 1971 inhabitants of the region aged between 46 and 65 have risen from 19 to 25 per cent. In the same period 200,000 left the land but only 80,000 new jobs were created. Clearly the region's first responsibility is to find means by which people can be coaxed back into the abandoned hill-country by a combination of agricultural changes – a move away from cereals towards pasture and dairy farming with modern methods of farming and marketing – and a degree of inland industrialisation to give work but also to balance the seasonal tourism, employment in business and administrative offices and other secondary activities on the congested coast. Economic improvement without too high a cost in traditional ways is a reasonable aim: the Marches have after all produced Rossini and Raphael, Bramante, Pergolesi, Spontini and Leopardi and, among leading figures in modern Italian life, Enrico Mattei, chairman of E.N.I. Politically the Marche is as unbalanced as was its traditional society.

Not so Umbria, which politically forms part of the so-called Red Belt of central Italy with Tuscany and Emilia-Romagna. And, if the Umbrian Communists show less of the organising ability of their Tuscan and Emilian colleagues, they make up the deficit by expressing greater and more radical anger.

Umbria is small (784,000 inhabitants) and depressed, but it knew better days. The steel works at Terni, which were built in such an out-of-the-way place for security reasons before the First World War, flourished reasonably under Fascism because of the demand for war material, and agriculture responded to the stimulus of Mussolini's demands: about sixty per cent of the people of Umbria were engaged in the 'Battle of the Grain' launched by the dictator. Hence, both agriculture and what industry there was prospered under a closed system and languished when this framework was removed. Umbria is still suffering from this reversal of its fortunes as well as from the effects of social change common to the whole country. The system of share-cropping on which Umbrian agriculture was based had collapsed before the Government began intervening to replace it by straight rental: of the 208,000 share-croppers in 1955 only 72,000 remained twenty-two years later. It is one of the few regions which is losing population; in 1951 it had 804,000 inhabitants. Like Marche, it suffers from a lack of industrial development and, at the same time, an exodus from the land of peasants looking for work in the towns. The bad state of the economy has brought from resentful Umbrians the lament that they belong to a third Italy, neither the congested north with its industrial prosperity, nor the south which is lavishly helped: once again similar as a problem to the Marche but, also once again, expressed with more anger. Curiously, to the ordinary traveller Umbria is best known for the splendid tranquillity of Assisi and such beautiful country towns as Todi and Spoleto. The anger at social conditions may be unexpected but it is certainly there and its symbol may well be that the first head of the regional administration with its seat in Perugia, Pietro Conti, was a Communist trade unionist rather than primarily a politician. It will be his business to attempt to stop what Umbrians feel to be an unjust but very real threat – that their region will exist largely to provide fresh air for people who can afford to leave Rome at the weekends.

Tuscany has a similar form of left-wing administration to that of Umbria with the slight difference that the regional government is led by a Socialist rather than a Communist, despite the fact that the Socialists have only three seats in the legislature to the Communists' twenty-three. But the politics of Tuscany have only a relative importance. The Marxism theoretically followed by a majority of Tuscans is due as much as anything else to the Tuscan habit of mind of wanting to be able to supply the answer to everything. They like to give the impression that there are no secrets of the stars or the earth that cannot be explained by philosophy and knowledge. To this they add a naturally radical basis of mind. They are as far as can be from dry ideologues. They are ingenious, independent and hard-working, with a particular talent for practical work, qualities which accounted in the past for the formidable heights which they reached in the arts and their surviving skills in artisan production which they combine with a sturdiness of temperament. No Tuscan will permit doubts that Tuscany is the most beautiful and the most Italian part of Italy and they can justly claim that Tuscan is regarded as the most proper way of speaking Italian. They have one of the supreme treasure-houses of the arts in the regional capital of Florence and a countryside which some of the world's greatest painters have made the background to the greatest events of the Christian religion and to Paradise itself. Nowhere could angels more fitly be found nor immaculate virgins smile in mysterious pride.

Only the Tuscans seem anxious to leave it: in fact, the abandoning of the countryside in Tuscany has been one of the most massive phenomena in the region's recent experience. An average of 200,000 people a year have been giving up the soil. In all it has a population of 3,460,000 and has nine provinces of which Florence is the largest with a population of 1,130,000. Scarcely nine per cent of the surface area is plain, and southern Tuscany has a good deal of poor forest and grazing-ground which suggested to the Umbrians that southern Tuscany and parts of Lazio might form their own 'Third Italy' movement – an idea rejected in Tuscany, which prefers to look at the better prospects rather than harp on less-happy circumstances. Tuscans on the whole have faced up to the reality that post-war living has brought huge changes in traditional life and the new conditions must be met. They have some unique assets.

The first is the gift of imagination and hard work. This combination, however, is not best suited to heavy industry and the assembly line. Though Tuscany has some heavy industry such

as the steel mills of Piombino, the main efforts at economic
expansion are to be seen in the growth of small factories.
About one-third of Tuscany's industrial workers are employed
in wool and textiles around Prato, fabrics at Empoli, Florence,
Montevarchi and Arezzo, marble at Massa Carrara and other
such traditional types of production. And about eighteen per
cent of the total labour force of 1,300,000 is engaged in artisan
trades, particularly in and around Florence and Pistoia, a field
in which the Tuscans claim a national pre-eminence. Another
gift which is natural is the beauty of the countryside itself and
parts of the long Tuscan coast (unlike Umbria, which is
Italy's only region to have no direct contact with the sea) which
means that tourism is a natural asset of long standing and
could well be better exploited. Tuscany as the garden of
Europe is an old idea but more necessary than ever, as are
measures to protect its beauty from pollution, which is another
of the region's responsibilities. And finally the departure from
the land of so many traditionally minded peasants gives the
opportunity for a rethinking of Tuscan agriculture on modern
lines.

A good deal of what is said of Tuscany can be said of
Emilia-Romagna, the stronghold of the Communist Party in
Italy which lies across the other side of the Apennines. But
comparisons are inclined to be misleading in central Italy, and
the most interesting aspects of the character of Emilia-
Romagna are exactly those which most clearly differentiate
it from anywhere else.

Its inhabitants are famous for good eating and drinking, a
robust appreciation of physical pleasures, strong feelings about
politics and religion and a radical tradition of anti-clericalism
which the Communists have inherited. The average Italian at
the end of 1971 was estimated to spend 193,250 lire (£132;
$322) a year on food while the average in Emilia-Romagna
was 229,000 (£150; $381). One writer estimated that an Emil-
ian eats as much in a day as a Roman eats in a week and
a Genoese (regarded as parsimonious in the same way as
Scots) in a month. The physical attractions of Emilian women
have always been famous among those who are attracted by
the robust type, and both Boccaccio and the Marquis de Sade

have recounted their adventures in search, certainly not in vain, of girls under the arcades of Bologna, the provincial capital. Bologna itself is the physical opposite of Florence. The architecture is impressive in a weighty way: the whole city breathes solidarity and seriousness of purpose, whether in terms of work or of enjoying one's self. Gaiety is genuine but not to be taken lightly. The delicacy of Florence, set so unobtrusively among its hills, is another world, and this splendidly bucolic region of Emilia-Romagna where pleasures are taken with so broad-shouldered an approach dissolves to the north through the mists of the Po delta to the even finer delicacies of the Venetian lagoon.

About half of Emilia-Romagna is low-lying and its principal plain is bordered to the north by the Po, Italy's one navigable river and the waterway which, in its course from high in Piedmont, through Lombardy and Emilia, marks the course of the country's prosperity. Hence, the region has more than a foothold in the prosperous northern plain though historically it has tended to look more to central Italy and to Rome, mainly because the popes ruled about two-thirds of it, the remainder belonging to the duchies of Modena and Parma.

Prosperity in the region is real but inclined to be haphazard. The increase in population (eight per cent from 1951 to 1969) is one indication: the total is now around four million. About a quarter are still dependent on agriculture. The sight of the rich farmlands of the Emilian plain is stirring because they look prosperous and well run even if a touch with the ancient past is suggested by the way in which some of the rural towns and roads still follow the old Roman grid pattern of colonisation. Much of Italy's sugar-beet is grown in the area and much – too much – of the country's fruit, to the extent that in the province of Ferrara in particular the destruction of apples and pears is now a sadly familiar sight. Despite the impression of abundance, Emilia-Romagna produces less than Lombardy if agricultural produce is reckoned in proportion to the number of people working the soil. One explanation is that farming is still tied to the old system of smallholdings. Tiny farms are understandable in the parts of Italy where mountains or difficult terrain hold back modernisation or where poverty dictates a laborious approach tenaciously clung to because for generations it has at least provided a living. It is less understandable in a region in which not only a half is plain but another third is hill-country. Yet the average size of farms increases very slowly: from 8·1 to 9·3 hectares (from 20 to 23 acres) between 1961 and 1971.

A great deal of energy expended in small concerns is equally true of Emilian industry. Ravenna has its huge refinery and petro-chemical works based on its natural-gas fields, but much more typical are the small and medium-sized engineering works at Bologna and Modena (where Ferraris are made): shoe-factories, tractor-making, ceramics, woollen goods and furniture, effectively run in many cases by men with a farming background and the tradition of hard work which tilling the soil has left behind. The average size of factories is increasing slightly, but little more than forty per cent of them employ more than ten workers, which is below the national average. Bologna itself is an imposing city without rivals as the region's natural centre, but the capitals of all eight provinces of Emilia-Romagna are true centres of their own neighbourhoods and their area of influence follows to an unusual degree the provincial borders.

As in almost every part of Italy, families have been leaving the soil, especially the difficult terrain of the Apennines. The growth of industry has offered some of them work. Others have tried their luck at the huge business of entertaining summer visitors, an industry in itself which Emilia-Romagna, with its miles of broad sandy beaches, has shown energy, but little taste or planning, in its development. Rimini, Cattolica and the newer lidos in the province of Ferrara are now bywords for an acceptable level of mass accommodation in the summer season which has effectively destroyed the character of much of the coast except for those who enjoy the sight of endless groups of humanity beneath their coloured umbrellas on the beaches: in four years the number of beds in hotels rose from 108,000 to 140,000 in 1971, and the industry was estimated to be worth about 50,000 million lire (£34 million; $83 million) in foreign currency. Another destination of the former peasants and farmers is the small shop. The small shop in Italy is a national problem: there are far too many of them. The record for the whole country is held by Forli, and the region in general is above the national average with 8·8 food shops for every thousand inhabitants and slightly more than eight shops selling goods other than food.

All of this economic panorama brings one to the main point of the region's future: How does a Communist administration propose to deal with the problem of an electorate which votes Communist but shows the virtues and vices of the typical bourgeois? They should obviously set about reforming the distribution and marketing system and do away with a lot of the small shops, which simply serve to keep their owners financially stable and prices high. But 85,000 people in the region have retail licences and if to this total is added their families and dependents they represent a large part of the electorate and one with which only a brave or foolhardy politician would tamper. The same can be said for farming. Agrarian reform could greatly increase the productivity of Emilian farms and the regional authorities have, indeed, stated that agriculture will have a high priority in regional planning. Industry will probably be able to follow the artisan tradition for some time yet because Emilian businessmen have shown shrewdness in placing their products on the international markets. The mistakes of the tourist trade cannot be undone but the region already has a creditable record in expenditure on anti-pollution measures which are vital to the survival of its massive resorts, and it is fair to say that the most recently developed resorts, though by no means fair and beautiful, are an improvement on those which grew up in the fifties and sixties.

By historical accident, Italy's most strongly Communist region merges to the north – literally merges because of the oddly nebulous atmosphere of the delta – with Veneto, which is the fortress of Christian Democracy. The old anti-clerical, radical, Jacobin tradition of the Emilia-Romagna, due in part to the effects of papal rule, vanishes like a ghost across the silver waters of the Adriatic: in its place is Venice and the region in which the Church is held in most respect, traditionally rich in vocations and in votes for the Christian Democrat Party which on 7 June 1970 won its expected over-all majority. So great was the Christian Democrat preponderance that one might say, without being unfairly malicious, that Venice itself was sinking beneath its weight. There is not much doubt that, if there were more competition for votes among the various parties, Venice's problems and those of Veneto as a whole would have been faced with greater promptness and sympathy. In the period of Italy's greatest prosperity, the decade from 1951 to 1961, emigration from Veneto reached its highest figures: 401,000 people left the region.

The dilemma of Venice is internationally famous. The city is sinking and the water rising, two distinct phenomena. The first is largely due to the pumping of large quantities of water for the mainland industries from the subsoil. The rising of the waters is common to the Adriatic and is due to the melting of glaciers. It is possible that, apart from the effect of the artesian wells, the upper Adriatic is sinking because it is at the fold of two upward movements of the soil, to the south and the north. To these natural, or semi-natural, difficulties must be added the effect of the industries on the mainland across the causeway from the old city. They are industries of a dirty kind which cause pollution of the atmosphere and of the lagoon waters: hence, the structure of the old city is constantly being subjected to toxic effects which increase in scope because of the higher tides caused by the rising waters and subsidence. The mainland industries have two other painful effects. The first is that they have attracted immigrants not only from the Veneto countryside but also from the south, people with no interest in the preservation of the old city, with shocking problems of their own of atmospheric pollution, but powerful because they are a larger reservoir of votes than the old city. Clearly, they would not in the slightest be moved by appeals to save Venice when their own parts of the same municipality (the old city on its island is only a section of the municipality of Venice which includes the mainland towns) need help to make them habitable. And, finally, the mentality of the industrialist and the industrial worker – though more the former – is in no way moved to grasp the delicacy and costliness of the problem of safeguarding the old city, which has about as much importance to an industrialist as a Picasso hanging in the boardroom of an armaments factory.

Venice is essentially a problem of the balance between the natural and the artificial. The rulers of the Venetian republic were severe in imposing respect for the finely balanced lagoon and in keeping the sea-walls in good repair. The Italian republic has failed to do so and there are some excuses for this conduct. The materialism of the years of industrial expansion meant that Italians in general were scarcely interested in the fate of Venice and industry was creating huge problems elsewhere, such as the immigrant populations of Turin and Milan and the shanty-town dwellers of Rome, which could justly be regarded, in human terms, as demanding more urgently the Government's attention. This explanation would have comforted those unconvinced about the necessity to save Venice if anything comparable had been done to solve other problems. Instead, other problems were not given priority because they were not faced and in Venice a deep-water canal was dug across the lagoon with no regard for the effect it might have on the ecological balance; plans for still greater increases in industrial production were put forward while Venetians, typically, quarrelled among themselves as to what should be done about the old city. Only at the beginning of 1973 did the government obtain approval for its bill for spending the 30,000 million lire (£205 million; $500 million) international loan which was supposed to provide the basic measures to safeguard Venice and which immediately aroused a controversy concerning the respective competences of the State, the region and the municipality in the business of spending the money.

Veneto to most people means Venice, which is just because of its associations. But the farmers in the low-lying Po delta live each winter under the threat of floods, either if the river bursts through the reinforcements of its banks, or, as in November 1966, the sea itself rolls across the flat fields, leaving not only a problem of flooding but also of salination of the soil. The Rovigo province is frequently described as one of the depressed areas of the north comparable with depression in the south. Apart from the concentration of industry around Venice itself, the main zones of industrial expansion are in

the west, around Vicenza and Verona. But these cities nowa-
days look less towards Venice as their natural centre than to
Lombardy and Milan, an unhappy reversal of Shakespeare's
sail-maker in Bergamo who no doubt was working in the
Lombard heights with an eye on the ships in the port of
Venice.

Lombardy is the heart of Italy's industrial expansion. A
third of Italian exports originate in this one region: it provides a quarter of the gross national product. Its population
has risen at a great pace: in 1951 the region had 6,560,000
inhabitants: in 1961 some 7,400,000 and in 1971 more than
8,500,000. In the period 1951 to 1966 the increase in population (23 per cent) was almost double the national average. In
twelve years from 1955 to 1967 almost 1,500,000 immigrants
came to Lombardy first the Venetians (246,000) then the
southerners. They went where work was to be found, and
Lombards followed them: over the last twenty years, Milan,
Como and Varese have increased their populations by a total
of 1,600,000 whereas Pavia, Cremona and Mantua lost 65,000.
In 1971, Lombardy had one computer for every 3700 workers,
a higher proportion than Britain or any of the other members
of the European Economic Community and only a little way
behind the proportion in the Ruhr. But Lombardy has the
great advantage over the Ruhr or any other pure concentration of industry of variety. More than half (fifty-one per cent in
1971) of its income came from industry but it has some of
Italy's richest agricultural areas. Almost half the region is
plain. The extent of this plain can be seen on a good day
from the top of Milan Cathedral when the Alps to the north
and the Apennines to the south are just visible. Because Italy
is generally regarded as a north–south country, with a backbone of mountains and plain along the coast, it is easy to
forget the huge extent of this east–west plain: it is practically
as long as the Alps from which, from the beginning of time,
it must have seemed like the promised land, a great carpet of
potential prosperity. As indeed it has been, and still is. But
in a way it suffers from its diversity. No one in Italy has solved
the problem, the essential problem in Italian development,
of how different civilisations can go their own ways and pre-

serve their own values in face of the imposition of values which
are fashionable but unconnected – practically a virtue in itself
– with the immediate past. The result is that the rich variety
that gave Lombardy its manufactures, its crafts, its ricefields,
its lakes, its mountains, its valleys and its lowland has been
crudely levelled into acres where people are kept busy in factories and areas where comparative illbeing has caused emigration. Lombardy has the worst pollution problem in Italy.
Milan is a gigantic, suffocating lesson in how great cities
attract more and more people and become more and more
uninhabitable. Prosperity is there in the lavish shop-windows,
in the queues of cars forming at weekends to reach ski-resorts
and villas, in the shocking overcrowding of the hospitals (in
1971 the estimate of additional beds required was 8500), lack
of homes, of schools, of nursery-schools and a desert of development of factories and blocks of flats, particularly in the area
to the north of the city. Milan is making one great contribution
towards social development, with Turin, the other great manufacturing centre overwhelmed by the problems which it has
itself created: it has brought a revulsion, particularly among
young southerners who hear of the life of immigrant factory-
workers from fathers and uncles and brothers, against the conditions of living which undisciplined industrialisation has
brought with it. The reaction has come too late but it is there.

The cost of development and how it can best, instead of
worst, be paid is the great problem facing Italy's most powerful region. The dangerous level of pollution of the atmosphere
in Milan and elsewhere is a problem which the regional administration inherited after a quarter of a century of industrial
expansion. Social services ought to function better in the energetic north than in the more soporific south. But in Milan the
University was described in 1971 by its rector, Romolo Deotto,
as in a state of semi-paralysis. With more than 25,000 students,
its membership had doubled in four years and so lecture
halls, teaching staff and money were all completely insufficient. It has since had the equally paralysing experience of
student violence. The city's famous polytechnic with 11,000
students had one-third of the space it needed. In the field of
pollution, it was estimated that the cost of undoing as far as

possible the damage to Lombardy's lakes and rivers would cost 500,000 million lire (£344 million; $833 million), or five times the whole current budget of the regional administration.

But against the problems one must set the confidence of the Lombards that they will at long last be able to tackle their own problems in their own way without constant recourse to Rome; the central bureaucracy is soundly hated by the leaders of Lombard regionalism.

However strong their efforts, they will be unable to maintain the traditional variety of the region. The sub-Alpine civilisation in Italy is practically dead and the mountains are resorts for city people rather than the background for the harsh life of villagers who attempted to draw a little agricultural blood from the stone heights. To the south of Milan, the gentle, measured landscape of the countryside around Cremona and Mantua, still centres of a more leisurely love for living lost long ago in Milan, shows the signs of the farmers' plight. They have not been able to maintain their position against industrial prosperity. Nothing was done to create the essential reforms which would have usefully preserved communities with much to offer the region as a whole: reforms such as the formation of efficient co-operatives, the placing of rents on a modern basis, improved social conditions such as better houses, schools and transport which would at least have convinced those who decided to stay on the land that their work and their standards of living were being sympathetically thought about. The result of the failure to do so was that between 1958 and 1970 the number of Lombards engaged in agriculture dropped from 469,000 to 206,000. It was not so much the statistical loss that counted but the fact that it included a high percentage of young people. An indication of the abandoning of the land by the rising generation which could have adopted new measures for increasing its prosperity is that the inhabitants of Milan have an average age three years beneath the national average, because it attracts young people. The pyre could be its symbol.

Lombardy itself is the symbol of the truism in Italian society that massive prosperity brings social problems as surely as does massive poverty. The region suffers from both. It has its own internal differences which have inexorably been crudely reduced to the heights of production and of consumption in the main cities and the rejection of more traditional life as insufficiently rewarding. That is why the sounds of Bacchelli's phantom hunting-party on the shores of the Mantuan lakes, presaging destruction, had so heart-rending a quality. Especially now that those lakes are seriously polluted. But Lombardy does not have only Lombard problems: life would have been relatively simple without the trainloads of southerners, poor men thinking that, if not Eldorado, at least the chance to work was a day away in a second-class railway-carriage. While the reservoir from which they came remains unused in the south, Lombardy cannot stop what eventually is the frustration of expansion. While the rivers and lakes are ruined by the outpouring of 60,000 industrial concerns and of the towns and cities, the stimulus to follow a wrecking course is inevitable because of the constant need for more development. Partly this need is in the system itself which cannot, in order not to give ground, do anything but expand. The more it expands the more people are caught in the vortex of its teachings, which are to spend more in order to take up the extra that is being produced at constantly higher costs, because to be able to spend more means to be paid more so that the process is not just an expansion: it is a spiralling delusion. Lombardy has this basic condition aggravated by the fact that the army of those willing to be deluded has increased proportionately with the boom itself so that satisfaction was always beyond society's grasp. To some extent Lombardy's future depends on whether enough southerners have yet been convinced that the north is not the solution to their problems.

All this applies as well to Piedmont but, in general, in an attenuated way. Piedmont is larger than Lombardy but has fewer inhabitants, 4,379,000 instead of 8,500,000. It is the second largest region after Sicily and supplies about ten per cent of the national product. Average income is well above the national average, 900,000 lire (£614; $1500) a year compared to 700,000 (£480; $1166), but the figure varies from well over a million in Turin itself to little more than 600,000 lire (£410; $1000) in Varallo. There is less plain but more breathing space. Agriculturally it is advanced by Italian standards but it does not have the legendary fertility of parts of Lombardy and of Emilia-Romagna. It has far more hilly and mountainous country than Lombardy but shows the same move to the lowlands and in particular the cities. More than two and a half million people live in the plains of whom about two million have settled in Turin or its dependent municipalities whereas the hills have 1,220,000 and the mountains about half a million. The disproportion is once again evidence of a failure in the prosperous years to plan development and devise the incentives which would have maintained a more balanced variety of social conditions, at the same time saving the cities from new industrial slums and the overcrowding which industrial expansion forces on them.

Piedmont is suffering, if the term is exact, the after effects of its own creation because it was the state which united Italy. Now it is feeling the consequences of a massive influx of labourers from the south as well as from its own countryside. Turin is Italy's greatest centre of the engineering industry. It is almost entirely dependent on the presence of the Fiat factories and other initiatives of the Agnelli family, and they in their turn are dependent now on a mass of immigrant labourers. History could hardly have demanded in a more ironical manner that the Piedmontese and in particular the Piedmontese industrialists finally recognise their responsibilities, because if history has a logic Turin and the former grand duchy of Piedmont should have been investing for centuries in this moment in which unity for the first time is taking on a meaning instead of being an exhalation of *Risorgimento* rhetoric.

Of all the states of Italy, Piedmont was the only one not to be occupied by foreign powers except for brief periods. History had taught its ruling house of Savoy – Europe's oldest ruling dynasty when the post-war referendum sent them finally into exile – to preserve the country's integrity and form its character by a long process of diplomatic ingenuity. This ingenuity was based on the Savoys' control of the Alpine passes, which were essential to invaders seeking to plunge down into Italy, especially the French. The name itself is indicative of Piedmont's destiny. It comes from the low Latin *pedemons* and *pedemontium* which reflected the position of Piedmont at the foot of the mountains (overlooking the point that much of it was, in fact, amongst the mountains). It is a comparatively recent invention as Italian names go. Localised place-names in the Po valley became more frequently used in the tenth and eleventh centuries and Piedmont was one of them. The name referred originally to the territories at the foot of the Maritime and Cottian Alps. By the end of the twelfth century a group of feudal nobles with territories between the Po and the Chisone valleys called themselves 'Lords of Piedmont'. The term still had little exact definition. The crucial step in its future consolidation was taken in the fifteenth century when Amadeus VIII, the first of the Savoys to possess the title of duke, created a principality of Piedmont in which he gathered some of his territories on the western side of the Alps. Piedmont, because of its geographical position and the fact that its ruling house possessed territories on the French as well as the Italian slopes of the Alps, received a strong French influence. But one of the more fascinating elements in its history is the gradual shift towards an Italianate rather than a French character which was accompanied by the disposal of the dynasty's possessions on the French slopes and the consolidation of the territories looking naturally to Turin as their capital. The decisive step came in 1563 when Emmanuel Philibert, the greatest of the Savoy dukes, placed his capital in Turin rather than Chambéry. He had defeated the French six years earlier at St Quentin and went on to the logical decision that the future of the duchy of Savoy lay on the Italian side of the Alps. French influence was to be a recurring factor, but Piedmont's course had been set. Careful diplomacy and freedom from foreign occupation were to make the highly disciplined little state of Piedmont the catalyst which forced Italy into unity little more than a century ago.

Some historical background is necessary because Piedmont had this cardinal part in creating unity. The man who fashioned unity was Cavour, and he was at heart a regionalist. He did not live long enough to impose his views and, largely because of the lack of other ideas, Piedmont's highly centralised style of government was imposed on the rest of Italy. This is the real historical lesson provided by Piedmont. Italy could be united without much bloodshed largely because the diplomatic situation at the time was favourable. But unity was not enough. A concept of regional development was required but could scarcely have been successfully applied when the mode of thought was the liberal, centralised nation. The writers of the present Italian constitution rectified the error. The politicians kept the country waiting another quarter of a century before applying the constitutional articles on regionalism. In the meantime they managed, as Italian politicians are so adept at doing, to make a drama of whether regionalism was right for the country or not. The result was that the new institution started under bad auspices. Piedmont, if anywhere, should give it a fair trial.

Historical responsibility is simply the background to urgent modern requirements. The regional administration will first have to face the acute social problems of Turin itself. Immigration turned it within the space of two decades from a provincial city of great charm which knew how to preserve an elegant centre, while factories around it were supplying Italians with most of their cars, into one of Italy's acutest problems. The city has expanded in the worst way possible. New inhabitants have settled in the historic centre of the city, much of which has been turned into slum dwellings, and in outlying communities. These outlying areas suddenly found themselves with far more inhabitants than they could handle, people whose life was largely a coming and going to and from the Turin factories. Their presence has gradually filled in the space between suburb and centre and at the same time helped to destroy the individual character of both. What might be called 'greater' Turin, with ironic undertones, consists of the old capital itself with a suburban belt of twenty-three municipalities and a second suburban belt of twenty-nine municipalities all requiring a massive effort of development and planning to make them function according to the demands of the post-war social revolution.

The countryside superficially has the same problems of a flight of the younger and better farmers. But agriculture in

Piedmont has a special connotation. The ricefields in the province of Novara have their own fascination though the number of persons concerned with them dropped in the decade up to 1971 from about a quarter of the province's working force to little more than a tenth. But the genuine specialities of Piedmont's agriculture are the wines and the famous white truffles of Alba. Nowhere in Italy is the making of wine taken so seriously as in Piedmont and nowhere are such great efforts made to protect the good name of a recognised wine. The responsibility of the regional administration is clearly to protect these efforts as best it can, but even a unique patrimony such as the wine-making skills of the province of Asti nowadays needs more than protection. Life in the farms which nestle so solidly into the Piedmontese hills but are, in fact, extremely uncomfortable has to be improved if young people are to be persuaded to stay. Holdings are too small. In the Asti province the 130,000 hectares (32,110 acres) under cultivation are split up among 33,000 smallholdings with an average of between 3 and 5 hectares (between 7 and 12 acres) each, far too small for efficient working. And even the countryside feels the burden of the immigrants. The province of Cuneo, for instance, to the south-west, has more people employed in agriculture (100,000) than in industry (65,000) but has to deal with the problem of some 7000 landless labourers most of whom have found their way up from the south.

The bulk of Piedmont, and in particular the stolid amiability of Cuneo itself – one of the great centres of the Resistance movement – rather strangely merges to the south-west into the narrow somewhat exotic strip between mountains and the sea which forms the region of Liguria. Its shape is delicate in itself: nearly 250 kilometres (155 miles) in length and between 10 and 30 kilometres (between 6 and 20 miles) wide, hugging the sea-coast like a brightly coloured ribbon. The gentle climate of the narrow coastal plains allows the cultivation of olives and citrus fruits as well as an abundant production of flowers. Much of the agriculture is horticulture, and as much of the coast is a continual series of villas and resorts the first impression of Liguria is that it is one long garden. But its trees and its flowers and its villas are simply the ornamental border dividing the two great elements in the region's life: the mountains and the sea.

This geographical shape has driven Ligurians to look out on the world. It was no coincidence that the discoverer of America was Genoese. Genoa as Italy's greatest sea-port is the economic centre of Liguria and the natural capital. But it does not sum up the region in the way that Turin is the essence of Piedmont. Whereas history made an entity of Piedmont, geography has prevented such a thing happening to Liguria. The rise of the mountains is steep and immediate, so that contact with the hinterland has never been easy. The broken coastline is beautiful but made communications by land extremely difficult. Until the mid-nineteenth century the principal way of travelling from one place to another in Liguria was by cargo-carrying sailing-boats which dealt with coastal traffic. Hence, once outside Genoa there is no great pull towards the capital and the same can be said of Savona or La Spezia or such smaller places as Camogli and Varazze and Loano, now resorts but one-time small ports with a life of their own.

The regional conscience may come, but it is certainly not being stimulated by the massive social problems such as are found in Lombardy and Piedmont. Genoa as a port does indeed have problems, but they are largely organisational and must depend for their solution on the possibility that the central government will adopt serious measures for improving the way in which all Italian ports function. The organisation is slow and expensive. But that is beyond the competence of the Ligurian region. As far as Genoa is concerned, the region will have to face the difficulties of its development. The extremely limited space has to be used to best advantage. Part of the business of making Genoa a genuine capital of its region will be a greater insistence on cultural activities accompanied by continued modernisation of the port and the replacement of heavy industries, which are wasteful in space and carriers of pollution, with specialised factories in such fields as electronics instead of its steel works and its oil refineries. Another part of the business will be open communications through the mountains equivalent to the coastal motor-highways.

An urgent problem which touches every Italian region in any way dependent on tourism is pollution and preservation of natural beauty. Liguria is outstanding in the damage done to its sea and beaches and landscape. Building speculation like everything else in this narrow but extremely beautiful coastal strip of land is dominated by the sheer lack of space and the value of what there is. The Italian Riviera deserved better than to have its coasts polluted and its enchanting coast-line buried beneath reinforced concrete. Take Rapallo: it must have been a charming resort even if Max Beerbohm's decision to live there was regarded as eccentric. It has now become the shrieking example of bad urban development and has given its name to the process. To speak of a town which has been *rapallizata* means spoilt by undisciplined expansion.

Does the north present a unity? On the whole it can be described as a region made up of smaller regions. The inter-national border largely follows the main Alpine watershed and for most of its length passes through uninhabited moun-tain-country with such exceptions as the Ligurian Riviera, Trieste on the east and the projection of the Swiss Ticino. Its heartland is heavily populated lowland almost encircled by the Alps and the Apennines except for the east where it runs down to the sea. Its southern borders are real and do not simply mark an approximate point of change between north and centre. In the west, the narrow Ligurian coast so strongly and immediately supported by its mountains widens into the coastal lowland of Tuscany. In the east the Apennines com-plete their frame of the northern plain and touch the coast at Cattolica, exactly where the regions of Emilia-Romagna and the Marche meet. Geographically Emilia-Romagna forms part of the north whereas historically it belongs more to the centre.

North and south (but not the centre) have their own regions with special statutes: in the north the three border regions with particular ethnic or historical problems are Valle d'Aosta, Trentino-Alto Adige and Friuli-Venezia Giulia; and in the south the two great islands of Sicily and Sardinia. These regions had all been in existence for years before the normal regions were established. All had problems of their own. Valle d'Aosta forms a natural part of Piedmont but feels a strong

French influence. Trentino-Alto Adige saw years of a bitter struggle on the part of the German-speakers to preserve their ethnic identity, a struggle which brought with it spasmodic terrorism. Friuli-Venezia Giulia had to await the settlement of the Trieste issue before its own regional status could be considered. Sicily was hurriedly given semi-autonomy after the war because Rome feared the strength of the separatist movement. And Sardinia, or at least the central mountainous area which is its heart, has never become a part of anything despite the waves of invaders duly chronicled by the textbooks.

Valle d'Aosta is Italy's north-western mark. The valley was somewhat isolated until the two great tunnels of the St Bernard and the Monte Bianco were opened, respectively in 1964 and 1965. These huge projects combined with the Autostrada through the valley itself solved the problem of isolation. So far the valley has gained more in transit traffic than any great number of visitors who come to get to know it despite its dramatic scenery (including Mont Blanc itself) and romantically placed castles as well as a well-organised gambling casino. It comes at the bottom of the list in several of its more favourable features. It is the smallest of Italian regions with an area of 3262 square kilometres (2022 square miles): it has the smallest number – 108,000 – of inhabitants and the lowest figure of density of population. It has the highest peaks in Europe and glaciers cover 200 square kilometres of its area, so that agriculture begins at a serious disadvantage. The region nevertheless has an annual average income of 900,000 lire ($1500) for each inhabitant, which is higher than any province of neighbouring Piedmont with the exception of Turin itself. Some 44 per cent of the population is engaged in industry of which one-half in terms of manpower are employed by the Cogne steel works; 26 per cent are farmers and 30 per cent in other activities of which the most important is tourism. This last figure explains why, as elsewhere, there has been a flight from the mountains, but in Valle d'Aosta the flight has affected the slopes between 2500 and 3600 feet whereas the higher slopes are still populated because of the success of the tourist industry. The valley suffered particular neglect under the Fascists and on 6 October 1944 the National Liberation Committee in a clandestine statement affirmed its right to semi-autonomy. On 4 January 1946 its first regional council was nominated by the Government and by the parties making up the National Liberation Committee and its statute was promulgated on 26 February 1948.

Politically the valley has known its theatrical moments. In May 1966 the local French-speaking party, Union Valdôtaine, which had ruled with the help of the Communists, sealed the doors of the government building in an attempt to prevent the transfer of power to a centre–left administration, and a commissioner had to be sent from Rome to help solve the crisis. The alliance of the Union with the Communists was an odd marriage. The Union was fundamentally conservative. Its followers, for instance, were against industrialisation because industries would attract immigrants and other people from outside. But they remained together from 1958 to 1966 with the additional support of the Socialists. Politics are complicated by local alliances and interests but the valley can hardly be called politically unstable: from 1948 to 1970 it had seven different regional governments while in the same period Sicily had twenty-six. According to its own administrators, the region in the first twenty years of its life had managed to achieve at least double what would have been possible by going through the centralised administration in Rome. There has also been a marked closeness between local politicians and the electorate, more than is to be found elsewhere in the country, a result which depends to a large extent on the limited size of the region and its homogeneity with such special features as the widespread use of French, which is the valley's second language.

The people of Trentino-Alto Adige frequently seem as conservative as those of Valle d'Aosta but history and social developments sharpened all their problems. Until 1918, the region belonged to the Austro-Hungarian Empire and was known as the South Tyrol. In 1918, mainly on President Wilson's promptings, the South Tyrol went to Italy, which thus received its border on the Brenner Pass. A tidy solution, but one which would have required the most delicate handling from the Italian side to make it workable. And, to give the Italians their due, the Brenner was not one of their primary aims at the Peace Conference. Baron Sonnino, the Italian Foreign Minister, was much more concerned with inheriting from the break-up of the Austro-Hungarian Empire a part of the old Venetian possessions on the Dalmatian coast because of his overriding interest in gaining control of the upper Adriatic.

The Fascists could hardly have expected to deal delicately with the question of a powerful ethnic minority within Italy's borders but on the national frontier, and a minority used to the easy-going ways of the Austrians in handling a multi-racial state. Mussolini attempted to Italianise Alto Adige. From 1920 to 1940 there was enforced immigration in an attempt to make the Italian element in the population predominant. The Italians during that period became the majority in the two leading cities of Merano and Bolzano. Housing and work were required for the new inhabitants and industry was established there. The German-speakers remained in the fields and the mountains and the industrial workers and the bureaucrats were Italians brought from elsewhere in Italy. This policy had two dangerous features. It exacerbated ethnic quarrels and made future clashes inevitable. At the same time, Alto Adige went ahead economically while the other province of the region, Trento, which has a majority of Italians, was a centre of Italian resistance to the Austrians and produced, in Alcide De Gasperi, Italy's greatest post-war prime minister, remained poverty-stricken. The first of these dangers was made worse in 1939 by an agreement between Hitler and Mussolini. On top of Mussolini's campaign to extirpate German from Alto Adige and turn it into a reliable border-province of Italy, the two dictators agreed that German-speakers could opt for Austrian citizenship and move away. Many wanted to do so and some managed to do so before the outbreak of war: after the war the Italians allowed them back, full of the extremist views which border people feel when engaged in a patriotic and, in this case, racist war.

At the peace conference after the Second World War, Italy and Austria came to an agreement on Alto Adige. Italy undertook to allow German-speakers access to public office, to allow the return of German surnames and place-names, to allow schooling in German and to give the area a wide measure of autonomy. And, implicitly, the Italians had admitted that Austria had a certain rightful concern about how these Italian citizens were treated. The promise of semi-autonomy was immediately taken in hand by De Gasperi, who produced a solution which, according to the Austrians, was deliberately out of keeping with the agreement. He combined Trentino with Alto Adige as two provinces of a semi-autonomous region. The machinery was complicated in the effort to appear equitable. Three administrations were set up, each with a legislative assembly, one to represent Bolzano with its predominantly German-speaking population (two-thirds at the time), another representing Trentino and the third the region itself. The provincial governments met in their respective seats whereas the regional administration spent half of its four-year term in Bolzano and the other half in Trento. Each time it moved it elected a new president and vice-president, alternatively of German-speaking and Italian-speaking origin. Members of the provincial administrations were chosen to give an exact representation of the two linguistic groups. Despite these efforts, the region was born in the eyes of the German-speakers with the taint of original sin. They maintained that the Austro-Italian agreement was meant to give Alto Adige itself a status of semi-autonomy. De Gasperi, by adding his native Trento province to form the region, assured it an Italian-speaking majority.

Post-war developments could only irritate the conflict. Alto Adige was an attractive, expanding province. The immigrants arrived. The German-speakers felt more and more threatened by the rising seas of *Italianità* around them. Temperamentally they were not equipped to enjoy the more generous concessions gained from the Italians. They were farmers and did not want to be officials or judges any more than they wanted to be factory-workers. Officialdom, as everywhere else in Italy, was in the hands of southerners. And so one saw the clash of the frontiersmen: the sharp-witted, shrewd, rather contemptuous southerner, exaggeratedly Italian for these northern, Swiss-like reaches, face to face with the heavy-minded, heavy-footed, resentful arch-German wearing his *Lederhosen* in the way a Sicilian socialist would wear a hibiscus.

The German-speakers had Austrian sympathy as well as German extremism. The sixties saw the conflict turn to systematic violence which in ten years brought 47 deaths and 250 terrorist incidents of one kind and another. Austria took its case to the United Nations but abandoned this tactic after appraising Italy's usefulness in helping Vienna's association with the Common Market. The two sides settled down to work out a modified version of the region which had brought substantial progress to Trentino and confusion and violence to Alto Adige. The result was a confirmation of the pattern of three separate administrations but with greatly enlarged powers going to the two provinces. As an indication, the regional budget dropped from 35,000 million lire (£24 million; $58 million) to 6000 million lire (£4 million; $10 million) with the balance going to the provinces.

The eastern mark, Friuli-Venezia Giulia, had to await the settlement of the Trieste dispute with Yugoslavia and then overcome the diffidence of the bureaucrats before it was established as a region. The law by which it was set up bears the date of 31 January 1963. The region consists of three provinces and is a constitutional invention. The provinces of Trieste and Gorizia are what remains of Italy's much larger Venezia Giulia which between the wars included the Julian Alps and the peninsula of Istria. The *de facto* settlement of the Trieste question left that famous city in Italian hands but deprived it of much of its historic hinterland. The addition of the large province of Udine, known as the Friuli, was an attempt to give the city a supporting territory though in the past the people of Friuli were much more inclined to look towards Venice than to Trieste. Friuli was an agricultural world: that of Trieste a world of port-workers and commerce. More to the point, Trieste was developed to serve the Austro-Hungarian Empire. It has yet to find its function in Italy. Gorizia suffered even more dramatically from the loss of its hinterland. The new border cuts so close that it shares cemeteries and sewers with Nova Gorica across the border in Yugoslavia.

The Italians are frequently blamed, and constantly blame

themselves, for having failed to find a role for Trieste. It was the great port, a century ago, of central Europe. Its aspect is still Austrian and it has the air of a fine city. But when the Austro-Hungarian Empire came to an end its function as a great city was over. No one could admit as much because it was the subject of rival claims from Italy and Yugoslavia. Trieste itself does not admit as much and blames the national government for not having helped it find a second vocation as central Europe's port even if, because of historical circumstances, it is now a part of Italy. But, in fact, Venice is better placed to serve northern Italy, with the exception of Friuli-Venezia Giulia itself, and the Yugoslav ports are more convenient for the countries of Eastern Europe and they have been expanded, in particular Rijecka, to continue this function with efficiency. Much of central Europe, moreover, looks towards northern rather than southern ports, especially after the closing of the Suez Canal. Hence, Trieste is an insoluble problem if one expects to see a revival which would take it back once more to the heights it reached in the nineteenth century. Its population as a result is advancing in age: young people look elsewhere to make a career. Its standard of living remains high but at the same time Trieste has enjoyed more help from Rome than any other Italian city.

Trieste is helped by one of the real successes of post-war Italian foreign policy in establishing for the first time a cordial relationship with Yugoslavia. But it has been slower than Gorizia to press ahead with the exploiting of a useful friendship. Perhaps because in the past Gorizia's prosperity was based on co-operation between Italians and Slavs. This co-operation was sound until 1918. It could make no progress in the atmosphere of the inter-war years and the immediate post-war period until the memorandum of agreement on the Trieste question was signed with Yugoslavia in 1954. Gorizia immediately settled to the question of cultivating friendship with Croatia and Slovenia as well as Austria.

Udine's problems have little to do with those of Trieste and Gorizia. One of the effects of the loss of territory to the north-west was that the province of Udine accounted for ninety-one per cent of the territory of the region and sixty-four per cent of its population. This anomaly was reduced when Pordenone, a swiftly developing industrial centre, was made a provincial centre, bringing the total to four. Udine itself has some industry, and if new industrial jobs are still not keeping pace with the exodus from the countryside the region plans sufficient industry to stem the flow of emigration to other countries. The people of Udine are regarded as quiet, serious and industrious and sought after as seasonal immigrant-workers in Europe. Though the region is a long way from solving its difficulties, it is regarded as one of the more creditable experiments in this practice of semi-autonomy, all the more so given the lack of a regional history behind it such as that felt, for instance, by Piedmont or Tuscany. Like its Venetian neighbour, though to a lesser extent, it is generous towards the Christian Democrats: 44·5 per cent of the total at the 1970 elections.

And where, where, does it matter less whether one votes Christian Democrat or for the moon than in the remaining two special regions: Sardinia and Sicily? Nothing could be more distant than the difficulties of German-speaking minorities, of French influence, of how to live with the Slavs because the poor old Austro-Hungarian Empire is over. To be in central Sardinia is to live among people who have rejected every element of what is proudly called European civilisation: the Phoenicians were there and the Romans and the Byzantines, and the Genoese and the Spaniards and the Piedmontese and now the Italians, and it is as though they had never been. They have all been rejected. Sicily is the opposite. It has had the same visitors, with a rather large Greek and Arab influence, and reacted by absorbing its visitors. Sicilians are a marvellous amalgam. Sardinians have a dignity that only long periods of suffering and a refusal to be netted by Europe have combined to preserve as one of the few pure anachronisms remaining: not old-fashioned or prompt to break into folksong, but a genuine civilisation which has survived in its everyday form for 2000 years or more. And against tyranny, privation, religion. This is the description of the local religious festival at Lula: 'We kill some animals, and a few goats and sheep. Then we go to Mass. Then we open a barrel of wine and get drunk.'

Sardinia is the second largest island in the Mediterranean, Sicily being the first. Geologically it is older than Italy. Psychologically it regards the Italians as interlopers though, because of the awareness of its backwardness, there has never been a strong feeling of separatism on the island, never as strong as in Sicily where separatism was overrated. It has two centres of modern development: Cagliari, the capital, and Sassari to the north. Much of the country in between is the hilly or mountainous setting for an extraordinary pastoral life, made ugly by its vendettas and conflicts, which is the form of primeval man still with his reactions ready to oppose the encroachments of modernity. The basis of life is the herd of sheep and goats. The protagonist is the shepherd. There are about 2,300,000 sheep in Sardinia and the island accounts for about a third of the flocks of the whole of Italy.

The constant preoccupation of the shepherds is to find pasture. Ollolei, for instance, with its two neighbouring villages, has 200,000 sheep of whom 30,000 can be supported by the territories of the three villages. Sustenance for the remainder must be found elsewhere in the island so that much of the year the shepherds are nomads, renting pasture where it can be had from the landowners. If there is drought, they must find fodder as well as pay the landowners. This fundamental structure, broken-backed to begin with, dominated by strange and cruel laws of its own, is the background of efforts both to put an end to Sardinia's notorious primacy in banditry and to attempt a regional plan of development. Sardinia had its first regional election in May 1949. No one doubts that the region has brought improvements. The average income in the island more than doubled (from 150,000 lire (£102; $250) a year to 335,000 (£280; $558)) in the decade and a half from 1951. At the same time banditry came increasingly into the news. It was at its height in the late sixties. Huge reinforcements of police and troops arrived just as earlier they arrived under the Romans and the Piedmontese and equally failed to remove the basic causes of a phenomenon which was not a conflict of justice with outlaws but of two forms of injustice.

The real fugitive from justice in Sardinia, in the words of a Communist deputy from the island, Ignazio Pirastu, was the State. And its accomplice was the region. So argued the dreamers and planners of a genuine Sardinian Renaissance after the war, who were destined to see the same politicians take over control of the region who had shown no interest in the past beyond wanting the advantage of power. There was no real break and the region was a reflection of the central government. It did not lead Sardinia into great new adventures nor did it wholly neglect the requirements of the island. An indication of the conduct of the Sardinian regionalists was given by the first important debate which aroused the interest of the political class: in an island suffering from the accumulation of centuries of social problems, including illiteracy from which one-quarter of the Sardinians suffered in 1951, they debated whether representatives at the regional assembly should, like a member of the national parliament, be entitled to the title *Onorevole*. These complaints have to be judged at the same time as expensive efforts made by Rome, from the 400,000 million lire (£274 million; $666 million) voted in September 1961 for improving the Sardinian economy over the following fifteen years, to the possibly decisive parliamentary commission under the chairmanship of Senator Giuseppe Medici which reported in early 1972. The Commission called for the approval of a series of bills which would have the effect of changing the structure of the pastoral economy and of making more money available for social development.

Sardinia has almost nothing to do with Italy in the sense that its real life has nothing to do with anywhere else at all. Sicily is sometimes regarded as the heart of Italy, Goethe's 'key to it all', or the distorting mirror in which all Italian vices and virtues, but mainly the vices, appear in even worse forms than elsewhere. Compared with Sardinia it has had a kinder history and remains more favoured. It is larger, with five million inhabitants compared with Sardinia's 1,500,000. Palermo, its capital, has for centuries been a famous European city which various viceroys and invaders were happy to come to whereas they shunned – and bureaucrats still abhor as a punishment-posting – any city in Sardinia. It was granted semi-autonomy in May 1946, before Italy even had its own new constitution, at a time when the bandit Giuliano described himself as a colonel in the 'voluntary army for Sicilian independence'. An incident involving the famous bandit gives an indication of feeling immediately after the war. He was present at a meeting, so it is said, two days after the referendum by which the monarchy was ended in Italy. Also present were a Piedmontese general and representatives of the separatist movement. The meeting took place in the house of a priest in Palermo. The general asked if the Sicilians would welcome the proclamation of Umberto as King of Sicily. He was assured that the Sicilians would rebel against the republic in the King's support. After the meeting, however, the priest told the general that the reverse was the case but no one dared say so because they were frightened at what Giuliano might do.

Semi-autonomy substantially wider than that given to Sardinia was rushed through without a clear idea of the situation in Sicily. Application of the statute was far from complete. It allowed, for instance, for the setting-up of a high court to judge charges of misbehaviour on the part of the regional government. This court was never established so that the regional government theoretically was immune from punishment from crimes committed in the exercise of its duties. Only in 1970 did the Constitutional Court remove this privilege. The Sicilians were clearly in no condition to think seriously about what regionalism meant. In a quarter of a century they have made of it the cautionary tale of how regionalism should not be conducted. Relations with Rome have been a constant problem, not least because many of the bureaucrats in the central government with whom the Sicilians have to deal are, because of the vagaries of recruiting civil servants, Sicilians themselves. The region was modelled on the State and produced a bureaucracy even worse than that of Rome itself. The expenses for the personnel of the region rose from 2646 million lire (£1·8 million; $4 million) in 1956-7 to 31,608 million (£21 million; $52 million) in 1970, and as a natural result their work became slower and less effective. Not that effectiveness was the aim. The bureaucrats are a privileged group brought together by the old principle dear to southern Italy of *clientelismo*. The region has 7500 civil servants and 600 different offices. They are paid more than national civil servants, and members of the regional assembly at Palermo pay themselves more than members of the national parliament. Palermo has 2500 dustmen, 300 more than Milan which has double the population, and the city is dirty.

Malpractices are monumental. In the absence of any lead from the State in regional development, investment in industry and public works has largely followed the promptings of power, local, electoral and client-interests. Half-finished hospitals, abandoned villages built as part of the agrarian reform movement and the most appalling forms of speculative building are common throughout the island. Palermo itself is one of the great examples of building speculation which was to a large extent financed with Mafia funds with the connivance of the local authorities. But the most painful example was Agrigento. The town was poor – its province is one of the poorest in Italy – and its fame was mainly due to the Greek temples in the plain beneath Agrigento itself, which was largely a medieval town. The temples are huge and, as any visitor can see, impressive but the typical product of colonists who built more massively than they needed. But they had the sense to build down in the valley where there was no chance of a collapse. The post-war speculators took no such pains when they built shoddy but weighty blocks of flats in the medieval centre, taking advantage of the fact that Agrigento had no urban-development plan and the exclusively Christian Democrat administration was open to any form of connivance. The result was that on 19 July 1966 a large part of the city collapsed and 7543 people were homeless. Greed, maladministration and a total ignorance of civic responsibilities literally brought the city low. This is what the special correspondent of a northern newspaper, *La Stampa*, wrote:

> Years and years of abuse and violations of every kind such as those revealed by the regional enquiry (shelved) which were known to everyone here, the impunity accompanying them, the Mafia-style paternalism of the old landowners, the

insolence of those made newly rich by building speculation, the constant rotation of power within the ranks of the same party (the Christian Democrats) have produced these results.

The temptation to make of Agrigento a microcosm of what was wrong with Italy as a whole was not resisted: especially by the Communists.

It is customary to draw a line through the centre of the island (it passes through Agrigento) and regard the east as comparatively free of Sicily's worst historical burdens, including the Mafia. This distinction is just. The east was settled by Phoenicians and Greeks whose influence lasted, while to the west, across the mountains of the Madonie, Palermo and its surrounding countryside has absorbed more from the Arab and Spanish influences. Certainly the people of the east are more open, less grave, less tortuous of mind than those of the west and are proud to point out that their part of the island is scarcely touched by Mafia crimes and suffers from the *malgoverno* to which they are subjected by Palermo. Logically enough the east has been more intensively developed by northern industrialists. Nevertheless Catania, the main city in the east, a charming, vibrant place, has *malgoverno* of its own. So bad, in fact, that the protest against Christian Democratic rule has given it proportionately the largest Neo-Fascist vote of any Italian city. The result of the concentration of industry is that the province of Syracuse has almost double the average annual income of the Agrigento province. Even so, industrialisation has proved a mirage, another reason for Neo-Fascist gains. The labour force in 1951 was 1,466,000 and in 1969 was down to 1,391,000 despite an increase in the population over the same period from 4,489,000 to 4,780,000. In the year 1968-9 the labour force dropped by 51,000 and in the decade from 1960 about 500,000 Sicilians emigrated. In the ratio of the number working out of the whole population, Sicily comes last in the regional count. And this despite such massive expenditures as the 340,000 million (£232 million; $566 million) which Montedison and E.N.I. have spent between them in the island, the first mainly for its huge factory near

Syracuse and E.N.I. in its petro-chemical works at Gela. There is still a terrifyingly long way to go before the accounts of history are settled and islands such as Sardinia and Sicily can begin life without the weight of centuries of misrule and lack of development. And so far it has not been helped by the performance of the regional administrations of either of these islands.

Of the two Sardinia is more strongly Christian Democrat. Sicily is normally more to the right than Sardinia, but in June 1971 the island helped deliver a massive and unexpected shock to the politically conscious by giving a large increase to the extreme right. It was the first serious sign that once again reaction was a threat to Italy.

CHAPTER FOURTEEN

Reaction and Revolt

NORTH and south in a broader field was the essence of the reaction of a Danish traveller whose encounter with Italy is described in one of Isak Dinesen's Gothic tales. The encounter takes place in an inn near Pisa:

> While talking, the youth rested his left arm on the table and Augustus, looking at it, thought how plainly one must realise, in meeting the people of this country, that they had been living in marble palaces and writing about philosophy while his own ancestors in the large forests had been making themselves weapons of stone and had dressed in the furs of the bears whose warm blood they drank. To form a hand and a wrist like these must surely take a thousand years, he reflected.

The youth turns out to be a girl, but the conclusion is correct nevertheless. In the course of a quarter of a century since the end of the Second World War, progress or industrialisation, the advance of the consumer society, emancipation, the entry into a modern world, the choice of civilisations, Americanisation, whatever label is placed on Italy's experience, have challenged a form of life which in its essentials is very old indeed. Much of it has been swept away. A fresh consciousness has replaced some of the old mores. But the old defensive processes still function strongly because at no other time in their modern history have Italians felt so much in the midst of turmoil. History helped them devise a set of reactions when confusion and lawlessness threatened to destroy life's pattern.

The feeling of confusion and vulnerability is caused by the failure of any of society's institutions to provide that feeling of security such as is given by a crucible in which changes can be seen to be taking place before our very eyes, but within the limits set by the walls of glass. Italians have had to watch and experience transformations which they knew were in no way being kept in shape. This is a disconcerting feeling. Nerves snap after a while. And the strain is greater when people realise that there is no going back to how things used to be. Southerners cannot abandon the northern cities and go home. Apart from the shame of it, they would not be able to settle again to the stagnant life from which they had fled. They cannot go back to the land because, under the pressure of the European Economic Community, Italian farming is becoming more like that of the rest of Europe which means larger holdings and far fewer people employed on farms. This was the aim of the 1,000,000 million lire allotted in March 1972 for Italian agriculture by the Community. Carts need no longer be painted with the naïve skill of the Sicilian artisan: the potter's craft will soon be extinct except among amateurs: the magicians still pass on their incantations to the sick and unlucky in the remote villages of the south but they will not withstand the advance of the chemist's shop. There is no way back. There has been an emergence of what for want of a better word can be described as the modern spirit. But it has proved too weak and too inexperienced to shape society's transformations. It may in the future show that Italian humanity can be combined with an industrial society. For the moment it is simply the victim of a boundless conservatism which is trying to deal with a beleaguered form of life. It is instructive that in the immediate post-war years the Christian

Democrats constantly impressed themselves on the public as the 'dam against Communism'. By 1972 the Communists were appealing to the electorate in practically the same terms, but as the one true defence against reaction. The dyke mentality is as strong in the average Italian as ever it was in a Dutchman.

As a result of this sense of beleaguerment, pure reaction has indeed been strong. For instance, the opposition to divorce and the insistence of conservative Roman Catholic opinion on calling a referendum against the divorce law surprised people who felt that in Western societies no one challenged the principle of divorce anymore, but regarded it as a social service. Italian opinion was by no means convinced. The Catholic answer, quite apart from religious teaching, was that Italy's post-war recovery, on which the country's subsequent expansion was based, owed its resilience to the strength of the family. In the future, they argued, Italy would still require this strength even if the country now felt it had become a part of Western, industrialised society. On a completely different plane, the internal migrations and in particular the dreadful conditions of southerners in the big cities, brought a revival of the old-fashioned methods of self-protection and exploitation. The Mafia not only grew in its native Sicily because of the weakness of the political forces and, in some cases, their collusion, but also saw some of its leading figures move north: the methods polished to perfection by centuries of experience began to appear in Piedmont and Lombardy, in Rome itself and parts of the south. In the factories, alienation grew with the same speed that production fell, and the first signs of genuine revolution began when the extreme left exploited the disgust and confusion felt by elemental rustics to the harsh tedium of the factory and the insupportable social conditions outside it. With the certainty that night follows day, or the other way about depending on one's political views, the far right reacted to the new-found aggressiveness of the workers. New problems arose for the myopic political class – was left-wing violence as bad as right-wing violence? – a subject which was lengthily debated: and the essential issue of what they were to do as the two extremes encroached more and more on the terrain within the chalk circle known as the democratic area, consisting of Christian Democracy and its occasional allies.

The frame of mind of the Italians as, one after another, their worlds begin to shatter, including the newly created world of the consumer society, is as varied as the regions themselves. As had to be the case in a country becoming, despite itself, increasingly united, the old forms of reaction added new features to their masks and new forms of reaction took their places amongst the old. Bandits in Sardinia have behind them the same social causes which drove them in the past to kidnapping and shooting, even if their banditry now is better organised. Sheer poverty and the feeling of old resentments still drive men to open revolt in the south. The class-struggle still remains ostensibly the driving force of change from the left despite the social conservatism of much of the latest Communist thinking, and some of Italy's most extreme social reformers believe they are applying the teachings of Catholicism, ignoring, apparently, the continued conservatism of the Italian hierarchy during the pontificate of Paul VI.

The Sicilians are credited with having invented, in the Mafia, the most effective institution of those originally improvised to make up for a lack of authority on the part of the public powers. Its transplantation ought to have been a sharp warning to the politicians that a new Bourbonism was not going to be enough.

The real origins of the Mafia, like the name itself, are obscure. The Sicilian writer, Leonardo Sciascia, inclines to the view that it takes its name from that of the Arab tribe, *Ma afir*, which governed Palermo during the Arab domination of the island. It was certainly used by the inhabitants of the ancient centre – the *borgo* – of Palermo to describe a proud, handsome personage; a girl referred to as *'na carusa mafiusa* meant a girl notable for a particular type of proud beauty. The fact that originally the Mafia was closely confined to the extreme west of the island and that its stronghold coincided with the area in which the Norman conquerors from 1099 to 1190 forced the surviving Arabs to live has suggested a racial solution to the mystery of its origin. To particularise so much may be a mistake, but the Mafia probably owed as much as any surviving phenomenon to the effects of the Arab occupation. It was first brought to the knowledge of the Anglo-Saxon world by Brydone, whose account of his travels in Sicily included a description of the 'honoured confraternity'; and its first literary use was the play *Mafiusi di la Vicaria* by Giuseppe Rizzotto which was published in 1863 and was a great success, with some 2000 performances in twenty-one years. The geographical restriction of the Mafia in its heyday to a closely defined part of the island is shown in a topographical study of the Mafia published in 1900, which traced the relative density of the Mafia's presence in the island.

Whatever its exact origins, the Mafia is not simply an artificial organism created to make up for the lack of security. It is rooted in two of the basic principles of life in the south: the vendetta and the refusal to co-operate with the authorities. The vendetta is one of the principal springs of delinquency, just as it is the only motivating force on the structure of traditional society. The vendetta is one of the principal components of Sardinian banditry which has some general lines in common with the Mafia though is very different in other ways, as Sardinia itself is so different from Sicily. Its great importance is the persistence which it imposes on the conduct of the avenger. A sense of justice would give no such drive. Nor, except in the remotest cases, would the need to do good. But the conviction that an insult calls for blood and that blood can be washed away by more blood, and only by more blood, namely that of the enemy or one of his family because the family after all is the basic unit, is relentless, reliable, logical, mystical, awe-inspiring, everything that appeals to the southern mind. It is a law, unlike the law of the land, of which they can be fearfully but somehow contentedly in awe. It distinguishes southern life more than any other habit, and the Sicilians were able to harness it to the protecting power and the killing power of the association which came to be known as the Mafia. The refusal to speak to the authorities is equally typical but a negative rather than a driving factor. It is called *omertà* which means manliness, and the deaths of those who break this law are particularly atrocious. They have to be. The whole framework would collapse if for a moment someone dallied with the notion that society's official institutions should be respected.

Originally the Mafia was feudal in the sense that it protected society as it was. Hence the beneficiaries were property-owners and those with something to defend, which in Italian thinking even today usually means property – the most sacred concept in society. There was, for instance, a tremendous upheaval within the Christian Democratic Party itself when the housing law of 1971 introduced the idea of long leases as an alternative to outright ownership. The thought that in ninety-nine years' time a man's descendants would not be able to enjoy the whole inheritance which he had left them after a life-time of work was to many conservatives a scandal. Many modest Italians go through life paying off the debts incurred through buying a piece of land which frequently they can do nothing with, except take their picnics on Easter Monday (the one day of the year on which Italian families seriously set themselves the task of picnicking, which is not a habit which comes naturally to them). Things which can be touched and carry a market-price have great value, which is why such an extraordinary example is St Francis, who renounced all worldly goods, to say nothing of his love for animals, is so impressive; and also incidentally why the Church in Italy can be so deeply involved in worldly considerations, mainly the business of property-owning, to the scandal of all races but Italians. Property-owning is next to Godliness and in its way perfectly clean. It was no coincidence that brought the Vatican deeply into the property field.

To return to the Mafia, this deeply conservative character marked its ideology and activities. Many of its most prominent victims after the Second World War were Socialists and Communists, especially those who attempted such heretical activities as the organisation of the peasants into unions, or properly functioning labour-exchanges. One of the tragedies of the aftermath of the Allied invasion of Italy was that many of the most reactionary sections of Italian life were helped, or revived and encouraged. The Mafia was one of them. Ironically, the Fascists before the war had seen the danger of the Mafia in its challenge to the Party and the strong state, and attempted its extermination. They drove it out of sight but failed to exterminate it. The Allies, in one of the most simplistic and damaging decisions for Italy's future, made use of the Mafia to facilitate the invasion of Sicily like weak men now who make use of the drugs which the Mafia is prominent in trading, just to help themselves over the immediate difficulties. The result was not only a revival. The Mafia's influence in post-war Sicily was stronger than at any time in its history and was one of the factors that discredited the island's regional administration. Its power was demonstrated in many ways – not least by ensuring a charmed life to Salvatore Giuliano, the greatest of the post-war Italian bandits, until he was no longer of use to them. He was then killed and his body, in the generally accepted version, handed over to the despised authorities, who claimed to have shot him themselves.

Banditry as such has no direct part in the Mafia's work. Bandits are outlaws who act alone at the head of their own band. The Mafia bends the law, ignores the law, depends on a tightly knit organisation, sends its killers as an extreme measure, but spurns the splendid personality and prefers to work surreptitiously but all the more effectively for that. The acknowledged heads of the Mafia have normally been unobtrusive men, certainly unglamorous, usually rough rather than suave, with an occasional gesture such as that of sending over a bottle of wine to your table in a restaurant to let you know that they know of your presence and do not mind your being there. There was no place in such an organisation for the bandit and the two types of delinquency have little in common, as the fate of Giuliano showed. An outstanding example of the difference is provided by the remark of a famous Italian industrialist intent on placing an assembly plant in the south, in Sardinia or Sicily, who decided on the latter because, as he said, an agreement with the Mafia could be relied on as binding whereas in Sardinia, where delinquency centred on banditry, there was no one single personality whose word would bind the rest.

The immediate post-war activities of the Mafia were mainly agricultural. It controlled such crucial points in the system as the markets and the water-supply and guaranteed protection to the peasants who obeyed its rules. The centre of its power was in Palermo. Its hold over life depended on the impotence or acquiescence of the public authorities and its power was inflated by the urgent needs of the newly installed democratic processes. Italy had never before known a system by which everybody had a vote. Pre-Fascist democracy was based on an *élite*, and never in a reactionary's wildest dreams could anyone have imagined that fears of Communism in Italy would drive the democratic parties into alliances with any powers in the land able to produce votes for the Christian Democrats and their allies. The Mafia could produce votes. Any candidate in western Sicily with a hope of success had first to arrange to obtain votes from the local Mafia chief, and arrangements of this kind were not limited to the west of the island. The price paid was connivance.

This system lasted until about 1960. By that time progress had had its own effect on the Mafia. The shift from the country-side to the towns meant that control of the agricultural world was less lucrative and attention was turned instead to the marvellous field of undisciplined building speculation. This was the period in which Agrigento collapsed under the weight of illegal constructions. But speculation left its real mark, and a small army of bodies, in the building boom of Palermo. Rivalries for enrichment were strong. The advent of younger, more ambitious men, who were more willing than the tradi-tional type of Mafia criminal to turn to straight gangsterism, meant that more blood was spilt in public than ever before and an unknown number of victims met the fate of being buried in the wet cement of the foundations of some huge and hideous block of apartments in the island's capital. In 1962 in Palermo alone, in less than two months, fifty-six people were shot. The great age of building speculation was the period from 1959 to 1963. In those years, 4000 building licences were issued: 3400 went to four people, one a coal merchant, another a janitor, the third a carpenter and the last a building labourer. All were, of course, simply agents of Mafia leaders, most of whom had already boosted their fortunes in the drug traffic which, again as modern life called more desperately for the help of narcotics, became increasingly lucrative. Italy, and Sicily in particular, was on the traditional route of drugs from the Middle East to New York. This traffic in itself grew; at the same time more drugs were stopping in Italy.

Italians are far from having a problem of drugs comparable to that of the United States or Britain. Estimates vary bewilderingly to a maximum of 600,000 who use drugs. Much nearer the truth were Ministry of Health figures in 1970 that only 8000 were addicted to 'hard' drugs with about 80,000 on hashish and marijuana. Legislation against drugs is harsh and indiscriminate; it allows no distinction between use of drugs and trafficking, which is absurd. Nevertheless, drug-peddling and drug-taking are crimes against which the Italian authorities concentrate their attention, and if it were not for the fact that the penal code is unintelligently inflexible, these efforts could be regarded as one of the better achievements of the Italian police. The main preoccupation was naturally with the young.

In early 1971, Vito Ciancimino, a Christian Democrat who had been in charge of the municipal department for urban development, found himself somewhat surprisingly proposed as mayor of Palermo. He constantly denied accusations of connexions with the Mafia and sued those who said or implied otherwise, including Angelo Vicari, the then national chief of police. In May 1971 Ciancimino lost this case. At the time the case was arousing great interest the regional election campaign was being fought and it was noted that Arnaldo Forlani, National Secretary of the Christian Democrat Party, managed to complete his tour of speaking engagements in Sicily without once mentioning the Mafia. His reticence did not help him. The Mafia much resented the repressive measures taken against them and anyone suspected of having anything to do with them in Palermo. The Christian Democrats made the same mistake as the Fascists in believing that repression was the answer, and were less thorough. The Mafia, like any other association feeling that it had something to protest about, shifted its support to the extreme right. This change of policy from supporting certain Christian Democrats and making use of their acquiescence to backing the new party of protest –

the M.S.I. as modified by Giorgio Almirante – is one of the causes for the big increase in the Neo-Fascist vote in Sicily in the 1971 regional elections.

The authorities had been stimulated into increasing ruthlessness against the Mafia by a series of spectacular crimes: spectacular not only because of what happened but also because they broke new ground. In September 1970 a Palermo journalist, Mauro De Mauro, who worked for the left-wing newspaper *L'Ora*, was kidnapped outside his own home and was never heard of again. He was an expert on the Mafia's interest in the drug traffic and at the time of his disappearance was investigating the last few days of the life of Enrico Mattei, on behalf of the director Francesco Rosi who was making a film about the life and death of the late chairman of E.N.I. Leading journalists are not as a rule the type of target for the Mafia. They would have other ways of dealing with tiresome journalists. In May 1971, when the Ciancimino scandal was still fresh, gunmen shot Pietro Scaglione, chief public prosecutor of Palermo, as he left the cemetery which he visited daily to pray by the grave of his wife.

Increased pressure on known or suspected members of the Mafia in Palermo and the demand for narcotics in the northern cities accounted for the opening up of Mafia activities in Milan. The Italian police in the north understandably preferred to look on crimes committed in Milan or Turin as simply a part of the difficulties arising from the unhappy social conditions of the newcomers rather than stamping them as Mafia crimes. Police are conservative everywhere and nowhere more than in Italy. But new factors had to be faced. Immigration had attracted to Milan and its suburbs alone more than 250,000 Sicilians and inevitably among them were some members of the Palermo underworld, who brought with them the techniques they had learned from their contacts with the Mafia. These unpleasant elements among the immigrants exploited their fellow-southerners by organising a squalid imitation of the Palermo building speculation, renting rooms in semi-derelict blocks which they re-let to immigrants in conditions of up to ten a room. They also took a hand, if a modest one, in drug traffic and currency smuggling into

Switzerland, the protection of nightclubs and the organising of prostitution.

All these ventures were minor copies of Palermo activities and showed little sign of the true Mafia flair. The real connexion became clear in 1963. On 23 May a man called Angelo La Barbera was shot, but not killed, outside the flat which he rented in Milan. He was one of the leading figures in the Mafia of the Palermo building industry. He had left Palermo after his brother Salvatore had been kidnapped, never to be seen again. Like other Mafia personalities, he was finding Palermo too difficult for him: rivalries and the increasing harshness of the police were denying to Palermo and its surrounding area the historical monopoly in Mafia affairs, and the organisation was being forced to spread elsewhere. This connexion of Milan with Sicilian crime was confirmed dramatically on 30 April 1971 when Antonio Matranga was killed. He was a close friend of Gerlando Alberti, one of the most feared Mafia gangsters, later to be hunted on suspicion of having planned the De Mauro and Scaglione crimes. His murderers were never found but enquiries were conducted among suspected Mafia contacts. In theory Milan should have taken over the patrimony of crime which the Mafia offered in the way that Rome took over the Athenian heritage. In practice this could not happen because of one essential difference: the Sicilian Mafia at home could rely on the connivance of officials and politicians. In Milan it could not.

Piedmont developed an expatriate Mafia of a different kind from that which settled in Milan. Nothing could seem more absurd when sitting in Piazza San Carlo in the elegant centre of Turin, amidst the orderly type of baroque which should have appealed deeply to Gibbon but surprisingly did not, than to imagine that a brutal evil such as the Mafia was at work. Once again it arrived with the immigrants. The speciality in Piedmont is recruiting groups of poor immigrants into gangs of cheap contract-labour to be hired out to constructors. The existence of this Mafia type of activity was brought to the public eye on 1 May 1971 when an illiterate Calabrian immigrant building contractor, Carmelo Manti, shot four men dead in Turin. These men were supplying him with cheap immigrant-labour. Their claims for payment, as they delivered more cheap hands, had been steadily rising to the point that on the day of the shooting he was about two million lire in debt. And so he shot the men who he felt were charging him unfairly. Less than a year later a group of Piedmontese employers went to Rome to report on the situation directly to the parliamentary anti-Mafia commission.

The south itself was not unaffected. Calabria had its own tradition comparable with the Mafia, as did Naples with its Camorra. Calabria remains desperately poor. It has ruthlessly been used as a reservoir of votes by local politicians in exchange for public works and promises. This is a familiar southern pattern. The same could be said of its semi-criminal organisations, dating from Bourbon times with somewhat similar aims as those of the early Mafia. The Calabrian 'honoured society' was less effective than the Sicilian Mafia because of the Calabrian propensity for intricate intrigue, strange rites and a natural bent for conspiracy. These groups made most of their money at harvest-time, during agricultural fairs and at points in the process of selling property, anywhere when a substantial amount of money in an agricultural community was changing hands. One of the uses for which this money served was to help widows and orphans of former members and to pay the judicial expenses of a member who came up against the law. In this rudimentary form of social-security system, the Calabrian type of Mafia showed itself wiser than the Sardinian bandits who behave in a far more individual way and find themselves faced with the prospect of having to carry off increasingly lucrative enterprises in order to pay legal fees while they are tried in contumacy. The fundamental elements were present in the Calabrian organisations – distrust for the law, a conviction that the State was the enemy, that co-operation with the State's agents was harmful and damaging and, as the motive force, the habit of the vendetta.

This modest Calabrian rural Mafia was given a fresh lease of life when in about 1960 the Sicilian Mafia decided that the Calabrian coast would be ideal as a base for landing contraband, in particular smuggled cigarettes. The Sicilians traditionally used their own strip of coast between Palermo and

Trapani but were forced to look further afield because the Sicilian coast was being too closely surveyed. The first of these arrangements was made between representatives of the Sicilian Mafia and leaders of the Calabrian groups. Both prospered. But for the Calabrians the experience was stimulating as much as lucrative. They began to understand how their old methods could be used in modern conditions. They took a hand in building speculation and made a prosperous business of demanding payments for allowing the construction without interruption of the motor-highway to Reggio Calabria, a perfect case of an old form of delinquency adapting itself to modern opportunities for extortion. Once the motor-highway was finished, they took to kidnappings. From May 1970 to August 1971, the period which saw the high point of this new venture, ten people were successfully kidnapped for ransom and three attempts failed. Families are reticent about how much money they pay in ransoms, but those ten kidnappings are thought to have brought in the equivalent of £450,000 ($1,080,000). The Calabrians had learnt from both the Sicilians and the Sardinians, who are the acknowledged experts in kidnapping for ransom. Geographically Calabria lends itself well to this form of crime because of the great expanse of the Aspromonte mountains where victims can be hidden with almost the same facility as in central Sardinia. Not only geography was against the police. The population refused to help in enquiries. Families would not even tell the police whether or not they had paid ransoms and if so how much. The police could only reply with the traditional methods of repression. (There are times when one can sypathise with the difficulties of the police in Italy.) The province of Reggio Calabria by late 1971 had the highest number of persons (4600) in proportion to the population under special orders of surveillance issued by the judiciary of any province in the country, not excluding that of Palermo.

The geographical spread of the Mafia's activities is less important than the spread of the Mafia mentality. Rome has suffered from both. In September 1971 the general public discovered that a venerable Mafia personality, Frank Coppola, then aged seventy-two, not only lived close to the capital, near

Pomezia, but was suspected of arranging for an alleged contact of the Mafia to be installed as a functionary of the newly established Lazio region, which has Rome as its capital, and was even said to have penetrated the Rome public prosecutor's office to tamper with tape-recordings (10,000 metres of them) made of his telephone conversations. The functionary was Natale Rimi, son of Vincenzo Rimi, an old colleague of Coppola sentenced to life imprisonment, who was arrested as a result of investigations into the disappearance of Mauro De Mauro. Coppola was also under suspicion of illegalities in speculative building along the Lazio coast, of having had a part in the escape in December 1969 from a Rome clinic of Luciano Liggio, one of the most ferocious of post-war Mafia killers, and of being involved in the narcotics traffic. His daughter's reported comment on her father's troubles was: 'Everything bad said about my father is an invention of the Communists. My father is a good man, respected and loved, a great benefactor of Sicily. For years those sitting in the Chamber of Deputies bowed before him. Now they have left him alone. They are going to feel it at the next elections.'

Apart from the real presence, there is the symbolic presence of a frame of mind not far removed from the attitude in Sicily which originally produced the Mafia. The law is not there for the public good and in any case is weakly applied: the official institutions do not function and cannot demand confidence. There is a seeming failure to seek out the truth without fear or favour, as was shown so tragically in the Valpreda case and all the unhappy circumstances of the Milan bombings. At a more humble level there is too widespread a feeling that a powerful friend is one's only salvation: it is who you know, not who you are, that matters and you too, if compromising recordings have been made of your telephone conversations, might be able to rely on someone within the law-courts building itself to snip away the worrisome stretches, or, as happened in February 1973, to enter a judge's office and simply steal a set of tapes. But if you are an unemployed labourer you will go to prison for stealing a chicken. The relationship is increasingly that of client and patron. The moral centre has, at least temporarily, been lost in the reaction to administrative incompetence. This incompetence and the reaction to it becomes more evident and more positively damaging when caught up in a rush towards what now can only ironically be called Western values. The liberating forces of technical and industrial progress have had the effect of turning the human mind in on itself, constricting its growth and its proper play and excellence, as if some flower about to bloom received a blow and its petals closed and withered.

Morality is a difficult concept to talk about in Italy. By nature Italians are born with much of what constitutes morality. When touched they do not, individually, curl up like a stricken rose and let their goodness wither. They are very human, capable of acts of extreme individual kindness as they are capable of acts of extreme individual bravery or sanctity. They are at their best when their actions, or reactions, depend on their own spontaneity. Corporate morality is much more difficult for them, and of no great interest. That a man makes money out of a public office is still not quite taken for granted but causes no surprise – any more than do statistics which show the appalling extent of swindling of insurance companies by motorists and mechanics. It is recognised that some people have been punished for corruption when their principal crime was to break the rules which they felt it impossible to obey because they were too antiquated. Though they live far more public lives than Anglo-Saxons, village-lives in the centre of huge cities, Italians paradoxically refuse to accept what elsewhere would be regarded as the obligations of living in a community. Right and wrong are concepts seldom applied to public life. Hobbes is a more disgraceful writer than Machiavelli but it is Machiavelli who became the symbol, or synonym, for the devil at work in affairs of state, though he did no more than express, with perhaps more cynicism than was called for, the Italian attitude towards the conduct of public business and the question of where morality is relevant, producing a highly intelligent analysis which excludes all consideration of Christian values.

No one has the right to try to probe into the moral feelings of others but in the case of the Italians an attempt must be made in order to explain the apparent moral indifference marking their reaction to the changes brought by modern conditions. They are frequently accused of following superstition and not religion. Their critics presumably mean by this that superstition is religion without morality. This is so. But not because the Italians are prone to immorality. It is so for two reasons: the first, self-evident, that where there is great poverty and ignorance and a tradition of legend, as is the case in much of the south but not only in the south, superstition is inevitable. The second reason is that the most Centaur-like characteristic of all Italian traits is the distinction between theory and practice. They are taught morals in the way they are taught everything else, with almost no encouragement to see a practical application. To study law does not mean that you want to practise law: to study teaching does not mean that you intend to teach. There is no close connexion between studying and doing in the Italian mind (and the 200,000 unemployed primary-school teachers in early 1972 should have brought the point home). Clearly thousands of devoted parish priests through the ages have done their best to instruct their flocks in the ways of right behaviour. But the results are not so noticeable, for this simple reason – that Italians, more than other races, are constantly being told one thing or another. They listen respectfully and then go their own way. This attitude explains why Italians were incredulous or, rather, pitying when Catholic opinion elsewhere was so incensed by Pope Paul VI's confirmation of the ban on birth-control.

And in the field of public morality they have surprisingly little guidance. For largely historical reasons, the ecclesiastical hierarchy feels it has much more to impart than simply religion as such or morality. The bishops, when speaking as a whole, talk at length about the collapse of values, the corruption of morals, the direction in which Catholics should think when casting their vote in elections, but references to public morality are rare indeed. It would be unusual to hear a prelate recommending a person's candidature because the man was of outstanding moral worth, and even if he did the recommendation would carry little weight. To say that a candidate could obtain favours for individuals once he was in Rome would be taken as much more serious talk and, fundamentally, a moral reason, because a candidate of this kind could think of the good of one's family and friends.

Periodically the Italian public is subjected to upbraidings about the sad state of morality. On 29 February 1972, for instance, the Council of the Italian Episcopal Conference called for 'a more intense and unanimous recourse to prayer' to face the dangers threatening Italian society. The statement was a strange mixture of lamentation and political hinting. The bishops maintained that disquiet and malaise were spreading throughout the country as a result of the increasing amount of agitation, some of it legitimate in origin and some of it damaging. A lack of confidence in the effectiveness of institutions was making headway, encouraging irresponsibility towards the common good, and even economic progress seemed in no small way compromised; work for the humbler classes was marked by growing insecurity, widespread economic and psychological uneasiness, while at times the temptation emerged of an almost desperate reaction to problems which were becoming permanent and apparently without solution.

The statement went on to point out that delinquency and criminality were becoming steadily more frequent and worrying. Violence was touching the extreme limit at which violence bred violence. Damaging elements had entered or were threatening to enter family life, such as divorce, on the gravity of which the bishops had expressed themselves clearly. School life was profoundly disturbed. Various forms of injustice were being perpetrated at the cost of the weak and the unprotected while the rules of morality were frequently overlooked in professional conduct and at times in the field of public responsibilities. All this was accompanied by a crescendo of thoughtlessness and hedonism going as far as to include drugs, which were an indication of a vast and profound moral decadence. Apart from calling for prayer (which is a generical suggestion rather like a general's call for bravery and a good turnout) the bishops opposed trade union unity and proposed unity among Catholics in meeting these problems, an obvious suggestion to vote for the Christian Democrats in the general elections which at that time were known to be imminent. It is difficult for the ordinary believer to distinguish in such messages a genuine Christian element which will help him face a complicated world. There is no recognisable religious substance.

Somewhat surprisingly, given the Communist Party's respect for the Church, the Communists answered this statement with an angry lecture to the bishops on morality. This answer appeared on 2 March and accused the hierarchy of complicity in the admittedly shabby state of the country. While agreeing with the seriousness of the country's economic and other ills, the Communists, in a leading article in *L'Unità*, sought specific responsibilities. 'For twenty-five years this country has been governed by politicians who describe themselves as democratic and Christian. For twenty-five years Italy, at every general election, is faced with men who hide behind the cross and the shield, the symbols of the Christian Democrat Party, and talk in the public squares about justice, liberty and moral values.' The point of the Communist argument was that Italy was about to face a general election in a situation denounced in harsh terms by the bishops but which was the responsibility of a governing party supported since the end of the war by the bishops themselves.

Certainly, economic progress was compromised. But thousands and thousands of milliards of lire had been absorbed in

unworthy speculation, by shameful swindles, by absurd and ill-considered expenditure lacking in any form of productive usefulness. Certainly the weak and the defenceless suffer injustice. But they suffer injustice at the hands of powerful men: of the great capitalists, the parasites, the speculators who are the very people who finance the Christian Democrats, the Fascist groups and anyone else intent on being a nuisance to the Communists. Certainly crime is spreading, even if Italy in this respect is in the last place in our happy Western world. But the Italian police, the most numerous in the world, is permanently mobilised against the workers calling for a just wage: and it is mobilised in vain. Because never, and we repeat never, has a trade union or Communist demonstration been anything but a lofty and civilised protest.

And when, this Communist sermon continues, someone was in fact arrested for such matters as drugs the people concerned were not metal-workers or textile-workers, but the so-called 'polite Rome', and those arrested were the victims, not those who make millions out of drug-peddling and who, 'well turned out and with well-bred elegance bow to a bishop or bend to kiss his ring'. Hectoring from both sides scarcely offers a helpful guide. This is one of the reasons why, despite talk of morality, the Italians remain great pragmatists where moral behaviour is concerned.

No one should be misled by the penitential processions on Good Friday. (The most famous is in Taranto, and prominent places in it – such as carrying the cross – are purchased: the procession each year is preceded by an auction at which the objects under the hammer are positions of honour in the penitential rite.) Or by the apparent predilection for pomp or, where it is still possible, liturgic fussiness in religion, or the queues at the confession-boxes, or the white-dressed girls at their first communion. They will all decide what they think is right by very mundane standards. They will not sing:

And priests in black gowns were walking their rounds
And binding with briars my joys and desires.

The explanation is not simply that a natural outlook outweighs what seems to be no more than another set of imposed teachings. For much of recorded history, the Italians have had the seat of Christendom in their midst. By force of circumstances, the Holy See has had to accept being shaped by mundane considerations. 'It has been perhaps profound wisdom on the part of the Church not to make itself the paladin of all the great human causes, and even to sanction certain crimes, such as slavery, but it is certain that this conduct has alienated from her all generous hearts, all those who thirst for justice.' So wrote Rémy de Gourmont in the 'Dust for Sparrows' as translated by Ezra Pound. The remark may be true if applied elsewhere but it is not true of Italy. Certainly the Church has not taken up the great human issues (and on that of slavery one might add that there were slave markets in Piedmont and Genoa as well as Palermo as late as the fifteenth century). But Italians do not thirst for justice. They want a bare minimum of institutions which function reasonably well. If they thirst for anything it is injustice in their own favour. And at the same time they are tolerant in judging the behaviour of their Church, far more tolerant than other people would be. They understand so well the claims of power. They sympathise even when they do not agree with what the Church has done. They, and they alone, are intimately aware that the Church which they see bears on its shoulders not only the burden of providing priests for Italy but also the whole government of the Church Universal. With this awesome responsibility, how could it not sometimes be seen to disadvantage and even seem to be taking attitudes and performing actions which appear distant from the mere application of the Christian message. Facts are facts. A girl might be a voluptuous beauty, desirable in every way and the very embodiment of love, but many Sicilians would still feel cheated if she were not a virgin. Italians refuse to be shocked or discouraged by what might seem earthbound attitudes in what is supposed to be something celestial.

The crucial point in relations between Italy and the Vatican is frequently overlooked: that Italians made the Church what it is, or rather its central government. For centuries it has been an Italian preserve, created by Italians in the Italian image, in thought, in style, in architecture. To talk of interference is thus highly misleading. This feeling was implied but only half expressed in the meeting between President Leone and Pope Paul VI on 22 September 1972. This call at the Vatican was the President's first official visit to a foreign head of state, and was clearly intended to convey that the political situation in Italy had changed and more intimate relations between the two courts could be expected. The Pope made clear that he did not like the introduction of divorce and Leone made no response. The Pope might have been accused

of tactlessness, but if Leone had answered him by reference
to the sovereignty of the Italian Parliament in such matters
the whole point of the visit would have been destroyed. This
issue attracted the most attention, but the really interesting
passage in the Pope's speech was his warning to Italy not to
seek to imitate others. Here he was stepping on ground that
was far closer to the heart of the Italian problem. The Pope,
of course, is no impartial observer of the Italian scene. Perhaps
nobody is, but certainly not the Pope. He could not accept
challenges on his own doorsteps from critical Italian Catholics.
This is another point which has to be weighed when the
Italian failures in dealing with modern life are assessed. But,
accepting the Italian responsibility for the Church as it is, the
Pope was in a sense merely returning the compliment when
he enjoined Italy to stay in the known ways and not to change.

I know that if I were an Italian I would not have written
that. But deep down I would know that it was true. I know
that I would resent it even if I were a faithful Catholic. But
I would not know what to do about the situation. The majority
chooses acquiescence. Ideally the country should be true to
itself. But more than any other country in Europe Italy cannot be. History decreed centuries ago that Italy could never
be left out of Europe's affairs. A country which has Gothic
cathedrals and Arab–Norman architecture, pious hermits and
popes, Greek ruins beneath the castles of the Swabians, Sicilian
quarters in sight of the Alps, protestors as far to the left as
the political spectrum spreads, and the blackest of Fascist
conspirators, anarchists and Jesuits – the list could be long
but the point is clear that life is inclined to be one dilemma
after another, which is why the degree of acquiescence is so
high.

The wisest words on the problems of Italy's relations with
the Vatican were never spoken. They were included in a
speech which Sidney Sonnino, Prime Minister and Foreign
Minister before the rise of Fascism, prepared to read in Parliament but in the event never did. The text was found among
his private papers long after his death. Being an Anglican
Jew (and the only Anglican to be prime minister of Italy)
he was somewhat diffident about giving his views on the

316

problem of the Papacy and this may be why he never delivered the speech. He intended telling the Chamber that Italy should avoid coming to an agreement with the Vatican so long as the Vatican was in predominantly Italian hands. Once it had become more international, Italy could come to a lasting agreement with it, advice which Mussolini would have done well to heed before coming to his arrangement with the Pope in 1929.

Sonnino had little time for religion in his own life. But he could see that the religious question in Italy had at least two sides. The religious life of ordinary Italians ought to be quite distinct from the relations between the Italian Government and the Vatican. To some extent they are, and it would be wrong to overlook the strong stream of a simple form of Christianity which exists historically and presently in the Italian mind; the automatic connecting of a good man with a Christian which is far from being the case when one is dealing either with the high prelates of the Curia or with the third element in Italian religion, the superstitious element. Silone saw the Vatican in these terms: '... we see a complex historical product, the product of a given culture, or rather the amalgam of various cultures, the millennial elaboration by a closed community, in constant inner turmoil and also in competition and conflict with others. Finally, to put it charitably: a noble, a venerable superstructure. But what happened to poor Christ in such a superstructure?'

The Italians support all but the insupportable, and frequently their estimate of insupportability is so low as to approach fatalism. But when the point of protest is reached the eruption is violent. The south produces the most dramatic examples of this sudden explosion of rage. It is a tradition which has been sustained in the post-war period despite all the money invested and the planning intended to raise the standards of living for southerners. Just as modern conditions revived the Mafia and gave it a different character but one based on its historical origins, so the handling of the southern problem has given fresh meaning and intensity to the south's propensity for suddenly flaring into revolt: spontaneous anger rises from the accumulated grievances of centuries like the bursting into bloom of a scarlet hibiscus rooted in rank compost. And

usually it dies as quickly, with passions soon spent. There have
been exceptions. The rebellion in the south against the new
northern masters immediately after national unity was achieved
claimed more casualties than all the other *Risorgimento* wars
despite the official reading of events that the fighting was an
operation against bandits. The immediate post-war period had
some dramatic clashes, notably at Melissa, which has entered
left-wing lore as the symbol of police repression against the
peasantry, and the name still brings respectful applause from
Communist congresses.

But the crucial uprisings were those that took place from
the end of 1968, when two striking peasants in Sicily were shot
by the police, to the epic of Reggio Calabria's revolt. They
were most of them misinterpreted when they happened. The
Italian habit of seeing the world through spectacles coloured
by cliché is well established. 'Beautiful legends', as Giovanni
Giolitti said when prime minister, 'should not be destroyed' –
a feeling which explains why Italians expect a conventional
interpretation to be given them of any event and are prepared
to accept it, though aware that if anyone were tiresome enough
to apply rigorous methods of checking the theory could be
readily challenged or destroyed. Giordano Bruno and Galileo's
fate are taken subconsciously as object-lessons. Pious legends
and official accounts of controversial events are outwardly
accepted. That is how the Government could claim credit for
shooting the bandit Giuliano while public opinion maintained
that he was betrayed by his lieutenant, Pisciotta (later poisoned
in his prison cell); or keep Valpreda and his alleged fellow-
conspirators locked up for years without trial for the Milan
bomb-murders. '

Occasionally reality raises its questioning head. That is what
happened at Avola in eastern Sicily in November 1968. Two
men died. A Victorian picture was promptly painted of two
poor peasants who ran into trouble while desperately looking
for the means to subsist. Both Communists and conservative
opinion were intent on placing haloes of sentimentalism around
the victims. The later southern revolts, at Battipaglia, Caserta,
L'Aquila and Reggio Calabria, were in their different ways
given an aura which made them readily understandable to the

public at large but avoided showing the criticisms they contained of policy towards the south and modern developments in society.

Avola was a serious trade union struggle in which the farm-labourers of this part of the province of Syracuse were intent on establishing a principle. The details of the struggle are worth recalling. For the purpose of setting agricultural salaries, the province was divided into two zones. In one, regarded as more profitable, the farm-labourers were paid 3580 lire ($5.90) for a seven-hour day: in the other the pay was 3210 lire ($5) for an eight-hour day. This part of Sicily is among the most advanced, and even farm-labourers were no longer the helpless semi-serfs of recent memory. The strikers were pursuing two aims: first, the end of zonal pay, which they wanted replaced by a basic sum payable anywhere, on the grounds that a man's work was his work wherever he might ply it; second, the establishment of mixed commissions to check that a man's hours and days were properly recorded. The point of this demand was to give the men full social security. By law, a labourer had to work one hundred days a year in order to qualify for unemployment pay. Once over that total he was entitled to 400 lire (c. 30p; c. 65 cents) a day when out of work. Some of them had been willing to omit registering days on which they had worked, after they had reached the total of one hundred, because they saved the employers' having to pay their share of social contributions. In order to be relieved of this burden, the employers would pay more than the agreed wage, especially at harvest-time and other busy periods. But by late 1968 the labourers wanted to put an end to these informal understandings and give up a little ready cash in order to enjoy their full social-security benefits like any other type of full-time, properly registered worker. And so they insisted on the establishment of the mixed commissions to supervise registration.

This second demand was the harder of the two for the employers to accept and the one on which the negotiations had become deadlocked. A clash between strikers and police at a roadblock on the road between Avola and Syracuse on 2 December brought about the tragic pitched battle which ended with the deaths of two labourers, apparently the victims of panic on the part of the police. The strike had by then lasted ten days. A settlement came almost immediately after the violence and the workers obtained practically all that they wanted. The new contract represented a remarkable advance. Zones were abolished and the labourers received 3780 lire (£2.58; $6) for a seven-hour day and the committees were to be set up to watch over their interests. A decade earlier, the Syracuse province had been poor. The arrival of industry and the reorganisation of agriculture helped raise the average income to 465,000 lire (£317; $775) a person. And with this advance there clearly went a maturing of the outlook of the farm-labourers, usually regarded as the rearguard of the workers' movement. The battle was taken up elsewhere. In June and July 1971, the farm-labourers of Apulia went on strike under the leadership of all three main trade union federations, who were co-operating in a strike in Apulia for the first time since the critical days of 1948. The labourers not only insisted on the application of the law by which they were entitled to have from the employers a clear indication in advance of plans for the whole season so that the amount of work available could be accurately estimated, but demanded social security similar to that of industrial workers. And for the first time they organised themselves like industrial workers. Employers anxious to have their crops of ripened fruit were prevented from sending to the Molise and the Abruzzi for labour by constant picketing of the farm-buildings. They were guarded by strikers day and night. Finally, in March 1972 some 1,700,000 farm-workers came out on strike while nego-tiating a new national contract and industrial workers throughout the country struck for brief but symbolic periods to support them and building labourers struck for a whole day. For the first time the farm-labourers could feel themselves to be something better than the least privileged of the working class and the seed was sown in Avola.

As if in the wake of Avola, but actually for widely different reasons, the town of Battipaglia rose in revolt on 9 April 1969. By doing so it set the pattern for the urban guerrilla which was to become a part of Italian life, in the north as well as the south. Rebellion broke out when the news spread that the tobacco factory was to be closed. First the inhabitants simply went on strike: a general strike which brought all activities to a halt. After ten days of rising anger, more dramatic measures were adopted and streets were blocked, the railway line blocked, the police station besieged and the town hall burnt. Police reinforcements were sent to the town, and two people died: a young schoolmistress called Teresa Ricciardi, who taught French, was shot as she stood on her balcony watching a demonstration, and a youth called Carmine Citro fell with a bullet through his head in one of the main streets. Flowers were placed at the door of the schoolmistress's house and a tyre outlined the point at which the boy fell, with a vase of flowers within it.

The cry was raised of another Avola. There was some similarity in the number of victims and the fact that both were taken to have been killed by the police. The mayor, in fact, had to negotiate the withdrawal of the police reinforcements from the town, which was then left in the hands of the *carabinieri*, who were quick to say that they could well have maintained law and order if it had not been for the arrival of police reinforcements. An effigy of a policeman, with a captured plastic riot-shield was set up outside the smoking remains of the town hall to symbolise those who, in the words of the inhabitants, 'betrayed us'. But there was little other comparison with the bloody events of Sicily.

Battipaglia is near Salerno. Its history is short by any, not only Italian, standards, but marked by strains. The Bourbons founded it little more than a century before the revolt in order to encourage the growth of a populated centre in the marshy Cilento plain where there had been unrest. Shortly after its foundation, the House of Savoy replaced the Bourbons and purloined the funds set apart for the development of Battipaglia. Hence the inhabitants were left to manage for themselves in the midst of a malarial plain, in a town without roots. One of the slogans of the revolt was: 'You have owed us everything for a century!' It had 40,000 inhabitants at the time of the revolt; in 1959 the total population was 14,000, an indication of the problems brought by sudden expansion to a town with no traditions except the tradition of resentment. It was a town based on improvisation, another familiar aspect of Italian life. Even more so because Battipaglia, in the period of its expansion, could rely on the support of a right-wing Christian Democrat, De Martino, a rich tobacco-importer, to look after its immediate interests. His death coincided with, and exacerbated, economic difficulties. Battipaglia felt these difficulties more sharply because the protector had gone. Three fruit- and vegetable-bottling factories were forced to close. A sugar factory was in serious trouble. Then came the announcement that the tobacco factory would close. This factory comes under the control of the state monopoly. It was true that the demand for cigarettes made with Italian tobacco had been dropping for years and in terms of the market this factory could reasonably have been closed. But there was also the feeling that, as the State owed them a living anyway, it should keep the unprofitable factory open.

The protest was against a life which lacked security unless some powerful protector was available with his good offices in Rome. One of their constant complaints was that Potenza was looked after by Colombo, Naples by the Gava family, Bari by Moro, but they had no one. Even the good times in Battipaglia were precarious and the bad times brought a conviction of hopelessness. Unlike the protest of Avola, the whole community was involved, not just a particular class. There was no political colour to the revolt, and when representatives of the extreme right tried to exploit the situation they were promptly forced to desist. Like Avola, Battipaglia learnt that by having two of its people shot by the police the town could look forward to a better future.

In September 1969, it was the turn of Caserta, outwardly a completely different place to Battipaglia. It still shows signs of the grace which it enjoyed as the summer seat of the Bourbons, no hastily-run-up little town without a past. For two days it was gripped by violence after the news was heard that for the sixth consecutive season the local football team had been denied promotion to the second division. This distinction had gone instead to Taranto on the grounds that the Caserta stadium was not up to second-division standards.

The mayor himself led the first demonstrations of protest.

Just as at Battipaglia, the presence or otherwise of a great protector, was an issue. Caserta believed in the protective powers of Senator Bosco, a Christian Democrat belonging to Fanfani's faction. No doubt the belief exceeded what the Senator could with the best will in the world have done for them. But they insisted on abiding by the legend and blaming him if they failed to obtain what was their due rather in the way that southern women harangue a religious image which refuses to perform its miracle for them. They were particularly demanding in the question of promotion to the second division not only for what they felt were reasons of popular justice but because they believed that Taranto was unfairly favoured by the support of Aldo Moro, then Prime Minister. Thus, when the humiliating result was heard, posters appeared on the walls through the dust raised by the rioting and the smoke of the burning tricolour flags which said: 'Moro beats Bosco six to one.' And the Communists, who refused to have any part in the violence, had angry crowds under their party offices shouting: 'You have been bought by Moro! He will bring you to power!' To that extent there was a political aspect to the violence.

All this was colourful and in many cases deeply felt. But the real issues were two. The first, that violence was now becoming recognised as a part of modern life in a way in which a decade or so earlier would have been unthinkable. On 10 September the Milan newspaper *Corriere della Sera* commented: 'The public power inspires neither confidence nor fear; this is the authentic drama.' And that was true. After the behaviour of the police at Avola and Battipaglia, the forces of law and order were kept firmly leashed. Their inability to deal effectively with social unrest was straining the coalition partners, the Socialists in particular finding their position in a government which used its police forces as an arm of repression increasingly embarrassing. They looked with envy across the floor to the Communist opposition which could make its unbridled protests. But the fact remained that the police, who in any country must be regarded as the guarantors of law and order, the instrument of a state based on law, inspired hatred without fear. The second aspect of the Caserta riots was that the noisest of the demonstrators were people who had drifted into Caserta from the surrounding countryside as part of the great move from the fields to the streets. Of the eighty-two persons charged with offences arising from the violence, fifty-seven had been born in the province but not the city. They now either lived in the city or returned after their shift in one of Caserta's factories to a country village. Psychologically the apparently stupid protest against the failure to be promoted to the second division was a protest of countrymen who could not digest the life which industrialisation had imposed on a city which in the past had been largely bureaucratic and ornamental, and a city which could not digest the changes imposed upon it. Caserta had felt the effects of industrialisation, but fewer factories than were promised had actually been built. At the time of the revolt, the active labour-force was 11,000 out of a population of 66,000 and at least 5000 people lived in the city without having placed themselves on the civic lists as residents.

The southern protest reached its culmination with the remarkable revolt of Reggio Calabria, which began in the autumn of 1970 and continued fitfully, but frequently with much violence, well into the following year. It coincided with the most turbulent strikes which the northern industrial cities had seen since the end of the war, the decisive 'hot autumn' which was to change radically relations between workers and management, workers and their environment, and the whole system on which Italy's industrial prosperity had been based. But the Calabrian revolt was more comprehensive in the way it demonstrated the reasons for desperation.

The pretext for the uprising was the choice of Catanzaro instead of Reggio Calabria as capital of the Calabrian region. It was not at all a bad pretext. Reggio Calabria is by far the largest of Calabria's cities: historically it has always been looked on as the leading city in the area and its people have a more open-minded outlook on the world at large than either Catanzaro, set gloomily in its mountains, or Cosenza. Reggio Calabria felt that in the past it had been promised much and given little. That could just about be accepted with resignation because governments had always behaved in that way towards the extreme south. But the people could not accept lightly seeing what they regarded as their one sure right taken away from them for political convenience. Even more, they resented the picture presented to them (correct, in fact) of a meeting over supper in a Rome restaurant between Giacomo Mancini, the leading Socialist from Cosenza, and Riccardo Misasi, a left-wing Christian Democrat from the same city, and other Calabrian notables who agreed among themselves on the sharing-out of political spoils in Calabria: Catanzaro should have the regional administration, Cosenza the projected university (projected for about fifteen years but now apparently about to take shape) and Reggio Calabria would have I.R.I.'s next steel mill somewhere in its province. The answer was a general strike in Reggio followed by demonstrations which frequently ended in violent clashes with the police. Two people died.

The old ills were there: the habit of feeling abandoned; of suffering injustice; poverty; the conviction that the police were no more than the repressive arm of an unsympathetic state. To which others were now added. For the first time a generation had grown up since fathers and brothers had gone to the northern industrial cities to find a living. These relatives told them of conditions up there, and young Calabrians were beginning to show a new determination to stay in the south and reject the humiliation that Turin and Milan offered them. There was little work to be found in the south, and it was symptomatic that many of the leaders of the revolt were young people who had had a higher education and were protesting against the neglect of their city, which meant neglect of their own claims to the right to work in their native region. Most people in the city were not impressed with the promise of the steel mill. It was no more than a promise, and governmental promises were not, to say the least, regarded as holy writ. It had, after all, been offered to Sicily as well. Moreover, the southerners were now far less impressed with the theory that industry solved all. A look at the north had taught them what it did to the human condition. They were also impressed with what it did to natural surroundings. Southerners are more sensitive to pollution than northerners for obvious reasons. They are shrewd enough to see that industry would only be worth their while if it really did solve all their problems, because the cost is heavy in what it destroys of life and life's surroundings. What little they had seen in Reggio Calabria of industrial development had been a dismal semi-failure. The most likely place, they were told, for the site of the steel mill would be the plain of Gioia Tauro, Calabria's richest agricultural area and one of its most beautiful stretches of countryside and coast. All this explains why Reggio Calabria preferred to have the offices of the regional capital, in themselves representing a source of jobs and of spending, with development of a tourist industry and forms of light industry, combined with measures to take local agriculture in hand.

At the height of the revolt, Reggio Calabria was like a city under occupation by a foreign power. Police reinforcements were housed in requisitioned schools (which had the secondary effect of closing the schools), and jeeps and riot squads kept a constant and massive guard on the offices of the prefect and of the chief of police. Protest marches were broken up with quite unnecessary violence, and on the outskirts of the city units of the Regular Army awaited orders to part the combatants. Mothers protested that their student sons were arrested without cause and maltreated by the police. The population objected especially to the condemnation of their revolt in many sections of the Italian Press as a rising by the extreme right. They pointed out bitterly that Reggio Calabria did not have a Fascist tradition and the Neo-Fascists had a small showing there in the first regional election. But the truth was that the extreme right was the first to grasp what was happening and moved in to exploit the rioting. The other parties were practically absent because of self-disqualification. The Socialists were hated because Mancini was regarded as the main culprit. Effigies of him and Misasi hanging by the neck were carried through the streets. The Christian Democrats were, as usual, divided and largely concentrating on their own factional quarrels in which the mayor, Pietro Battaglia, was himself involved. The Communists misjudged the whole affair from the beginning and then fell back on denouncing the revolt as Fascist-inspired. Not only was their attitude based on a misjudgement: it was also dictated by the Party's increasing claim to be a proponent of law and order, because the Communist leadership had grasped the danger of becoming identified with violence of which the public at large was growing weary. This weariness with violence was mainly to be felt in the north where the Communists have by far their greatest following. But they were sufficiently shaken by the Calabrian revolt and by the Neo-Fascist gains in the south in June 1971 to pay particular attention to the southern problem in the 1972 electoral campaign. A left-wing party could appreciate the extraordinary resistance of people who were ready to bring all business to a stop in a city plagued with poverty and economic uncertainty but convinced that their cause was just, despite increasing financial embarrassment, tear-gas and truncheons. In the end the city gained some concessions. The regional assembly would sit there on occasion, and economic help was sent. But by then the situation had passed beyond the point at which it could be put right by concessions and regrettably the extreme right, in political terms, was the gainer. In a minor way the same must be said of the rioting in L'Aquila in March 1971, which took the form of a protest against the sharing of the regional offices with the rival city of Pescara.

The fundamental question behind all these disorders is that of the clash between man and his environment, if one includes in the environment the governmental failure to provide the minimum softening by way of social reforms of the clash between the two. There is no centaur-like distinction between north and south on the extent to which the problem was felt. The north's version of the southern revolts was the overturning of industrial peace which could be seen to have begun by mid-1968 when demonstrations in Turin turned violent, and the clashes of extreme groups which were still acute in early 1973.

The northern protests could in many respects be compared with those of the south. Southerners took a leading part in them. Injustice and bad social conditions were an element and the only difference from injustice and bad social conditions in the south was that in the latter case centuries had passed while they accumulated, whereas in the north scarcely two decades were required. This in itself is a measure of technical progress. But the differences are greater than the similarities. Industry itself was the moving force in the north, just as it had been the moving force in bringing about the huge changes in Italy since the war, including naturally the great advances in prosperity.

The climax reached at the turn of the year 1969 to 1970 depended for its timing on the fact that an unusually large number of collective contracts in industry required re-negotiation as they had run their agreed course. But the task of re-negotiation had been preceded by a whole series of events which were fatally to have their effect on what would happen at the Fiat works or at other large factories. First, the student protest was at full strength. One of the acutest writers on students' problems, Felice Froio, described their uprising from November 1967 onwards as 'the most important political and cultural event of the post-war period', and history may well prove him right. The students were a stimulus to the workers to make their own protests, and the effect was to carry some of the workers on to far more advanced positions than the trade unions favoured. And this despite changes in the outlook of the unions which in itself represented an unprecedented development as far as Italy was concerned. The unions increasingly adopted a purely political stance. They had always been political in one sense of the term: after a brief period in which there was a single trade union federation dominated by the Communists, it split into three main groups – the left-wing federation which was much the largest, the Catholic union and the small group led largely by Social Democrats and Republicans. The general shift within the whole movement throughout the year 1968 was towards reunification and a severing of direct links with political parties. But at another political level the unions became increasingly demanding: they insisted on the right to force the Government into adopting social reforms and to have a part themselves in devising these reforms. As a result, this period saw the beginning of national strikes called to back demands for such causes as higher pensions, housing for workers and improved social security. The unions had grasped the point that there was little use in obtaining increased salaries if workers could not find houses at rents they could afford and the lives of their families were made increasingly difficult by inadequate schooling and lack of social services in general. The sudden militancy of the unions was spontaneous. But it was allowed to expand because it came at the time when political power was at its weakest. Italy's serious political difficulties date from the election of May 1968, which was followed by the Socialist split and their departure for a time from the coalition. The unions were feeling their strength, and they came forward on to the national stage in a way they had never done before.

The aggressiveness of the unions had more than the students to stimulate it. Another quite new mentality had arisen with the formation of small, extremist groups. These groups were related to the student movement, but their interests went beyond student affairs. Like the student movement at its height, they were inspired by a form of extreme left-wing anarchy owing something to Maoist thought but more to a generalised feeling against all institutions. They were against Parties, Parliament, the law-courts, the assembly line and, in a particularly vindictive way, against the Communist Party, which they believed had betrayed its gospel of the class-struggle and the need for revolution to become just another moderate bourgeois party. Though split and hating each other as well as society, they held a common belief in the efficacy and necessity of violent revolution which would overturn the entire system.

Since 1967, when these *gruppuscoli* began to germinate, about one hundred have made an appearance. Not all survived. By early 1972 there were about sixty of them. They can be divided into two main categories: the Marxist-Leninists and the workers' groups. The first set adopts a form of Chinese Communism and had its origins in the founding at Livorno in 1966 of a party calling itself the Communist Party of Italy, Marxist-Leninist. The founders were dissident Communists and there was talk at the time that they had been helped to establish themselves by Ministry of the Interior funds because the Government thought that the Communists were the main danger and a left-wing anti-Communist extremist party would have a usefully divisive function. These groups are violently revolutionary but they are less extreme than the workers' groups in that they accept the immediate necessity for parties and recognise that the revolution requires time and organisation to prepare it. The workers' groups, of which the most important are Potere Operaio and Lotta Continua, argue the case for spontaneous revolution and only a rudimentary form of organisation which rejects a hierarchy. The workers' groups are at their busiest among the poor southern workers in the north, in the urban ghettoes, the shanty-towns and the suburban slums. A vague degree of co-ordination was provided by the group of former Communists which publishes the newspaper *Il Manifesto* and manages to plan joint demonstrations with two or three of them, at least one from the Marxist-Leninist side and the rest from the workers' groups. But essentially they are bitterly divided. The student movement, which by early 1972 was weakened but retained some degree of strength mainly in Milan, was inclined to co-operate more with the Communist Party than with the real extremists. The Communist Party denounces them regularly and – ironic when considered in relation with the rumours attending the birth of the Livorno party – readily co-operates with the police in identifying and handing over extremists. In return the *gruppuscoli* were not only responsible for a physical attack on a Communist professor in Florence, in July 1971, but threatened to attack the town hall in Bologna which is, of course, controlled by the Communists. The Party's denunciation of extremism reached its peak at the Central Committee meeting in February 1973, when Enrico Berlinguer attacked the agitators in terms which a Christian Democrat would hardly dare to use. And the Party astoundingly demanded the resignation of Senator Umberto Terracini from his post as leader of the parliamentary party in the Senate after he had signed a petition organised by the extreme left. He defended himself vigorously but unavailingly before the Central Committee. The extremist groups are at their strongest in Milan but the largest of them have followers in various parts of the country including the south. The Reggio Calabria revolt taught the extreme right that there were new possibilities for them in the deep south.

The pre-eminence of Milan in extra-parliamentary extremism can be explained by the city's nature as the heart of Italian business. Milanese are not interested in politics. Of the leading politicians from Milan only Giovanni Malagodi, the Liberal Party secretary, is of a calibre suitable to the immense importance which the city has in national life. Most Milanese are too engrossed in commerce and business to think of Parliament and politics, and when they do happen to think of public life in the capital they do so with scorn and contempt. Milan is the centre of Italian capitalism and sums up in its daily life the values of the post-war consumer society. The rejection of these values is what the extra-parliamentary left stands for, and that is why these groups were responsible for such escapades as the pelting of fashionably dressed crowds at La Scala with tomatoes and eggs. But reaction was quick to gain ground. Though many Milanese are indeed apolitical, this state of mind inevitably implies a leaning to the right. Once the right-wing extremists came into the open they were not liked by the Milanese but they could claim a degree of public support, even if at times subconscious, from public opinion when they erupted in violent clashes with the extreme left.

On 16 April 1971, two right-wing evening newspapers, in Rome and Milan, printed the text of a four-page letter written in confidence by the Prefect, Libero Mazza, to the Minister of the Interior, Franco Restivo. Presumably somebody felt that the public should know about the condition of public order in Milan and how better than through the eyes of the Prefect, who appeared to see the situation from a more anti-left than anti-right position. The part of the letter which made the greatest impression was the Prefect's estimate that Milan had 20,000 people belonging to extremist groups 'with organisations, equipment and armament which could be described as paramilitary'. Whether or not his judgements were correct, violence continued in Milan.

In April 1973 the balance was to some extent redressed when

the right-wing seemed clearly implicated in the killing of a policeman. This outrage was followed in May by the throwing of a bomb outside police headquarters. Several people died. The culprit was a self-styled anarchist with right-wing friends.

Behind the excess of activism, there was an element quite new to the Italian scene: an excess of absenteeism on the part of the workers. Italians have a high strike-ratio but they were known until 1969 as extremely hard workers when they were actually at their benches. But this, too, was to change. The Fiat works, for instance, had an average of five to six per cent of absenteeism in 1964-5: by the end of 1970 the proportion reached 12·5, and the eight million working-hours lost in 1969 had become thirty million by 1970. About 18,000 workers were absent each day. At Olivetti absences almost doubled in the four years up to 1970, by which time 13·6 per cent of the workers were absent and 9·4 of the salaried employees.

The reaction of management was to place the blame on legislation by which sick employees need no longer be examined by the factory doctor. By what is called the Statute of the Workers, one of the few laws passed during the rule of the centre–left coalitions which specifically favoured the working classes, the question of whether a man was fit enough to work rested exclusively with the doctors of the health service. Undoubtedly this innovation made absenteeism easier. But the real causes were much deeper, as is obvious when one recalls Saragat's dictum that Italy's great advantage was that the workers worked *con amore*. The first reason, as the unions were quick to point out, was that the increase in absenteeism was simply a process by which Italian workers were adjusting themselves to the behaviour of workers in the rest of Europe. Industrial society, once accepted, is industrial society and does not permit differences or various interpretations. This evolution in Italy incidentally washed away Italian industry's advantage over the rest of Europe but, as Italians quickly grasped, real competitiveness cannot exist in a modern industrial society, which must be uniform and, preferably, organised into constantly larger units. The old cry of free enterprise on which European capitalism was supposed to be based lasted about two decades in Italy. The unions and the absentees had by mid-1972 brought private industry practically to its knees, and only the massive firms and the State-controlled sections of industry could face the future with any confidence.

The second reason for absenteeism was that some seven million men who were working in factories had been recruited from among the farm-labourers of the south. It was obvious, or should have been, that these men would not be able to face so drastic a change of life without serious problems of readjustment of which health would be the first. They began without the remotest idea of what work on an assembly line entailed. They did so without the backing of efficient social services, or apparent sympathy either from employers or government. The one form of sympathy which they received, when their exasperation was at breaking-point, was to hear that their sufferings and difficulties were those which members of the European working class had already suffered before them, a not altogether satisfactory reversal of the tenets of the class-struggle. Workers of the world were united, but in alienation.

The gradual eruption of hatred of the productive process provided the element of human tension in the decisive 'hot autumn' of 1969. One can accept that the unions pressed too hard with their new political role. Their truculence happened to coincide with the decline in governing capacity of the politicians and as a result they could exceed the normal functions ascribed to unions. There was, moreover, no legislation by which their functions were formally expressed because, although the Constitution calls for a trade union law, no government had bothered, or dared, to produce an industrial relations bill. One can accept as well that the workers were subjected to a barrage of incitement from the extremist groups to demand everything immediately and press their point with violence. The atmosphere around them had the intoxicating tang of explosive, of occasional sudden death and of continuous tension. But fundamentally the lack of security was caused by a widespread disillusionment with what the new society was offering in exchange for the sacrifices which it required. And the workers were the first to react. That was why the period from the summer of 1969 to early 1970 was decisive: not only were industrial relations placed on a new footing but the men were demanding more humane conditions up to the stage of finding new processes for mass production which would do away with the assembly line: as well, of course, as shorter hours and higher wages. There was now no turning back, and one of the reasons why general elections were called in 1972, over a year ahead of the end of Parliament's term, was that a large number of industrial contracts were due for re-negotiation before the year was out and there was widespread fear that the situation would be too much for a weak government to face.

Shortly before Easter 1972, the Milan publisher Giangiacomo Feltrinelli was killed. His mangled body was found at Segrate near Milan beneath an electricity pylon. He appeared to have been killed by dynamite which had exploded too early as he set out to destroy the pylon. The man was a dangerous eccentric and as much a psychological as a political case: he was reported to be financing Milan's extremism and had planned to use Mesina, last of the great Sardinian bandits, to lead a separatist campaign which would have made Sardinia, in the reported plans of Feltrinelli, the Cuba of the Mediterranean. The extreme left and some of his friends immediately declared that he had been murdered. Candidates for responsibility were the Italian secret services and the C.I.A. Whatever the truth of how he met his end, the man blown up by the explosive forces which he was trying to use for his own purposes was in its way allegorical. Whether he died by accident or was killed, he had gone beyond his depth. And beyond what his nervous system could stand. If he symbolised anything he symbolised a country that could not live a myth, a country suffering from the fact that whole nations, when overstrained, cannot, like individuals, go away and rest.

I was with three friends, discussing the death of Feltrinelli. We looked at the likelihood of the hand of the C.I.A. The final comment from one of them, a leading financier and highly intelligent man, was: 'These people may be interfering, but they are no more than grave-diggers covering the corpse. The cause of the country's condition is suicide.'

The answer to such extreme pessimism is that Italy is a

country with great resilience and surely will somehow find a way back to the years of promise of the late fifties. The problem has ceased to be any centaur-like distinction between north and south because both have contributed equally to the extraordinarily rapid acceptance and rejection of a new form of life. To both the basic clash is between man and his environment, which is after all the century's principal theme. Probably they will in the end become accustomed to a new society. Not by surrender to it but by accepting certain of its conditions. More women will gradually shop at supermarkets. More men will stolidly go to work five days a week for forty hours and clean their cars on Saturdays. Young people will feel increasingly free from parental supervision and, having helped to destroy an educational system which no longer bears any relationship to their daily lives, will have nothing to put in its place. And little interest in devising a more practical system. With this degree of acceptance there will probably be a similar degree of withdrawal from the race. The condition of jaded nerves which was so apparent in the early seventies was by no means limited to workers and young people. It brought about a semi-conscious attempt to look back. That was the attraction of the newly refurbished political right. It was suggested in the reaction against divorce and the reluctance of the lay parties themselves to defend their own achievement of having introduced divorce, as if they themselves, instinctively, mistrusted the step into what is taken to be the modern world, which elsewhere appeared to be so normal a development.

Orpheus was no longer sounding his lute to entice Eurydice northward out of the underworld which, as everybody knows, lies to the south, near Naples. It was only artistic justice that the first work recognised in the textbooks as an opera should have treated the Eurydice theme, which is symbolically fundamental to the Italian experience in any age. But those early plots depended on a *deus ex machina* to provide the proper ending. There is, in the case of Italy's choice, no proper ending. Conservatism came back more strongly in the spring of 1972, but by European standards comparatively late. Italy persisted with its coalition of Marxists and Catholics long after her European partners had given up any pretence of looking left, and to some extent followed the prevailing pattern, not without the danger of slipping too far.

The real danger is not so much from extremism even if at times the climate looks disturbingly favourable to the right. Nor is it an answer to argue that Italy's difficulties originate in the denial of power to the Communists and that these difficulties would vanish if the Communists were brought into power. Apart from any dangers inherent in such a solution, the Communists do not inspire confidence that they have ready, waiting to be applied, a promising alternative. No: the danger is of a different kind. It is not a political question. It involves all of Italian society. To sleep. And not to dream. The sleep of the over-realistic. The rest not of the warrior but the relentless pursuer grown tired. The brilliant mind that ordered a coat and then could not pay for it. Songs of experience, not growing pains. That is why they are so worth listening to, even in repose.

Their own dilemma remained a psychological one. The immediate past was near, still real for many people, but already remote. The future was confused and uncomfortable: too remote in some ways and too near in others. There had been flashes of fresh colour. The student movement in its early days was one, and another was a more general feeling of the need for a new approach, for open discussion of problems, a rejection of taboo, all attitudes too readily suspect to the authorities.

Some seemed to want to call back something of the Middle Ages. But the Middle Ages had ended and neither faith nor tradition once gone can be easily recovered, and in the process even appearances change. Italy's past condition and present questioning was perfectly expressed by Webster:

Necessity makes me suffer constantly,
And custom makes it easy. – Who do I look like now?

It is hard to say. The new flowering was still awaited. There had been no cultural experience to accompany industrial expansion and its consequences, no spiritual guidance and no political enlightenment. When Forster's Middle Ages ended with the discovery of love in Florence, the couple heard the song of Phaeton which announced passion requited, love attained. 'The song died away: they heard the river, bearing down the snows of winter into the Mediterranean.' Italy's post-war experience has been the opposite: they have been moving upstream, away from the Mediterranean, towards the winter snows. It is a journey which must bring its hardships and discouragements. To look back would be to lose ground. To lose Eurydice, too. And the future would be still more uncertain. It is difficult to deny that Italy's travail and expansion, prosperity and unhappiness is a modern myth; the more studied the more instructive it is about life as it is lived in the second half of the twentieth century.

Index

Index

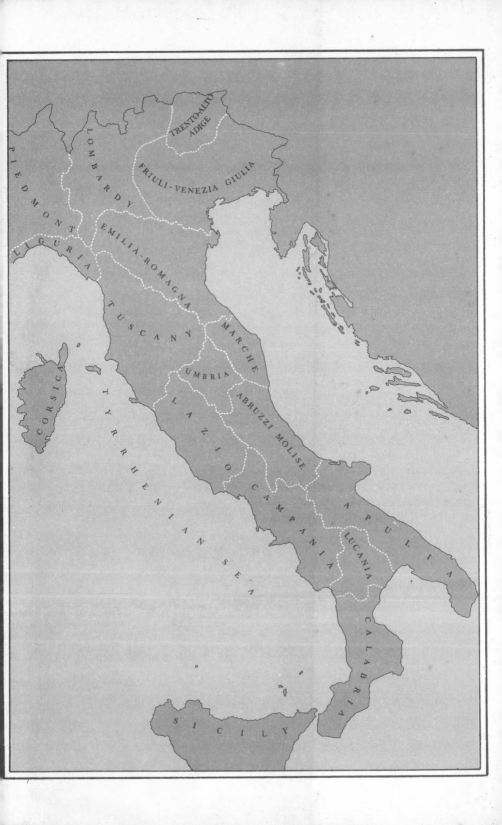